1950s (

Politics and Public Affairs

While the 1950s in Canada were years of social conformity, it was also a time of political, economic, and technological change. Against a background of growing prosperity, federal and provincial politics became increasingly competitive, intergovernmental relations became more contentious, and Canada's presence in the world expanded. The life expectancy of Canadians increased as the social pathologies of poverty, crime, and racial, ethnic, and gender discrimination were in retreat.

1950s Canada illuminates the fault lines around which Canadian politics and public affairs have revolved. Chronicling the themes and events of Canadian politics and public affairs during the 1950s, Nelson Wiseman reviews social, economic, and cultural developments during each year of the decade, focusing on developments in federal politics, intergovernmental relations, provincial affairs, and Canada's role in the world. The book examines Canada's subordinate relationship first with Britain and then the United States, the interplay between Quebec's distinct society and the rest of Canada, and the regional tensions between the inner Canada of Ontario and Quebec and the outer Canada of the Atlantic and western provinces. Through this record of major events in the politics of the decade, *1950s Canada* sheds light on the rapid altering of the fabric of Canadian life.

NELSON WISEMAN is a professor emeritus of political science at the University of Toronto.

NELSON WISEMAN

1950s Canada

Politics and Public Affairs

UNIVERSITY OF TORONTO PRESS
Toronto Buffalo London

© University of Toronto Press 2022
Toronto Buffalo London
utorontopress.com
Printed in the U.S.A.

ISBN 978-1-4875-5101-8 (cloth)   ISBN 978-1-4875-6335-6 (EPUB)
ISBN 978-1-4875-5545-0 (paper)   ISBN 978-1-4875-5880-2 (PDF)

Library and Archives Canada Cataloguing in Publication

Title: 1950s Canada : politics and public affairs / Nelson Wiseman.
Names: Wiseman, Nelson, 1946– author.
Description: Includes bibliographical references and index.
Identifiers: Canadiana (print) 20220274746 | Canadiana (ebook) 20220274789 |
    ISBN 9781487555450 (paper) | ISBN 9781487551018 (cloth) | ISBN
        0781487563356 (EPUB) | ISBN 9781487558802 (PDF)
Subjects: LCSH: Nineteen fifties. | CSH: Canada – Politics and government –
1948–1957. | CSH: Canada – Social conditions – 1945–1971. | CSH: Canada –
    Economic conditions – 1945–1971. | CSH: Canada – History – 1945–1963.
    Classification: LCC FC610 .W57 2022 | DDC 971.063/3 – dc23

We wish to acknowledge the land on which the University of Toronto Press
operates. This land is the traditional territory of the Wendat, the Anishnaabeg,
the Haudenosaunee, the Métis, and the Mississaugas of the Credit First Nation.

University of Toronto Press acknowledges the financial support of the
Government of Canada, the Canada Council for the Arts, and the Ontario Arts
Council, an agency of the Government of Ontario, for its publishing activities.

Canada Council   Conseil des Arts
for the Arts   du Canada

ONTARIO ARTS COUNCIL
CONSEIL DES ARTS DE L'ONTARIO
an Ontario government agency
un organisme du gouvernement de l'Ontario

Funded by the   Financé par le   Canadä
Government   gouvernement
of Canada   du Canada

Contents

Introduction: Reflections on Studying Canada of the 1950s

Why study a decade, any decade? And if studying a decade, why begin with a round number like 1950, and not 1953 or 1954? A "decade" is an arbitrarily imposed, abstract concept that organizes the passage of a period of time. We generally begin with a round number when we think of a decade: the 1930s, 1950s, 1960s, 1990s, etc. The period from 1955 to 1965 is also a decade, but the change from one year to the next involves only adding an increment to the last number, from 1955 to 1956. A decade beginning with a round number is meaningful only because we prefer to consider numbers as multiples of ten; thus, Canadians celebrated the 100th and 150th anniversaries of Confederation in a way that they did not mark the 97th, the 102nd, or the 153rd. So why study the 1950s specifically and why devote a chapter to each year as if it were a discrete period like the decade itself? My objective is to offer a compilation of some major events in each year, some statistics, quotes from leading politicians and others, and some press opinions. I have relied heavily on journalistic accounts, which journalists like to refer to as "the first rough draft of history."[1] My primary but not exclusive source was the *Globe and Mail*.

In such an undertaking there is the ever-present danger of drowning in an ocean of random facts. Unlike an analytical study or thesis, an annual review has no singular focus. Writers other than myself might well choose a different melange of particulars or details, assigning greater significance to their facts than the ones I present. That is hardly surprising. We make value-laden decisions about the particular facts we select. Using different facts and preconceptions to weave a quite different story to their own taste, others might reasonably criticize my inventory. The story of the 1950s can therefore never be what Voltaire called *un faible convenu*, a tale agreed upon by all.[2]

Because of ever-evolving alternative methods, styles, and approaches in the social sciences and historical studies, the story of the 1950s must be open and unfinished, subject to revision and reassessment. Future developments may cause one to look back at those years and see them in a different light, so we must be tentative and modest in our interpretations. We may think that the facts of what happened in the 1950s are what they are, that only opinions about them may have changed. However, new facts may emerge which change our understanding of what the facts were in the past. Moreover, we can never hope to know all the facts of what happened at a cabinet meeting, in the give-and-take at a federal-provincial conference, or what leaders said to one another at an international summit.

In dissecting public affairs in the 1950s we cannot escape the present. Without considering it, a retrospective study is merely antiquarian. Regarding the decade from the perspective of some of the prominent concerns of Canadian social scientists and policymakers of the 2020s – the role of women, racialization, the status and conditions of Indigenous peoples – we may note, for example, that images of women in the magazine advertisements of the 1950s usually showed them as dutiful, deferential housewives. Sex and sexual diversity are now openly discussed and studied, but they were kept in the shadows of public discourse in the 1950s, and they are barely mentioned in my account. Deemed scandalous in polite circles, *Playboy* magazine, which gained popularity as the years passed, was not once mentioned in the *Toronto Daily Star*. The only reference to *Playboy* in the *Globe and Mail* by a Canadian was by the newspaper's music reviewer.[3]

My orientation is that of an old-fashioned political scientist with an historical bent. Today's social scientists and historians, using software for quantitative techniques or discourse analysis, raise questions that could not have been pursued in the 1950s. Subjects such as Aboriginal affairs, multiculturalism, women in politics, and social and economic inequality were mostly neglected during and prior to the decade. Serious consideration of these subjects awaited the 1960s and the works of sociologists such as John Porter and others who drew attention to social stratification; they undermined the conventional view of Canada as an equal, homogenous, classless society. Porter opened new areas of inquiry by showing that an elite of predominately white men of British heritage sat atop an ethnic pecking order in Canadian politics, the economy, and the bureaucracy of government.[4] Their status had gone unquestioned and unstudied in the 1950s and was taken for granted earlier.

Soon after the 1950s, one of those men of British heritage, George Grant, dropped a depth charge under what had become the liberal foundations of the pan-North American ideology of the times. His invective, in the form of a nationalist cri de cœur, lamented the end of a distinctively conservative Canadian identity which could counter the influence of American liberalism and technology. Grant's conservative sensibility was rooted in the British conservative tradition championed by some Canadian leaders and authors who had, like Grant, expressed concern about social atomization and had contempt for crass materialism. However, the British-centric model of Canadian identity in the 1950s was destined to give way as Canada slowly became a more pluralistic society. Classical conservative thinking, despite the efforts of historians such as W.L. Morton and Donald Creighton, was fading quickly in the 1950s. Grant knew that he could only eulogize and lament a time that had passed.[5]

We cannot say of the 1950s, as we can of the 1940s and 1960s, that they represented a turning point in Canadian or world history. However, studying the decade does contribute to illuminating some of the fault lines or axes around which Canadian politics and public affairs have always revolved: Canada's subordinate relationship first with Britain and then the United States, the interplay between Quebec's distinct society and the rest of Canada, and the regional tensions between the inner Canada of Ontario and Quebec and the outer Canada of the Atlantic and western provinces.

Chronicling the 1950s requires sensitivity to previous events for they limited and made possible what political actors could do domestically and on the world stage. After American investment had overtaken British investment in Canada in the 1920s and economic integration with the United States continued to deepen, John Diefenbaker's Conservative government, which came into office in 1957, was unable to make good on its vow to reorient trade from the United States to Britain. No matter the skills of their political leaders, Saskatchewan and the Maritime provinces were relegated to have-not status because of declines in the 1930s in the wheat economy of the prairies and the fisheries of Atlantic Canada. In contrast, Alberta's oil bonanza beginning in the late 1940s enabled its government to fund generous government programs in the 1950s despite a stated ideological opposition to big government.

My study focusses on the what rather than the why of the happenings of the 1950s. The chaos of happenings in each year meant that I had to struggle, evaluate, and think about which facts to assemble. Marshalling facts and organizing events permitted me to identify unique or particularly notable trends. The emergence of jet travel accelerated the engagement of Canada's leaders in international summitry; the introduction of television facilitated the phenomenon that was Diefenbaker and the transformation of political campaigning; changing political conventions permitted the appointments of the first Canadian-born governors general as well as the first woman, Ellen Fairclough, and the first Ukrainian, Michael Starr (born Starchewsky) to the federal cabinet.

The backgrounds of Fairclough and Starr pointed both to Canada's British heritage and to the evolution of Canada's national identity, which took on a more polyethnic character as the 1950s progressed: Fairclough was an active member of both the United Empire Loyalists Association and the Imperial Order Daughters of the Empire; Starr, recruited by the CBC to speak on Radio Canada International's opening broadcast to Ukraine, was perceived by many Ukrainian community leaders as their spokesman in Ottawa on national and international issues.[6]

In the procession of Canadian political history, the 1950s may be considered as both a tranquil decade in which little changed or an era of transformation and adaptation. The Liberals and Conservatives continued as Canada's major federal parties, but the Conservative party scored a stunning, unprecedented majority victory in 1958. After winning more seats in Ontario than in all other provinces combined in all six elections since 1935, the Conservatives reshaped Canada's electoral map in 1958, winning every seat west of Ontario but one to become (to this day, seven decades later) the party of western Canada. Countries which were formally or actually at war with Canada in 1950, West Germany and Communist China respectively, were by the end of the decade either a close military ally (West Germany) or keenly pursued as a customer for Canadian wheat (China).[7]

The 1950s were part of a moving stream of events that make strict periodization – arbitrarily dividing history into specific chronological periods – awkward. Compared to the sorrow and then the hope of the 1940s, the 1950s may be characterized as an era of incrementalism; compared to the revolution in social norms of the 1960s, they may be considered a languid period. There was little in the way of social and intellectual upheaval; the public was not veering from an established path onto a new plane or direction.

The absence of a major calamity or crisis differentiates the 1950s from the decades before and after: there was no disaster like the Depression of the 1930s, no cataclysmic war like that of the 1940s, no countercultural upheaval like that of the 1960s, no critical juncture like the October Crisis and the election of a separatist government in Quebec in the 1970s. There was some constitutional tinkering, but no major renovation as occurred with the introduction of the Charter of Rights and Freedoms in the 1980s. And there were no national unity crises as occurred in the 1990s with the death of the Meech Lake and Charlottetown Accords followed by a referendum in Quebec that nearly sundered the country.

We may, of course, consider the study of the 1950s as an end in itself; it need not be justified as a stepping stone to present concerns, to evaluating those years as merely a prelude to the future. Nor must we think of the political personalities of the 1950s as simply precursors of their successors. As for the moral principles of the public, they were not either obviously and indubitably inferior or superior to those of today, although the values and mores of Canadians have certainly evolved and changed. In the light of shifting norms, the meaning and importance of some developments in the 1950s have changed as well.

The significance of some events in the 1950s may come to be altered as fresh knowledge and materials come to light. Reassessments of prominent figures generate new debate. For example, we learned much about the dynamics of the 1957 and 1958 federal elections and the thinking of Lester Pearson as a political actor on the world stage from books published in later decades.[8] Some obscure political actors during the decade, like one-term Progressive Conservative MP John MacLean, will remain obscure. Nevertheless, they may be worthy of note because, as the chapter on 1959 reports, he stood up in Parliament to publicly criticize his own government for the inadequate indemnity that MPs received.[9]

Prominent political actors of the 1950s may come to be both appreciated and criticized in ways that they were not or could not be at the time. The positive light in which many Canadians came to regard Tommy Douglas – they voted him the "greatest Canadian" in a 2004 CBC survey – is now darkened in the eyes of some because they have learned new things about him: that as a graduate student he had believed that eugenics and Christianity complemented each other and that his government's Métis colonies in the 1950s were designed to "rehabilitate" the Métis as "a final solution" to their destitution and marginality.[10] These are unfair criticisms because Douglas's views at the time, when the eugenics notion of "race betterment" was pervasive, were in the mainstream of North American progressive thinking. As mainstream values changed, he recanted earlier positions; as premier of Saskatchewan and minister of health, for example, he vetoed a eugenics proposal, and his Cooperative Commonwealth Federation (CCF) government extended the franchise to Indigenous people after he declared that they should enjoy full citizenship rights.[11]

A study of the 1950s engages the reader in a dialogue between then and now. The 1950s are of course in the past, but they are very much in the present as well, pointing to many of today's concerns. Immigration, natural resource development, pipelines, parliamentary democracy, health care, intergovernmental relations, civil rights, and relations with the United States are all issues of those years that continue as concerns today. Looking back to reconsider the 1950s places such contemporary issues in a broader historical context.

Climate change, a contemporary policy issue, did not get much attention in the 1950s. Nevertheless, it was not entirely ignored; scientists reported that the sun had become 2 per cent brighter and probably hotter between 1953 and 1958; the *Brantford Expositor* reported in 1955 that temperatures in North America had risen by two degrees in the previous fifty years; the *Oshawa Daily Times Gazette* told readers of a BBC report that "the whole world is getting warmer"; and, although it made light of the matter by titling an editorial "Palms in the Arctic," the *Globe and Mail* noted that Toronto's mean temperature had risen from forty-eight to fifty degrees Fahrenheit between 1951 and 1953.[12]

I am obviously familiar with subsequent events, and this is evident in various places in the material presented. Inevitably, this familiarity influenced what caught my eye in reading about the 1950s. For example, I note that Pierre Trudeau co-founded *Cité Libre* in 1950 and that the journal was, perhaps, an overture to Quebec's Quiet Revolution of the 1960s. A chronicler at the time might very well not have mentioned *Cité Libre*. That Trudeau eventually became prime minister throws even brighter light on his influential journal, although it never had more than a modest readership.

Similarly, I refer to twenty-six-year-old Paul Hellyer's presence in Parliament in 1950, his elevation to Louis St. Laurent's cabinet in 1957, and his criticism of the Conservative government's defence procurement policy in 1959. He caught my attention because I knew that he would in the future go on to have a long and unusual political career, demonstrating boundless ambition and fickle partisan allegiances. As a Liberal cabinet minister, he unified the Canadian armed forces and contested the federal party's leadership – in effect the prime ministership – in the 1960s; in the 1970s he became the star attraction at a Social Credit Party convention and contested the Conservative leadership; and then in the 1990s he led his own political party, the Canadian Action Party, which he continued to lead into the 2000s.

When the 1950s began, there was no plot or predetermined design to how the decade would unfold. I highlight figures like Trudeau and Hellyer because I knew they would become more prominent in later years. Conversely, some people who seemed to have a promising future found that their fortunes could take a turn to the sidelines. Minister of finance Walter Harris, for example, had a public profile comparable to that of Lester Pearson before Pearson was awarded the Nobel Peace Prize; on numerous occasions the press presented Harris as a potential successor to St. Laurent as prime minister. He was the only cabinet minister who could rival C.D. Howe, the "minister of everything,"[13] prevailing over him on such issues as the funding of a trans-Canada pipeline and the advisability of bringing down an expansionary pre-election budget as the economic outlook darkened in 1957. Harris also prevailed over cabinet colleague Jean Lesage, the natural resources minister and future Quebec premier, on the issue of subsidizing farmers.

However, political fortune soon eluded Harris: after being defeated in the 1957 election, he was defeated less than a year later in a contest to become leader of the Ontario Liberals, a weak provincial party with poor electoral prospects. He then quickly disappeared from the political arena and public consciousness. Harris and his federal cabinet colleagues could not foresee the disastrous consequences of their ill-considered behaviour in 1956, when the Conservatives outmanoeuvred them in the heat of a notorious debate regarding a trans-Canada pipeline. Their unconventional imposition of closure on parliamentary debate led directly to the end of more than two decades of uninterrupted Liberal government. Nevertheless, Harris did leave a significant policy legacy: the introduction of equalization payments for provinces, a provision which eventually became entrenched in Canada's constitution in 1982.

Structural changes in the international arena compelled some reorientation of Canadian foreign policy. As older imperialisms – be they British, French, or Dutch – collapsed, the two great powers were the United States and the Soviet Union. Geoffrey Barraclough identified the 1950s as the decade in which the "death-agonies" of the old-world order gave way to the "birth-pangs of the new." Asia and Africa verged on a resurgence; Europe's centrality in world affairs was no more and only vestiges of its domination remained.[14] Relations between whites and non-whites required readjustment as the developing world's revolt against the West gathered momentum.

There is no single "cause" for what happened in the 1950s or in any one year of the decade. The decade embodied an invisible chain of conformity with the past, but it may also be marked off from the decades immediately preceding and following. The 1950s had something of the culture that the war of the 1940s had ruptured but also came to represent the state of affairs opposed by the youth culture of the 1960s. Although many changes occurred in the 1950s, it was not a decade of transformative cultural change. Divorce, for example, remained frowned upon; there was no provision for it in Quebec's civil code and English Canada kept adultery as a prerequisite. Single-parent households were oddities.

The 1940s had been an internationalist decade; Canada was part of a multinational alliance confronting first fascism and then communism. The 1960s was a decade of rising national consciousness and nationalist pride; the centenary of Canada's Confederation and Expo 67 occurred in the context of English Canada's irrepressible anxiety over national identity as it stood in the shadow of the economy and culture of the United States. In Quebec, nationalist pride took the form of determination to be *maîtres chez nous*. In contrast, the 1950s was a decade of an uninspiring anaemic English Canadian consciousness as both the public and officialdom viewed the US as a benevolent imperial power, while in Quebec *la survivance* still served as the leitmotif, a stolidly calm disposition in the face of Anglo-American hegemony.

Ramsay Cook attributed the underdeveloped national consciousness of English Canadians to their lack of national myths and successful mythmakers.[15] Since that diagnosis, nationalist myths have been provided by storytellers such as Pierre Berton and John Ralston Saul among others.[16] Beyond the theme of survival in their histories of Canada, English Canada's historians could have, but did not, point to the eighteenth-century conquest of French Canada because that would have been divisive. It awaited the 1970s for Margaret Atwood's handbook of Canadian literature, *Survival*, to "place the literature of the country within the country itself," making the case that Canadian literature is a legitimate branch of study, "an entity in its own right."[17] In Quebec, Pierre Vallières's best-seller, *White N[******] of America*, claimed the moral high ground for the Québécois.[18]

Quebec historians, idolizing New France heroes like Dollard des Ormeaux and Jean de Brébeuf, had constructed nationalist myths by presenting the French Canadians as a divinely chosen people called by God to preserve the Catholic faith in North America.[19] This narrative offered Maurice Duplessis's conservative government leverage to champion a religious form of nationalism. Quebec's nationalist myths, however, became increasingly inadequate in the 1950s as bulwarks against modernization. The gradual demythologizing of Quebec's history turned the decade into years of unease and growing impatience with the foundations of Duplessis's ageing regime. Using his platform in *Cité Libre*, to which Vallières also contributed, Pierre Trudeau flogged his Québécois compatriots for their ethnically nationalist "wigwam" complex – that is, their attempt to shelter their culture through isolation.[20]

The public and the press were more inclined to accept what they were told in the 1950s than in later decades. The media showed little interest in inquiring into the veracity of politicians' discourse. There was virtually no investigative journalism or professional training of journalists. Toronto's Ryerson Polytechnical Institute, a pioneer in Canadian journalism programs, only began to supplement their course offerings to their printing management students in 1950 with a few lectures on "practical journalism." A full-fledged journalism program did not begin until years later.[21] However, the quality and breadth of political reporting did improve as the 1950s proceeded. By the second half of the decade, for example, the *Globe and Mail* engaged some regional correspondents to offer periodic insightful analytical columns.

Conservative partisans now rarely mention George Drew, their leader through most of the 1950s. In contrast, they burnish the image of the many-sided Diefenbaker as a visionary, although they rejected his leadership in the 1960s. Southern Saskatchewan's largest body of water was named after him. Similarly, Liberal partisans do not often refer to St. Laurent, their leader through most of the 1950s; they celebrate Lester Pearson who led them to their then greatest-ever defeat in 1958 and became their first leader since the 1880s who failed to lead them to a majority government. Nevertheless, they named the country's largest airport after him.

Political leaders, parties, and institutions cannot be understood apart from the social, economic, and geopolitical forces enveloping them. The accomplishments of some leaders, however, have arguably transcended such forces. More than mere vessels for larger influences, they were political titans shaping new forces in the 1950s. Unlike Drew and St. Laurent, Diefenbaker and Pearson proved to be such titans, along with Saskatchewan's Tommy Douglas, Newfoundland's Joey Smallwood, British Columbia's W.A.C. Bennett, and Manitoba's Duff Roblin: Pearson's peacekeeping initiative on the world stage, Diefenbaker's reshaping of the Progressive Conservative party's base of support, Douglas as a pioneer in health policy, Smallwood as a latter-day father of Confederation, and Bennett and Roblin as personalities who reconfigured their provincial party systems for the balance of the century.

This book will be of interest to readers with a curiosity for a political history that presents something of the rich fabric of Canadian society in the 1950s, a pivotal decade in Canadian political history. Readers may search but will not find a unifying theme because I did not set out to interpret or articulate a defining characteristic of the decade. For some readers, this book will be something to dip into like a reference book, rather than to be read as a continuous narrative. It fills a gap in the literature of the 1950s, a decade poorly served by works that provide a snapshot overview or stereotype of the period as mere backdrop to some more specific subject. Topic-focussed works generally fail to provide readers with the horizontal breadth this study offers. My purpose is to help the reader get a sense of the bigger picture that bears on an issue or question they are curious about. It is essential reading, a key reference work, for anyone interested in studying a political topic rooted in or related to the Canada of the 1950s.

Although I am sensitive to the impact of social factors such as gender, race, and ethnicity, this book focusses on traditional institutional themes in Canada's political history. In a context of social history dominant in contemporary historical studies, this book is a reminder that Parliament, elections, government policy, interprovincial relations, and foreign affairs remain vital subjects to be reckoned with in any effective political account. This study represents a revival of academic interest in political history but also bears marks of its renewal by harkening back to a more distinct historical and state-focussed tradition in Canadian political studies. It is offered as a helpful contrast and complement to the ahistorical, variable testing, and more quantitative work that characterizes so much of contemporary political science.

The inspiration and something of a model for this study came from two annual review series. The first was the *Canadian Annual Review of Public Affairs* (initially titled *Morang's Annual Register of Canadian Affairs*), authored by J. Castell Hopkins from 1901 until his death in 1923, and then by his wife, Annie Bonner, until 1936. The second series was the *Canadian Annual Review* (later the *Canadian Annual Review of Politics and Public Affairs*). Launched in 1960 and edited until 1979 by historian John Saywell, it runs to 2009. These series offer records of contemporary history, accounts of events within the lifetime of the authors.

Hopkins's initial publisher described him as unprejudiced, "absolutely impartial in political matters," and the series as "intended to afford the Canadian people from year to year a record of the principal events ... and to convey ... a summary of current progress in a country now steadily growing in national importance."[22] A profoundly conservative partisan Conservative and an imperial federationist, the Anglophilic Hopkins was a fierce opponent of more intimate relations with the United States, where, ironically, he had been born. When he began his series, Hopkins celebrated Canada as an imperial citadel connected to Britain, the world's leading great power.[23] Political scientist Stephen Leacock, an ardent imperialist like Hopkins and the best-selling humorist in the English language between 1910 and 1925, expressed the imperialist sentiment for a British Canada when he pleaded for "something other than independence, nobler than annexation, greater in purpose than a Little Canada."[24]

Canada, the world order, and the educational establishment had changed dramatically when the Harvard-educated Saywell, who was also editor of the *Canadian Historical Review*, began editing his annual review series. Canada, which had long departed from the cocoon of the British Empire, was firmly in the economic and cultural orbit of the United States. Saywell and his successor editors and contributors have been predominantly liberally inclined historians and social scientists. Saywell himself wrote the introduction to Pierre Trudeau's *Federalism and the French Canadians*, introducing the future Liberal prime minister to an English Canadian public.[25]

Like the Hopkins series, the Saywell series offers a reference guide and record of each year's more significant events and developments. It has had the imprimatur of the University of Toronto Press while most of the editions by Hopkins were self-published. The University of Toronto Press series has also included contributors from beyond the university; the initial 1960 edition, for example, included entries by a television critic, a librarian, a public relations officer, and a drama producer. Reviewing the 1961 edition, political scientist Norman Ward regretted its numerous errors and shortcomings; nevertheless, he concluded that it was "a most welcome and indispensable enterprise."[26]

This study seeks to fill part of the gap between these two series: the 1950s. The earlier series offer something of a model for this study but with significant differences. Most notably, the attention devoted here to each year is considerably shorter, a mere chapter; in contrast, the consideration each year received in the earlier series was a substantial, lengthy book; some of Hopkins's annual reviews ran for well over nine hundred pages. The short chapters offered here are glimpses and not contemporary reviews like those presented in the two series. Since much more time has elapsed since the 1950s than the time the earlier authors had to work their reviews, I could more deliberately sort out greater from smaller events. Events Hopkins and Saywell considered noteworthy in 1921 or 1961 may not be considered as particularly interesting or significant today. They did not have the benefit of posterity, greater detachment from the melee of events.

It is impossible to write of an historical era like the 1950s with anything like complete detachment. Growing up on the prairies, living most of my adult life in prosperous Ontario, and reading almost exclusively in English has, of course, coloured what I have compiled. An immigrant, I grew up in the Winnipeg of the 1950s and 1960s, when the Manitoba Club, the oldest private club in western Canada, which every Canadian prime minister visited through the 1940s, excluded Jews and visible minorities from membership. Manitobans like me are westerners, but Manitobans have never been as alienated as Albertans from Ottawa or as detached from central Canada as British Columbians.

The Manitoba I grew up in was "the Ontario of the prairies,"[27] more urban and more diversified economically than the other prairie provinces. Winnipeg, as Canada's then fourth largest city, had the largest manufacturing, commercial, and financial industries on the prairies. Winnipeg also had a rich cultural life: the Royal Winnipeg Ballet, the Winnipeg Symphony, the Manitoba Opera, and the Royal Manitoba Theatre Centre, Canada's oldest English-language regional theatre and the first of a network of regional theatres across North America. Winnipeg's Women's Musical Club was established in the 1890s, predating the establishment of Saskatchewan and Alberta as provinces.[28] Living in Ontario made me more sensitive than most westerners to neighbouring Quebec. Growing up on the prairies ought to have made me more sensitive to Atlantic Canada, the other half of outer Canada. Perhaps it did not because, unlike the prairies, as historian Frank Underhill once jokingly wrote, "nothing, of course, ever happens down there."[29]

There has never been a perfect historian and there can never be a "definitive" account of the 1950s or any period of Canadian history. I have attempted to convey, however imperfectly, some sense of the social, economic, cultural, and political forces at play in the 1950s. Sins of omission and commission are mine alone.

1950

We have enjoyed a higher standard of living than anywhere else in the world outside the North American continent.[1]

Louis St. Laurent

Canadians had been severely tested by the midpoint of the century that Wilfrid Laurier had proclaimed "the century of Canada ... the star towards which all men who love progress and freedom shall come."[2] In the decades that followed Laurier's heady prediction, farmers abandoned the major political parties, a general strike in Winnipeg captured international headlines, and a devastating decade-long depression occurred between two world wars in which thousands of Canadian soldiers died or were wounded. The brief recession of 1948–9 had ended and the government projected a modest surplus of $20 million in a $2.4 billion budget.[3] Canadians were engaging in a spending spree – vehicle sales increased by more than 10 per cent – and while the government acknowledged rising inflation, it was doing little to check purchasing power.[4] Canada was transitioning to post-world war conditions but also opted to engage in war again, in Korea.

Some signs pointed to continuing political stability. The federal Liberals, in their sixteenth year of uninterrupted rule, had won 191 of Parliament's 262 seats in the 1949 election. Long-term Liberal dominance led political theorist C.B. Macpherson to suggest that Canada's quasi-colonial status as an economic and political satellite of the United States could lead to the Liberals governing indefinitely, and that Canada, like Alberta, might have developed a "quasi-party system."[5] In such a system, one political party dominates overwhelmingly for a long time but much of the substance of democracy – the continued operation of free competing political parties, open parliamentary debate, and the conventions of cabinet government – are retained.

For the first time in fifty years, Mackenzie King, the recently retired longest-serving prime minister in Canadian history, did not attend the governor general's annual levee.[6] He died seven months later. However, the senior public servants his government had recruited and groomed during the Second World War carried on under the avuncular sixty-eight-year-old Louis St. Laurent. Sounding somewhat like Laurier's cheerfulness a half century earlier, St. Laurent boasted in his New Year's message that Canadians enjoyed "a higher standard of living than anywhere else in the world outside the North American continent." By year's end when Canada had committed to sending troops to fight in Korea, he was less sanguine, saying that while he did not expect to see another world war in his lifetime, his government was considering permitting women to enlist in the air force.[7]

Growing prosperity and technological advances were unmistakable. Canada was the world's third largest trading nation after the United States and the United Kingdom. Canada's farmers were enjoying an above average wheat crop. The economy, however, was becoming steadily less dependent on agriculture as oil, iron, and forests increasingly drove national wealth. New opportunities and amenities were on offer for consumers: the British Overseas Airways Corporation advertised return flights between Montreal and London on the fastest passenger airplane of the day, the propeller-driven Stratocruiser, for $500.02 ($5,734 in 2021); Canadian Pacific Airlines offered flights to Japan, China, New Zealand, and Australia in reclining "Loungaire" seats; the Westinghouse Electric Corporation promoted "the last word in modern refrigerator design" while cautioning that orders would be filled only "as fast as production permits."[8] Despite the economic expansion, the Supreme Court ruled that some wartime controls were still legally valid and the government gave serious consideration to limiting the construction of recreational facilities under the Essential Materials Act.[9]

Newfoundland had joined Confederation a few months earlier, adding 348,000 people to a national population of 14 million and 405,212 square kilometres, or three-and-a-half times the size of the Maritime provinces, to the country's land mass. The national rate of population growth exceeded that of the United States. Echoing Laurier's optimism, Progressive Conservative leader George Drew boasted to a British audience that Canada could easily feed, clothe, and house 100 million people.[10]

Parliament's standing committee on transportation carried the increasingly quaint title of Railways and Canals but other infrastructure was being built: Ottawa and several provinces signed an agreement for the construction of the Trans-Canada Highway, and construction began on an oil pipeline from the Edmonton region to the head of Lake Superior. Canada was also developing new links with other countries, concluding an air traffic agreement with faraway New Zealand, although Seattle remained the only city in the United States accessible by non-stop flight from Vancouver. An RCMP ship became the first vessel to circumnavigate North America.[11]

Canada had joined eleven other Western nations to become a founding member of the North Atlantic Treaty Organization (NATO) a few months earlier and now, three years after the International Monetary Fund (IMF) began its operations, Ottawa secured its permission to float the value of the dollar. British-born Viscount Alexander of Tunis served as governor general, but Canada's independence from Britain was continuing to grow: a few months earlier, the Supreme Court became the supreme authority in civil and constitutional cases, replacing the Judicial Committee of the Privy Council which was composed of British law lords. Westminster delegated the power to amend purely federal matters in the Constitution to Canada's Parliament. The term "Dominion" was still current, used in the media and by politicians, but officialdom subsequently stopped applying the descriptor "Dominion-Provincial" for the three first ministers' conferences held during the year, titling them "Conferences of Federal and Provincial Governments."[12]

Government policy dictated preference for British and American immigrants: 20,000 Britons and 7,600 Americans arrived. However, "northern European races" accounted for 86,000 immigrants and other "races" numbered 43,900. Some countries encouraged their citizens to immigrate to Canada; for the third successive year, emissaries of the Netherlands government requested the admission of 10,000 Dutch farmers.[13] The newly created Department of Citizenship and Immigration was charged with administering Canada's first Citizenship Act, which had come into force in 1947 and was previously the responsibility of the Department of Mines and Resources.

The centres of economic, demographic, and political gravity were slowly shifting westward. The city of Montreal outgrew the city of Toronto during the year, but metropolitan Toronto grew more quickly than metropolitan Montreal.[14] British Columbia's population exceeded Saskatchewan's population although Saskatchewan still had more seats in Parliament.

According to the Liberal government, the country was experiencing a labour shortage; others argued there was a surplus. On the same day that Labour Minister Milton Gregg pleaded with industries to hire more women, older people, and the physically disabled because of "demands

for greater defense production" and more soldiers, a group calling itself
the Union of Unemployed Workers, some of whose members had been
convicted of obstructing police, called for the suspension of immigration. The country's two national labour organizations deemed the post-
war high unemployment rate of 3.6 per cent a "national emergency." To
boost its ranks, the army advertised aggressively for recruits.[15]

Women played an auxiliary role in the political parties. St. Laurent said he "would like to have at least one woman on our side of
the House ... [it] would be a good thing for the other 190 of us," but
there was scant evidence that his or the other parties acted on that sentiment.[16] The year began with no women in Parliament, but a by-election
returned Ellen Fairclough. In British Columbia, Nancy Hodges became
the first woman Speaker of a Commonwealth legislature. To uphold
the moral order of society, the Imperial Order Daughters of the Empire
wanted the Criminal Code amended to include sex and love comics.[17]

Racial discrimination was common, and Indigenous people were
viewed as culturally inferior and susceptible to corruption. A letter
to the editor of the *Toronto Daily Star* signed "Coloured student" complained of prejudicial treatment by landlords, dance halls, and barbers.
Senator T.A. Crerar, a former minister responsible for Indian affairs,
contended that most Indigenous people did not want the franchise.
Senators were told that extending the vote to "especially the primitive
tribes" would produce an orgy of election bribery.[18]

Newspapers, radio, and magazines were the dominant media. In an-
ticipation of television's debut, the Canadian Congress of Labor lobbied in favour of a CBC monopoly because private ownership "would
be bad for our English-Canadian culture; it would be infinitely worse
for our French-Canadian culture." Private ownership of television
meant being "swallowed up by American programs."[19] The circulation
of newspapers – Toronto had three dailies – exceeded the number of
households as some subscribed to more than one paper.[20] Radio station
owners, unlike most newspaper owners, were intent on not limiting the
size of their audience by supporting a particular political party; they
provided all parties with the opportunity to purchase broadcast time.
MP John Diefenbaker, in a criticism Conservatives made often, used
one broadcast to attack the Liberal government for neglecting trade
with Britain.[21]

Winnipeg was the site of the largest mass evacuation and biggest
peacetime operation in Canadian history; a quarter of the city lay underwater for fifty-one days, leading a hundred thousand people to flee.
Five thousand army, air force, and navy personnel manned pumps, pa-
trolled dikes, and helped evacuate residents. Frogmen from Vancouver

and Halifax undertook underwater demolitions, and an American senator introduced a motion calling on President Truman to extend immediate aid to the city. At the same time, the army helped battle a fire that raged for thirty hours in Rimouski, burning down the house of the local MP, threatening the home of the lieutenant governor, leaving at least two thousand of the city's fifteen thousand residents homeless, and causing an estimated $20 million in damage.[22]

Federal Politics

Standings at mid-year in the multi-party twenty-first Parliament were 188 Liberals, 43 Progressive Conservatives, 13 CCF members, 10 Social Crediters, 5 Independents, and 3 Independent Liberals. The Conservatives had won nearly 30 per cent of the votes in the 1949 election but the Liberals, with nearly half the popular vote, captured the majority of seats in every province except Saskatchewan and Alberta. Only 2 of the CCF's seats were east of Manitoba and every Social Credit MP was from Alberta.

In the enveloping context of the Cold War, all the parliamentary parties attacked the pro-Soviet Labor-Progressive Party (LPP, a new identity for the Communist Party) and its affiliated groups. The Housewives Consumers League, considered little more than a women's wing of the LPP, resigned to the new Cold War reality, reconstituting itself as the Congress of Canadian Women to include several CCF women.[23] Parliament's external affairs committee recommended that the government reconsider granting passports to Communists after party leader Tim Buck travelled behind the Iron Curtain. The armed forces ousted some soldiers because decades earlier they had attended meetings of unemployed men organized by the Communist Party.[24] Conservative leader Drew proposed outlawing all Communist activity and attacked a University of Toronto professor who wished to teach in Warsaw because "anyone who is opposed to communism would not be permitted to teach in a Polish university."[25] Nevertheless, Communists retained some public support: one finished second in a Montreal by-election, Ontario and Manitoba had Communist MLAs, and the 360,000-member Canadian Congress of Labor contained a small but vocal Communist faction.[26]

Beneficiaries of prosperity, the governing Liberals attracted little public animus. A survey asking Canadians which of the three largest parties "would you be least likely to vote for" found only 9 per cent named the Liberals compared to 53 per cent for the CCF and 17 per cent for the Conservatives. A communist brush tarred the social democratic

CCF: the survey revealed that a major reason the public gave for disliking the party was that it "tends to communism."[27]

Nine by-elections during the year demonstrated continuing Liberal strength. Anticipated opposition in Quebec to Canada's participation in the United Nations' Korean War effort did not materialize. Indeed, a plurality of French Canadians supported a year of compulsory military training for young men. In the three by-elections held in October in Quebec, none of the opposition parties fielded candidates; a Liberal was acclaimed in one riding and Liberals ran against Independent Liberals in the other two. The two seats the Liberals lost were in Hamilton, where Conservative Fairclough replaced a Liberal MP who had been appointed to the bench, and in Nova Scotia where a court, finding irregularities in the soldiers' ballots, had overturned a Liberal margin of four votes in the 1949 election.[28]

The liberalism of the Liberals was harder to define than the conservatism of the Progressive Conservatives or the socialism of the CCF. The Liberals repeatedly reaffirmed their faith in "free enterprise," qualified with a willingness to resort to government intervention if, in their judgement, that was necessary for the public good. St. Laurent was fond of highlighting English-French amity, a "partnership ... between the two great races here in Canada."[29]

The Conservatives attacked the Liberals for adopting Keynesian cyclical budgeting, which required adjusting fiscal policy to economic gyrations. They promised efficiencies in government, lower taxes, and spending cuts except for defence. Drew proposed rationalizing services delivered by federal and provincial departments of health and natural resources by assigning responsibility to one level of government or the other. He also challenged the Liberals to keep their promise to introduce an old-age pension program without a means test.[30]

Like the Conservatives, CCF leader M.J. Coldwell called for more trade with Britain and less dependence on the United States. However, unlike the Conservatives, the CCF favoured reimposing some price controls and subsidies. The CCF also favoured government economic planning, which the Conservatives denounced as economic shackling. Calling for public health insurance, federal old-age pensions, and a tax on excess profits, the CCF wanted higher taxes on those earning over $3,000. The Social Credit Party issued its first-ever national manifesto, proposing a commission of monetary experts that would supervise the nation's finances. All three opposition parties talked of the need to tackle the rising cost of living.[31]

The parliamentary session featured the political debut of twenty-six-year-old Paul Hellyer, who went on to seek but not to find the leadership of the Liberals in 1968 and the Conservatives in 1976. In the Senate, there was no hesitation in criticizing behaviour in the Commons. One Senator proposed that MPs who spoke more than seven hundred times be called to order and become ineligible for future appointment to the Upper House. He wanted limits placed on "horseplay" and "clever aphorisms."[32]

Differences of opinion within party caucuses were often aired publicly with little rebuke by party leaders. Drew, for example, differed openly with future leadership contender Davie Fulton after Fulton advised men not to volunteer for service in the Korean War unless Ottawa imposed conscription. In the emergency session of Parliament held to end a strike by 125,000 railway workers – a strike of such severity that the government issued an order in council giving itself the authority to mobilize all commercial aircraft – six Conservatives and one CCFer disregarded their leaders' direction and voted with the Liberals, but none were expelled from their caucus.[33]

Parliament witnessed two particularly odd episodes. Drew, by uttering the archaic phrase "I spy strangers," manoeuvred to have the Commons gallery cleared in order to hold a secret session on establishing a Commons defence committee, away from the eyes of a delegation from the Canadian Peace Congress, who were lobbying for the recognition of Communist China.[34] A device dating to the time of Charles I, never before or since used in Canada, his gambit was defeated on division. In another peculiar incident, seven members of a Communist-linked organization, the Canadian Convention of Unemployed Workers, jumped up in the gallery one after the other in a planned attempt at disrupting proceedings. Parliamentary veterans could recall no such organized effort in the past.[35]

The government introduced no substantive bills between the beginning of the parliamentary session in mid-February and mid-May, at which time, without consulting Canada's 135,000 Indigenous people, the Liberals proposed major amendments to the antiquated Indian Act, something not done in seven decades. The changes would have extended local band control of their funding and enfranchised Indigenous people in exchange for their forfeiting some of their treaty rights. Coldwell expressed disappointment that the bill did not provide for non-sectarian residential schools to stand alongside church schools. The opposition parties together with a couple of Liberals advocated hoisting the bill, which was eventually done after Indigenous spokesmen expressed opposition.[36]

A two-month filibuster held up a bill to incorporate a pipeline company that wanted to transport some of Alberta's natural gas to Ontario through the United States. Conservatives argued for an all-Canadian route for the pipeline project while the CCF sought regulated pipeline tariffs and rates.[37] The debate foreshadowed the rancour and division of the 1956 pipeline debate, which contributed mightily to undoing a twenty-two-year-old Liberal government.

Intergovernmental Relations

Three federal-provincial first ministers' conferences were held, a first. The first two conferences dealt with potential constitutional amendment formulas so that patriation of the Constitution from Britain could proceed. Quebec premier Maurice Duplessis dominated both conferences, contending that constitutional amendment required the approval of all four of Confederation's original provinces. New Brunswick's John McNair dismissed this as a "compact theory" of Confederation that was "obsolete." Ontario's Leslie Frost proposed the American model for constitutional amendment – approval by two-thirds of the provincial legislatures and Parliament, which eventually became the general amending formula adopted in 1982. Duplessis discounted the Supreme Court as a neutral arbiter in federal-provincial disputes because Ottawa appointed its members. Several premiers wanted to know whether Ottawa and the provinces could delegate legislative powers to each other. St. Laurent put the question as a reference case to the Supreme Court and the court said "no."[38] Saskatchewan premier T.C. Douglas called for a permanent federal-provincial secretariat, regular first ministers' meetings, and an entrenched bill of rights; his province had adopted Canada's first such bill in 1947. In the end, the first conference resolved nothing, although on the sidelines of the meeting, Ontario and Manitoba agreed to study a $50 million power development traversing their boundary.[39]

The second conference, the first ever held outside of Ottawa (in Quebec City), was attended by more Quebec than federal delegates, reflecting Quebec's preoccupation with constitutional issues. (In contrast, only eight Quebec delegates had attended the 1945 conference on reconstruction at which Ottawa had seventy-five delegates and Ontario had thirty-five.) Some premiers endorsed Duplessis's position that provinces should have input to Supreme Court appointments. Douglas, concerned that a single recalcitrant province could block new national social programs, opposed Duplessis's insistence on giving every province a veto in such matters.[40] The conference ended as inconclusively as the first, and the issue of an amendment formula lay fallow until the 1960s.

The third conference was intended to focus on indirect taxation by provinces, old-age security, and the tax-rental agreements the provinces had signed with Ottawa during the war and renewed in 1947. However, anticipated federal expenditures for the Korean War effort weakened the positions of the provinces that wanted to revise the tax-rental agreements, and the conference focussed on old-age pensions.[41] With unanimous provincial support, the conference led to a federal pension for Canadians over seventy years of age through the established amendment mechanism, that is, a request in the form of a resolution by both houses of Canada's parliament addressed to the parliament of the United Kingdom.[42] Newfoundland's Joey Smallwood, a new father of Confederation, pleaded for more federal economic assistance, contending that poorer provinces were at least as entitled to assistance as countries receiving Canadian foreign aid. Disappointed, the conference for Smallwood represented "hopes postponed."[43]

The Provinces

Provincial party alignments were quite different than the federal alignment. Only in Atlantic Canada's capitals did Liberal governments, as in Ottawa, face Conservatives as the opposition party. In Quebec, the nationalist conservative Union Nationale held a commanding eighty-two of the legislature's ninety seats. Ontario had the only Conservative government in the land. Manitoba's coalition administration included Liberal-Progressives (themselves a coalition party formed in the 1930s) and Conservatives. The CCF and Social Credit parties respectively governed Saskatchewan and Alberta. British Columbia had a decade-old coalition government of Liberals and Conservatives facing a strong CCF opposition.

The spoils of governing were unabashedly delivered to victorious partisans in the game between ins and outs in the Atlantic provinces. Political quiescence and economic stagnation characterized the region with no essential policy differences between Conservatives and Liberals. Atlantic Canada's politicians acted as supplicants to the federal government, arguing that Ottawa's failures accounted for their region's poor economic conditions. Nova Scotia premier Angus Macdonald, reminding MLAs that Confederation had led to the election of anti-confederate MPs in the 1860s, described the Confederation bargain of 1867 as a curse, its consequences "onerous and galling." The Halifax *Chronicle Herald* reported on rumours that Prince Edward Island premier J. Walter Jones, who called on Ottawa to address PEI's transportation difficulties, might be appointed to the Senate. (He was in 1953.) New Brunswick premier John McNair reported, "Our hospitals now have actual cases of malnutrition," and Newfoundland's Smallwood criticized Ottawa for considering his province a "nuisance." He damned his Maritime colleagues with faint praise: "There is great leadership in these provinces, but ... not so much ... as in other parts of Canada and the rest of the world."[44]

Pierre Trudeau, who worked in the Privy Council Office, co-founded the magazine *Cité Libre* with Gérard Pelletier in Quebec. It became, perhaps, the overture to the Quiet Revolution of the 1960s. The journal debuted months after the Asbestos Strike that Trudeau considered "a violent announcement that a new era had begun"; the journal served as an organ of opposition to the illiberal, patriarchal Duplessis, who viewed the Québécois as his children.[45] Pelletier noted that before "1950 we were not concerned with ousting the government ... we barely thought about this."[46] Federal MP Georges-Émile Lapalme became the leader of the Quebec Liberal Party, which adopted a social justice platform calling for some of the same things as *Cité Libre*: the defence of academic liberty, freedom of labour association, and the end of political interference in the justice system.[47] At year's end, two years after all ninety-two of their candidates had failed in the 1948 election, Social Credit's Quebec affiliate, L'Union des électeurs, decided to withdraw from electoral politics, reasoning that elections were an inadequate method of bringing about Social Credit doctrines.[48]

Ontario's Leslie Frost, who had succeeded George Drew as Conservative leader and premier after Drew left to helm the federal party in 1948, exhibited a frugal, prudent governing style. He thought his government should operate like "a prosperous family-run firm that was managed cautiously, invested wisely in future expansion, and paid close personal attention to details." Signifying the post-war development of cooperative federalism, St. Laurent formally transferred Ottawa's water rights in the Niagara River to Ontario when he made the first official visit by a prime minister to Queen's Park.[49]

Although the official opposition CCF lost half its members between 1948 and 1950, and many of its constituency associations evaporated, the party's first truly women's committee was formed; the closest thing to the committee's constitution declared that "it is in the best interests of the people of Canada to establish socialism in this country."[50] The third place Liberals, whose ranks included candidates contesting elections as Liberal-Labour, were at first led from outside the legislature by federal MP Walter Thomson. He had defeated Harry Cassidy, a founding member of the CCF, for the Liberal leadership. Thomson characterized the CCF as prophets of economic doom and gloom, "creatures of distress."[51]

Progressive Douglas Campbell's coalition government in Manitoba was rocked by two crises, the first precipitated by the resignation of Conservative party leader Errick Willis from cabinet over a policy issue and the second over his party's representation in the cabinet. Campbell used his skills as a mediator to overcome the first crisis. Although Conservative party members then voted in convention to leave the coalition, their MLAs wanted to remain, and they prevailed. The CCF struggled with its public image, having months earlier expelled two MLAs as Communist fellow travellers.[52]

In contrast to Manitoba, where the party was a minor force, the CCF governed Saskatchewan, its base of voter support having shifted from the countryside and farmers to the cities and wage labourers. The Liberal Regina *Leader-Post* castigated the CCF as having "become the political voice of the labor movement – and the labor movement only."[53] Although characterized by the opposition Liberals as a proponent of state ownership because the government had created a stable of crown corporations, Premier Douglas announced that "vital problems of industrial and business expansion" required that his government would take "no steps ... to expropriate or socialize mining or the petroleum industry." While his government neither favoured nor opposed nationalization of Canada's railways, he opined that Ottawa ought to study the idea.[54]

Oil wells near Leduc, Alberta swelled the revenues of the province's Social Credit government. The Cold War had so undercut the CCF, which had only two MLAs, that the provincial Federation of Labour supported the government.[55] The Liberals, also with only two seats, jabbed at Premier Ernest Manning, calling him a "Judas" to Social Credit theory and William Aberhart its "Messiah." Manning, who also headed Calgary's Prophetic Bible Institute and had his own radio program, "Back to the Bible Hour," viewed religion and government as inextricably connected: "Anybody interested in political relationships would be seven kinds of a fool if he did not put God and Christ and the Bible back in their rightful place in the councils of our land."[56]

British Columbia's Conservatives, like Manitoba's Conservatives, drove tensions with their Liberal coalition partners. The parties caucused separately and retained separate party organizations. Unlike Manitoba's Conservative MLAs, however, many B.C. Conservative MLAs chafed at their apparent relegation to perpetual minority status in cabinet. Federal Conservatives pressed their provincial kin to leave the coalition, arguing that the arrangement aided the federal Liberals. Conservative leader Herbert Anscomb acknowledged that the coalition could not be permanent but argued that it should last until his party's "contracts" with the Liberals and the citizenry had expired.[57] For their part, the federal and provincial CCF parties claimed that the coalition demonstrated the absence of any difference between Liberals and Conservatives.

Canada in the World

In word and deed the Liberals committed Canada to internationalism, something that Mackenzie King had avoided. They did so however with some hesitation. Cabinet ministers argued about engaging in the Korean War: some asked, "'What would King do?' and [others] replied 'He wouldn't be getting involved.'"[58] Favouring involvement, St. Laurent carried the day. Canada became one of eighteen nations to volunteer troops to the United Nations effort. Although not a member of the Security Council, Canada participated actively in the fifty-nine-member UN and other international organizations; finance minister Douglas Abbott, for example, was elected to the IMF chairmanship.[59] On a world stage where the United States, the Soviet Union, and the United Kingdom dominated, Canada acted multilaterally on a number of other fronts including signing on to the Colombo Plan to assist Southeast Asian states battling Communist movements.

At the UN, Canada's hopes for the institution dimmed. External affairs minister Lester Pearson told a Ceylonese audience "something has gone wrong with a vengeance" at the UN because certain "forces" (i.e., the Soviet bloc) in the organization challenged international cooperation.[60] Nevertheless, Canada pursued cooperation, proposing that every member state earmark some element of their armed forces for a permanent UN military force. Pearson proudly announced that Canada was the first to have done so. Acknowledging there would be formidable problems in commanding such a "polyglot force," he nevertheless thought them surmountable.[61]

"The first aim of Canadian policy," according to the government, "was to prevent war." Earnestly if naively, Pearson implored the General Assembly's political committee to adopt a "Two year moratorium on bellicose and violent speeches" and "a two year effort to do something effective about peace."[62] Simultaneously, Canada was preparing for military activity; defence minister Brooke Claxton said that although the permanent army was small, the army's reserve forces had grown to forty-three thousand from thirty-three thousand two years earlier and were better prepared for a military role than they had been before the Second World War.[63]

Canada dispatched three destroyers and an air transport squadron even before Parliament endorsed participation in the UN effort in Korea. General A.G.L. McNaughton, Canada's former representative at the UN, urged Canada's engagement because refraining would be "a first step to our eventual subjection." Like Britain and France, but unlike the United States which was already fighting the North Koreans and Chinese, Canada urged caution and a negotiated settlement. Canada slated three infantry battalions for service in Korea, but the UN command cut its request to one after successful landings at Incheon by American and British forces. The war seemed about to end, but the introduction of 300,000 Chinese troops changed the conflict's complexion between the time the Second Battalion of the Princess Patricia's Canadian Light Infantry set sail for Asia in late November and its arrival in Japan in mid-December.[64]

The Conservatives, stressing the importance of military preparedness, repeatedly called for the establishment of a standing parliamentary committee on defence, which the Liberals repeatedly rejected. Future Conservative defence minister Douglas Harkness claimed that Liberal procrastination in deciding to send ground troops to Korea damaged Canada's international reputation. Future Conservative external affairs minister Howard Green suggested the expansion of NATO to include the Pacific and John Diefenbaker proposed Canadian participation in a separate Pacific pact to complement NATO.[65]

Henri Courtemanche, one of Quebec's two Conservative MPs, and two Independent Quebec MPs opposed engaging in the Korean conflict: Courtemanche questioned the cost and noted that Canada had not intervened when Communists had taken over Eastern European countries. The CCF supported entering the conflict, having voted 125–25 in favour at their biennial convention. Social Credit also gave their endorsement although one of their MPs indicated he had no enthusiasm for sending ground troops. The party's Quebec affiliate, L'Union des électeurs, urged Canadian neutrality, comparing the Korean War to the American and Spanish civil wars.[66]

Canada's military relationship with the United States became even more intimate once the war began. C.D. Howe, the American-born engineer known as the "minister of everything" because it seemed that nothing of significance the government did happened without his blessing, represented Canada on a joint Canada-United States industrial mobilization committee. This led to further coordination of defence production by eliminating virtually all barriers to the flow of arms and equipment between the two counties.[67]

As a member of NATO, Canada decided to station troops in Europe after the president of one of Canada's first multinational firms, Massey-Harris, among others, promoted the idea.[68] Ottawa made plans to end its still formal state of war with Germany and, as a gesture of friendship to the new West German federal republic, agreed that Bonn could send a consul-general to Ottawa to serve as the first German representative since 1939.[69] Canada was keen to restore trade relations with Germany so as to gain a new market for its steel and agricultural products.[70] In contrast, trade with post-war Britain was troubled; agriculture minister James Gardiner said "nice talking" to the British had failed to increase exports and "more direct talking must be done ... and I am quite prepared to do it."[71]

Canada was coming to terms with a reconfigured Asia. Like Washington, Ottawa banned exports to the new Chinese Communist state, but their positions were not identical on all issues related to China. Unlike the United States, Canada voted in favour of a recommendation by the General Assembly's political committee to invite China to discuss the US role in the Korean War.[72] All of Canada's Presbyterian missionaries in China had left, finding it impossible to work there because "anything to do with the Christian Church is suspected of working for a foreign power." In contrast, a United Church committee recommended that Ottawa recognize the new Communist regime so that missionary efforts in China could continue. However, the United Church leadership balked at proposing this to the government. Ottawa was not averse to recognizing the Peking government but held back partly because of US opposition.[73] Canada's good relations with the new Asian Commonwealth states of India, Pakistan, and Ceylon led to plans to train technicians from the first two. India however rejected a Canadian proposal to settle its dispute with Pakistan over Kashmir. India also disagreed with Canada about whether Communist Chinese representatives ought to be invited to a UN technical assistance conference.[74]

1950 typified much of the domestic calm that came to define the 1950s. It was not the best but far from the worst of times. The economy grew substantially as the standard and cost of living increased. Confederation had added a new province, Newfoundland, a few months earlier. Officials pointed to a labour shortage, but others spoke of an unemployment crisis. The federal and provincial governments were relatively modest operations; their combined revenues totalled $4.4 billion ($50.4 billion in 2021).[75]

The two levels of government failed, as they had in 1927 and 1935, to agree on an amending formula for a patriated Constitution. Quebec's insistence on a veto for Confederation's original partners proved to be a roadblock. Despite the failure, the provincial premiers agreed to extend social security for Canadians by transferring constitutional authority for old-age pensions to Ottawa, a sign of the warfare state giving way to the welfare state.

The dominance of the federal Liberals and the secondary status of the Conservatives, the norm in the first half of the century, continued.

With the federal Liberals comfortably ensconced as the "government party,"[76] political quietism prevailed. As the Red Scare raged at home and abroad, Canada's communist as well as its social democratic parties were in retreat. In contrast to the federal political scene, the partisan configurations in the provinces were remarkably diverse in the numbers of competitive parties and their ideological orientations. In no province beyond Atlantic Canada did a Liberal party govern on its own.

Internationally, Canada preached the politics of high purpose and multilateralism. It actively engaged in an older institution, the now expanded nine-member Commonwealth. Canada also contributed to the efforts of newer institutions like the IMF and NATO. At the UN where Canada played a patient, pragmatic, mediating role, it did not hesitate to criticize what it considered the Soviet Union's menacing actions on the world stage. Lester Pearson upbraided the Soviet ambassador for his "vicious and vituperative" speeches.[77] Ottawa decided to station troops in Europe, unprecedented in peacetime, and following the leadership of the United States, Canada went to war in Korea but under the umbrella of the UN.

1951

Inflation is today the Kremlin's strongest ally and unless we in Canada and the people of the other free nations bring it under control, we may be defeated by the Soviet Empire without being called to face in battle a single Russian soldier.[1]

George Drew

The 1951 census revealed how dramatically Canada had changed in a decade. Demographic firsts included the population of both Quebec and Ontario surpassing four million and British Columbia reaching one million. Saskatchewan was the only province to have lost people, and even with the omission of the new province of Newfoundland, national population growth was considerably greater than in any earlier decade. Most of the growth was suburban: metropolitan Toronto's population exceeded one million, another first, with the city's outlying municipalities accounting for almost the entire 22 per cent increase. Suburbanization contributed to reversing the trends of the 1920s and 1930s, and there was a significant shift from tenancy to home ownership. More supermarkets appeared, particularly in large cities, and small "corner stores" declined. Personal services establishments such as small shoe repair and barber shops also declined while theatres and bowling alleys proliferated, signifying more leisure time.[2]

The population grew, but established patterns of power related to social class, ethnicity, and gender continued to prevail. Although less than half the population was of British ancestry, economic power continued to belong almost exclusively to them; French Canadians were roughly a third of the population but constituted less than 7 per cent of the economic elite. Jews were also underrepresented. Educational patterns were slow to change as well: only two-fifths of fifteen-to-nineteen-year-olds were in school and less than one in twelve of the college and university aged were in college or university.[3]

As greater numbers of Canadians began driving cars, feeble jokes circulated about the shortcomings of female motorists.[4] However, there were two notable political advances by women: Ottawa's Charlotte Whitton – described by *Maclean's* magazine as "a modern symbol of the militant female" – became the first female mayor of a major city. Whitton, who had founded the Canadian Council on Child Welfare in 1920, championed women's equality but criticized married women who worked and opposed liberalizing the divorce laws. Thérèse Casgrain, who had led the women's suffrage movement in Quebec, was elected as the Cooperative Commonwealth Federation leader in the province, becoming Canada's first female party leader.[5]

Intermarriage among ethnic and religious groups increased, particularly between Catholics and Protestants outside Quebec. Indicating the British group's high social status, growing numbers of Germans, Dutch, and Scandinavians became adherents of English Protestant denominations. These trends led liberal historian Arthur Lower to speculate that tensions between ethno-religious groups would diminish in the future. Employment legislation in Ontario forbade discrimination based on "race, creed, color, nationality, ancestry, or place of origin." Similar acts introduced in the House of Commons by Ellen Fairclough and in the Manitoba legislature failed to get beyond first reading, while Kitchener and Hamilton, following the example of Toronto, Oshawa, and Windsor, passed by-laws barring racial and religious discrimination by business establishments.[6]

Three-quarters of the four hundred thousand immigrants who had arrived since the end of the Second World War were living in urban areas and mostly worked in manufacturing and construction. There were fewer family farms, and more farms were being managed by farmers who did not live on their farm.[7] Canadians of British ancestry were exiting agriculture more rapidly than others such as Germans and Eastern Europeans, but those of British heritage who remained in the agricultural sector were more likely than the continental Europeans to be farm owners than farm labourers.

Gross domestic product and disposable income per capita continued their steady rise that had begun in 1946. Predicting a record-smashing GDP for the year, government economists projected price inflation of between 5 and 10 per cent; at year end, inflation was almost 11 per cent.[8] Concerned, the heads of the country's four major national labour unions, representing more than a million members, drafted an unprecedented joint brief to the federal Liberal cabinet calling for the reimposition of price controls and the retention of rent controls scheduled to be lifted.[9] This semblance of organized labour unity concealed real divisions within and between the two largest national unions, the Trades and Labor Congress and the Canadian Congress of Labor. Inflation raged but price wars also broke out: in London, for example, gasoline retailers fighting for market share lowered the cost of a gallon to less than forty cents.[10]

Shortages of steel caused by the Korean War and delays in securing equipment undermined CBC's plans to launch television stations in Montreal and Toronto by year's end. Nevertheless, about sixty thousand Canadians bought television sets, receiving the signals from American stations via rooftop antennas. Electrohome, which had started manufacturing television sets in Canada in 1949, had four Toronto dealerships advertising "free demonstrations."[11]

In the context of Cold War hysteria, anti-Communist groups complained about some CBC radio programming. MPs received a rain of postcards and form letters from various religious organizations deriding the corporation's "anti-religious broadcasts."[12] Progressive Conservative leader George Drew called on the Liberal government to investigate allegations made by "very responsible individuals" that "men with known communist associations" were involved with the CBC's International Service. Conservative MP Agar Rodney Adamson protested the broadcaster's "leftist propaganda," a sentiment shared by Social Credit leader Solon Low. CCF MP Alistair Stewart retorted that "we have heard this every year, yet when it comes down to the point, we cannot get the charge documented at any time." Conservative frontbencher John Diefenbaker was more tolerant of the broadcasts: "So long as it does not constitute sedition or is not contrary to good taste, I can see no reason why various viewpoints should not be expressed." Social Credit opposed a five-year annual grant of $6,250,000 for the CBC and Conservative frontbencher Donald Fleming called for abolishing the $2.50 annual licence fee the corporation received for radio sets.[13]

The Royal Commission on National Development in the Arts, Letters, and Sciences urged the federal government to fund a wide range of cultural activities to preserve, nurture, and promote Canadian culture. Commission head Vincent Massey recommended that the CBC expand its International Service, control all television stations to avoid excessive commercialism, and encourage the use of Canadian content and talent. Intellectual provocateur and renowned historian Frank Underhill dismissed Massey's report as "merely another historical document" that would be "brushed aside by practical men as the work of long-haired highbrows."[14] Massey's recommendations however resonated with popular columnist Pierre Berton who trumpeted Massey's pedigree, setting the stage for Massey's elevation to the governor-generalship in 1952: "No Canadian family, past or present, has had a more profound impact upon the nation than the great House of Massey."[15] Six years after the release of his report, the government created the Canada Council for the Arts to promote and foster the production of works in the arts.

Prime minister Louis St. Laurent and his wife Jeanne took up residence at government-purchased 24 Sussex Drive, originally the home of an Ottawa Valley lumber merchant.[16] Ottawa and the provinces had different rules governing who could vote and compensation for politicians. Federally and in all the provinces except CCF-governed Saskatchewan and Social Credit-governed Alberta, where eighteen- and nineteen-year-olds respectively could vote, the franchise was twenty-one years of age. Eligibility to vote also varied provincially based on residency; Quebec required two years, British Columbia six months, Manitoba just three. Doukhobors were not eligible to vote in both federal and British Columbia elections. Politics was a part-time occupation for most politicians and their compensation was modest by contemporary standards: the indemnity for Ontario's MPPs was $2,600, Prince Edward Island's MLAs $1,000, and Newfoundland's MHAs $3,000 ($31,103 in 2021).[17]

A particularly popular major event was the two-month royal tour by Princess Elizabeth and her husband Philip, Duke of Edinburgh, who were described as "the young couple all Canada is waiting to meet." The Imperial Order Daughters of the Empire issued guidance on the proper manner of proposing a toast to the King. The Princess, claiming to be a fan of Maurice (Rocket) Richard, attended a Montreal Canadiens hockey game, saying she regretted that "we missed that knockdown blow of his [in a fight] last week." Caribou slippers had been promised to two-year-old Prince Charles, but none could be found until a pair were located in Stony Rapids, a Saskatchewan hamlet located just south of the Northwest Territories. Conservative leader Drew, who referred to Elizabeth as a "princess of Canada," proposed that members of the royal family be granted Canadian citizenship.[18]

A Canadian invention popularized under the name "Cobalt Bomb" revolutionized treatment for cancer, second only to heart disease as a cause of death. Machines in London and Saskatoon treated patients with cobalt-60 radioactive isotopes, which National Research Council scientists had identified as a radiation source suitable for cancer therapy. Safer and more powerful than the radium used in then-conventional therapeutic x-rays, cobalt-60 was also much cheaper, and the

Chalk River heavy water reactor was the only one in the world able to produce it. Separately, there was a large actual and potential market for cobalt as it was used in defence production during the Korean War. American investors lobbied Ottawa to lift restrictions on cobalt exports and there was talk of reviving the industry in Ontario's Cobalt district.[19]

Federal Politics

Mackenzie King was dead, but his spirit continued to dominate politics. St. Laurent, his chosen successor, retained many of the ministers King had appointed: C.D. Howe, Douglas Abbott, Brooke Claxton, Alphonse Fournier, Paul Martin, Lester Pearson, Milton Gregg, and Lionel Chevrier. St. Laurent's New Year and year-end messages blended optimism with concern, counselling Canadians to set aside fear, face the year with confidence, and "be thankful" that most Canadians were employed. However, he also acknowledged that "the cost of living has increased and caused real concern and even hardship." He described inflation as a painful but necessary sacrifice required by the cost of the West's collective security.[20]

Inflation preoccupied the three opposition parties because it preoccupied the public. The Civil Service Federation, representing most of the federal government's 120,000 workers, claimed inflation had skyrocketed by 18 per cent in less than a year while its members had received no increase in pay.[21] The dollar was worth less than sixty cents compared to its value in 1939, leading distinguished journalist Bruce Hutchison to wonder if it would sink to twenty or even ten cents.[22] Opposition leader Drew, repeatedly characterizing inflation in weird hyperbolic terms such as "one of the most powerful and dangerous weapons of Soviet communism," cited "Lenin who said that to bring about revolution it is only necessary to debase the currency ... Inflation is today the Kremlin's strongest ally and unless we ... bring it under control we may be defeated by the Soviet Empire without being called upon to face in battle a single Russian soldier."[23] Social Credit leader Low characterized threats of inflation and Communism differently: "Canadians have much more to fear from dangers that lurk inside our country and our economy than any possible external enemy, including Bolshevik Russia."[24] CCF leader M.J. Coldwell demanded stricter price controls while the Conservatives and Social Credit opposed extending controls beyond what existing legislation permitted.

Finance minister Douglas Abbott proposed a lengthened workweek to battle inflation and shortages. The major labour unions rejected the idea, although the president of the Toronto District Labor Council was willing to entertain it, "If the employer was prepared to make an equal sacrifice by reducing profits or sharing profits with the workers."[25] Supportive of economic planning, Coldwell proposed that the government "call in representatives of organized labor and representatives of other interested groups in the community" to solicit their views about stabilizing wages.[26] In sharp contrast, Social Crediter Low contended that organized labour's demands were at the root of the inflation problem: "Organized labor, under leaders with no real vision, instead of keeping their eye on output, prices and purchasing value, have fought blindly for higher wages and reduced hours of work."[27]

Farm issues dogged the government. The opposition parties criticized the Liberals for a $65 million payment to farmers as partial compensation for a bad trade agreement negotiated with Britain that obliged farmers to sell "ridiculously cheap wheat," according to CCF MP Ross Thatcher. The compensation worked out to $25 for every income taxpayer in the country according to the Conservatives; to underline how bad the agreement with Britain was, the party said full compensation would have required $250 per taxpayer.[28] The Liberals defeated the CCF's perennial proposal to permit a voluntary revocable check-off of union dues by workers in federally regulated industries which, unlike some provinces, had no mandatory check-offs. Nevertheless, some Liberals, including a parliamentary assistant to a cabinet minister, all the Social Credit MPs, and all but two Conservatives voted in support of the proposal.[29]

The Conservatives supported free enterprise, but party leader Drew said they were not prepared to worship at its altar: "too often the name of free enterprise is repeated as though it contained some mysterious quality ... free enterprise will be preserved most efficiently if the people ... are convinced that no one has been able to take advantage of the desperate plight in which we find ourselves."[30] All three opposition parties opposed the federal sales tax increase in the budget but the Conservatives were the only party to oppose price-fixing legislation. To fund defence spending, the CCF and Social Credit proposed increasing corporate and excess profits taxes, although CCF MP Thatcher opined that corporate taxes had reached a saturation point.[31]

The welfare state continued to be a work in progress. The CCF in particular championed welfare issues at a time when less than half the population had a prepaid hospital insurance plan and growing numbers of seniors were being housed in mental hospitals because they had no other place to live.[32] After a constitutional amendment permitted the federal government to enter the field of old-age pensions, MPs voted unanimously for a universal contributory pension of forty dollars per month for all citizens over seventy years of age with the CCF arguing that forty dollars was too little. The government estimated that seven hundred thousand Canadians were eligible to receive the pension.[33] With old-age pensions accomplished, the government committed to setting up a parliamentary committee to study health insurance. However, the cabinet was divided: reform-minded ministers including Paul Martin and Brooke Claxton supported public health insurance while more conservative ministers C.D. Howe, Douglas Abbott, and Alphonse Fournier were sceptical.[34]

Against the backdrop of the Korean War, the Liberals introduced legislation giving the government sweeping emergency powers, subject to parliamentary approval, to compel labour, suppress the publication of maps and photographs, make regulations deemed advisable for security and defence, and to impose price, wage, and rent controls.[35] However, the Liberals refused to enact more price controls when pressed to do so by the CCF.

Legislation also amended the Indian Act, permitting Indigenous people to practice their customs and culture, wear ceremonial clothing off-reserve without permission of the Indian Agent, go to pool halls, gamble, and hire lawyers to defend their rights. Indigenous women were granted the vote in band council elections. Citizenship minister Walter Harris said it was a mistake to assume that Indigenous people wanted to be enfranchised; they preferred, he said, to retain their status as wards and allies of the King. The curriculum at residential schools consisted of a half-day of classroom study and a half-day of learning a trade. Boys were taught carpentry, blacksmithing, and auto mechanics while girls learned sewing, cooking, and other domestic skills.[36]

The Gallup poll found that nearly half of respondents continued to support the governing Liberals.[37] Nevertheless, Conservative hopes were buoyed after the party won all five by-elections held during the year, gaining three Liberal seats, two of which were in Manitoba. The results were a significant setback for the Liberals, who had held forty-one seats in western Canada against the seven held by the Conservatives when the year began. A by-election in Prince Edward Island was somewhat different because it was held in a dual-member riding after one of its MPs died. Dual-member ridings had been created so that the Liberals and Conservatives could field both a Protestant and a Catholic candidate in the same riding.

Parliamentary collegiality went hand in hand with partisan jousting. Two weeks after Drew praised St. Laurent at an event honouring him for his public service, he led the forty-six-member Conservative caucus, unsupported by the other opposition parties, to stage an unprecedented eight-hour battle in the Commons in what the *Globe and Mail* parliamentary reporter termed a "most fantastic day." Many angry words and name-calling marred the debate, which dealt with price-fixing. Liberal James Sinclair, parliamentary assistant to the finance minister, contributed to the debate by attacking the oligarchic origins of the Conservative party: "since the days of the Family Compact, [it] has been the historic friend of privilege, monopoly and reaction."[38]

The Young Liberal Federation resolved to replace the Red Ensign and its Union Jack with a distinctive national flag featuring a green maple leaf superimposed on ten blue stripes representing the provinces. With some Conservative MPs objecting, the Liberal government gradually began eliminating the term "Dominion," which some associated with Britain's primacy in law and usage; the Dominion Elections Act, for example, was retitled the Canada Elections Act.[39]

Intergovernmental Relations

Paul Martin outlined the old-age pension legislation Ottawa was proposing for seventy-year-olds at a federal-provincial meeting of welfare ministers and some premiers. Martin estimated it would cost $250 million and suggested that for those between sixty-five and sixty-nine years of age, Ottawa was willing to share the costs with the provinces on a fifty-fifty basis for means-tested pensions. Manitoba's Liberal-Progressive welfare minister rejected the idea while Ontario's Conservative minister, like the federal CCF, opposed any means test and went further, calling for the disabled to receive pensions regardless of age. Quebec premier Maurice Duplessis opposed that idea, and Martin dismissed it as too expensive.[40]

All the provinces except Ontario and Quebec had tax-rental agreements with Ottawa under which the federal government collected personal income and corporate taxes on behalf of the provinces and remitted lump sum payments to them based on formulas tied to the gross domestic product, estimated at $20 billion. The renewable five-year agreements were in place for another year, but the provinces pressed the federal government to increase provincial access to fiscal resources at every opportunity. Constitutionally limited to levying direct taxes, the provinces argued that there was an imbalance between their social policy responsibilities and their fiscal capacities. Some federal officials thought the income tax was so powerful a fiscal tool that it should be reserved exclusively for Ottawa.[41]

Keen on enhancing their taxation powers, some provinces advocated a constitutional amendment permitting them to levy an indirect sales tax of up to 3 per cent. Ottawa agreed, but media commentary, the business community, and the federal Conservatives roundly condemned the idea, depicting it as a concealed tax on a tax because it would be levied on the federal sales tax at the manufacturer's level. Critics noted the tax would add to the bookkeeping and operating costs of businesses, increase consumer prices at a time of high inflation, and exacerbate revenue differences between the poorer and richer provinces. All the provinces except Quebec agreed to constitutionalizing the provincial right to such a tax, but a number indicated they would not impose it. Duplessis's rejection led Saskatchewan premier T.C. Douglas to compare him to Andrey Vyshinsky, the Soviet foreign minister who regularly cast vetoes in the Security Council.[42] The proposed amendment went nowhere.

Following the lead of Saskatchewan, Ontario asked the federal government to fund housing construction. Queen's Park wanted to accommodate the growing number of workers in the defence industries and new immigrants, about half of whom were settling in Ontario. Premier Leslie Frost proposed that Ottawa pay 75 per cent of the cost as it was doing in Saskatchewan, whose government, in turn, asked municipalities to contribute half the provincial share.[43] Ottawa agreed to share the cost of constructing a rail and road causeway across the Strait of Canso to connect the Nova Scotia peninsula with Cape Breton Island.

The Provinces

Three provincial elections took place and all three resulted in the re-election of governing parties. Newfoundland Liberal premier Joey Smallwood had the House of Assembly dissolved even though his government had two years left in its mandate. He claimed an election was necessary to get a popular mandate to extend government loans to European and North American firms wishing to establish new industries in the province. Marred by irregularities including a badly outdated voters list and a meandering ballot box eventually found at Liberal party headquarters, the election resulted in virtually no change in seats or popular vote. Led by federal MP Gordon Higgins, the Conservatives admitted that they had no expectation of winning. When a cabinet minister resigned two weeks after the election because of a disagreement with Smallwood, the premier decided his Liberals would not contest the by-election, offering the odd rationale that it would be a "bitter affair if contested by both parties."[44]

The Prince Edward Island election results, like Newfoundland's, were also virtually unchanged from the previous election: the vote for the governing Liberals crept up by 1 per cent. For the first time in the province's history, a woman, a CCFer, stood as a candidate, losing badly. A peculiar feature of the electoral system was that a resident who owned property in every one of the fifteen constituencies was entitled to cast thirty votes, one for councillor (the "property vote") and another for assemblyman (the "franchise vote").[45] Despite high voter turnout, just 1,298 ballots were cast in one race for councillor; PEI, with all the trappings of a provincial government – a premier, legislature, and courts – was a "Big Engine, Little Body."[46]

The Conservatives easily won Ontario's election, significantly besting their 1948 performance. They captured nearly half the vote and scored the largest majority of seats in provincial history. Opposition leaders Liberal Walter Thomson and CCFer Ted Jolliffe suffered defeats in their own constituencies. Premier Frost criticized Saskatchewan premier Douglas for campaigning on behalf of the CCF as "bad taste" and "bad politics." With little organizational capacity, the CCF was humiliated, reduced from twenty-one to two seats in the ninety-two-seat legislature. The party's campaign manager was delusional about the party's prospects, predicting, "We appear to be making *more headway faster* than in 1948."[47] Although the Liberals also lost seats, they regained official opposition status.

Provincial and federal taxation were major issues in both Nova Scotia and New Brunswick. Liberal premier Angus Macdonald of Nova Scotia repeatedly criticized Liberal Ottawa's policies, claiming that centralization of policymaking in Ottawa worked against his province. He fired off telegrams to St. Laurent and Paul Martin, criticizing them for raising the income ceiling for pensioners between sixty-five and sixty-nine years of age, and charging that Ottawa was violating provincial autonomy. His government raised taxes on gasoline, long-distance telephone calls, theatres, and other amusements and slashed expenditures to compensate for not having a sales tax.[48] Despite New Brunswick's extremely unpopular sales tax of 4 per cent, the government was compelled to practice fiscal restraint because its bonds were proving hard to sell; the syndicate marketing the bonds conditioned continuing to do so only if the government employed their advisors.[49]

Quebec's Duplessis continued his relentless campaign against Communists and Jehovah's Witnesses. Meeting with newsprint manufacturers ostensibly to talk about their rising costs, he insisted on discussing the alleged circulation of communist propaganda among woodcutters. A Supreme Court ruling stayed a charge of seditious libel against a Jehovah's Witness member, and a Quebec Superior Court ruled that Duplessis had been personally responsible for intervening without cause in the case which became known as Roncarelli. Nevertheless Duplessis, acting as his own attorney general, instructed prosecutors to continue proceedings against other Jehovah's Witnesses.[50]

Citing data in *Cité Libre* compiled by future CBC president Pierre Juneau, *Le Devoir*'s associate editor-in-chief, André Laurendeau, raised an alarm about "the mortal danger" that American media posed to Quebec's culture: the urban French Canadian family was seeing from two to four American films a month and had "a passion for the comics, and the comics are almost all American imports." Laurendeau described the French edition of *Reader's Digest*, the most widely read digest in the province, as "another American concoction."[51]

Manitoba premier Douglas Campbell, originally elected as a United Farmers of Manitoba MLA in 1922, agreed with the Manitoba Farmers Protective Association for a plebiscite to test support among oats and barley producers for compulsory marketing of their crops by the Canadian Wheat Board. By a margin of nine to one, the farmers opted to stay with the Wheat Board.[52] Like Manitoba, Saskatchewan protested a federally approved 12 per cent increase in rail freight rates, which came on the heels of a 21 per cent hike in 1948 and a further 20 per cent in 1949.[53] There were however signs of rural economic diversification in both provinces: refining began of the first crude oil produced in Manitoba, and Saskatchewan appeared to have one of the world's largest sources of uranium.[54] Saskatchewan's government stood apart from all the other provinces in its focus on public health care; provincial hospital infrastructure was judged unparalleled in Canada.[55]

Alberta's oil riches permitted the popular, well-ensconced Social Credit government – holding a commanding fifty-one of the legislature's fifty-seven seats – to project increased spending by over 20 per cent. Simultaneously, the government planned to run a budgetary surplus, reduce taxes, and generously fund municipalities.[56] All the party leaders in the legislature harangued Independent Social Credit MLA Arthur Wray for having attended the Communist-backed World Peace Congress in Warsaw; senior cabinet minister A.J. Hooke described Wray as a "rank Communist" and for having attacked Canada's rearmament and participation in the Korean War.[57]

British Columbia's Liberal-Conservative coalition government of twenty-two Liberals and seventeen Conservatives was showing more signs of fraying. Vancouver Centre's coalition MLA criticized his government for its natural resources policies and not requiring corporations to manufacture more in the province. A second government MLA, Conservative Tillie Rolston, crossed the floor to join former

Conservative-turned-Independent W.A.C. Bennett in opposition. The president of the Liberal Association blamed his party's MLAs for "the dangerous state of party affairs," scorning the cabinet's "weak-kneed Liberals" for raising premiums and introducing unpopular co-insurance charges for the provincial hospital insurance program.[58]

Canada in the World

Cold War anxiety fuelled by the Korean War and the presence of Soviet troops in several Eastern Europe states pervaded public discourse. External affairs minister Lester Pearson pronounced that Western Europe stood "open to Soviet conquest" while the CBC's International Service launched Russian-language broadcasting directed at the Soviet Union.[59] More than a third of Canadians believed a Soviet attack on Canada was imminent, and more than half expected a world war within five years. Magazine articles screamed with titles such as "If the Russians Attack Canada" and "The Russian Subs on our Coastline."[60] In turn, the Soviet government's official newspaper *Izvestia* described "Canada's ruling elite [as] the most obedient agents of Wall Street." Terming Pearson "an emissary of the American State Department," *Izvestia* snarled that "Britain's biggest Dominion nowadays reminds one of an American state."[61]

Pearson, an internationalist who promoted Canada's attachment to the United Nations and to world order, lamented that the UN was not able to undertake all the tasks imposed on it. The CCF's Coldwell, who had been part of the Canadian delegation at the UN's founding convention in San Francisco, supported Pearson's internationalism. Blair Fraser of *Maclean's* speculated that Pearson was on the rise in St. Laurent's cabinet and "may be our next prime minister."[62]

Whole-heartedly committed to multilateralism, Canada was navigating its way in a new bipolar world. Ottawa, generally toeing the American position on international issues, did so with significant public support.[63] However, Canada occasionally contributed to moderating some US positions, such as a provocatively worded American resolution at the UN condemning Communist China for aggression. Canada also did not agree with Washington's position on barring trade with China. Indeed, future cabinet minister Judy LaMarsh told the Young Liberals, who debated whether Ottawa ought to recognize the Communist regime, that "if the Chinese people want a communist government, Canada should recognize it."[64]

Pearson supported de facto recognition of the Chinese government in Peking but deferred to the objection of the US: "The Far Eastern problems could be more readily solved if diplomatic relations existed with the government of China which has the whole of the mainland of China under its control," he noted, but "differences of opinion with our friends in Washington" kept Canada from doing so. As hostilities in Korea intensified, however, Ottawa's position shifted to opposing even de facto recognition of the Peking government or to discussing the future of Formosa (Taiwan) so long as Chinese forces were fighting UN forces.[65]

Canada had committed to the UN effort in the Korean War in 1950 but Canadian troops were not battle-ready until well into 1951. To speed their readiness, the commanding general of US field forces invited Canadian soldiers to participate in American military manoeuvres and army schools. He also offered to help Canada transition from British to American military equipment.[66] In reporting from Korea, journalist Pierre Berton wrote of the superior astuteness of Canadians compared to Americans in some matters of warfare: "some sixty bodies of American Negro troops [were] slaughtered in their sleeping bags in a surprise attack [while Canada's] men sleep with their boots on … because they believe a man in a sleeping bag is too vulnerable to surprise attack."[67]

Canada continued its economic, military, cultural, and political pivot away from Britain and toward the United States. Many Canadian automobile dealerships were selling British-built Consul and Austin automobiles, but Britain, still in debt to Ottawa for a $700 million loan made in 1942, was no economic powerhouse.[68] Although Canada was increasingly in the orbit of the United States, it maintained intimate military and other links to Britain: anti-submarine exercises, for example, were scheduled with the British navy (but then cancelled on account of the Korean War requirements). And when Canadian troops advanced into North Korea in April and July, they did so as part of the First (Commonwealth) Division of the UN force along with troops from the United Kingdom, Australia, New Zealand, and India.[69]

St. Laurent described the Commonwealth as a precious instrument of international cooperation, but he differed with British prime minister Clement Attlee over how highly structured it should be and whether members should adopt a common policy whenever possible. At the ten-day Commonwealth heads of government meeting in London, St. Laurent, the only Roman Catholic in the group and "a man of Gallic ancestry cloaked in an appearance of Edwardian reserve," supported establishing some machinery for economic cooperation among member states, but to avoid a confrontation between the Indian and

Pakistani prime ministers, he agreed with others that the Kashmir issue not be raised.[70]

Canada dispatched army and air force personnel to Europe as part of its NATO obligations. Canadian delegates to NATO claimed that "Canada's role and contribution are never questioned, never criticized. Everybody, they vow, is happy about the way Canada is pulling her weight." However, some American officials differed: "We've got ten times as many people as Canada and fifteen times as much income. How come we've got thirty-seven times as many soldiers?"[71] To bolster their overall capacity, the navy, army, and air force reopened enrolment to women, but restricted them to roles in medicine, communications, logistics, and administration.

Ottawa was not expecting any large defence orders from the United States or Europe and considered its own security requirements small relative to the cost of production: "We must think in terms of, say, vehicle production of about five a day," said minister of defence production C.D. Howe, "rather than the hundreds a day we produced" during the Second World War.[72] Nevertheless, Ottawa committed to spending about $5 billion on defence production, mainly for aircraft, radar, and electronics. Some guns and ammunition produced were to equip divisions of the Italian, Belgian, Netherlands, and Luxembourg armed forces.

A major bilateral irritant with the US was the St. Lawrence Seaway project. Canada wanted to proceed, but the US hesitated to ratify the Seaway agreement made in 1941. The public embraced the idea of an all-Canadian project, but the government was determined to have the Americans participate. Howe, the main interlocutor with the Americans on the Seaway, told a Washington audience that because of the need to ease power shortages in the Quebec and Ontario manufacturing sectors, Canada would finance the Seaway on its own if American vacillation continued. He goaded the Americans to contribute to the project by saying Ottawa would toll ships carrying American-owned Labrador iron to Great Lakes mills to help offset the cost.[73]

The government was eager to conclude a peace treaty with Japan and it gave hunger-stricken India $10 million in wheat. The gift was part of a program in conjunction with other Commonwealth members intended to strengthen Asian states against the growth of Communist movements. Canada and India, however, did not agree on some major issues: prime minister Jawaharlal Nehru firmly opposed ordering UN troops across the thirty-eighth parallel into North Korea.[74] Unlike Asia and Europe – Ottawa resumed normal peacetime relations with West Germany[75] – Africa and Latin America did not figure much in Canadian diplomacy or in the consciousness of Canadians.

St. Laurent did not shy away from foreign entanglements and broke with Mackenzie King's low estimation of the UN. Still basking in the afterglow of victory in the Second World War, Canadians were at war again on Korean battlefields, but the economic impact and the cost in men, material, and money were substantially less. With the Red Scare shaping both policy and public opinion, St. Laurent lauded American leadership in the battle against "totalitarian communism."[76]

Inflation raged, people of British ancestry still sat atop Canada's ethnic pecking order, and intermarriage accelerated among members of religious and ethnic groups. As organized labour vied with organized farmers for the government's attention, agricultural interests, over-represented in Parliament, continued to command more sustained consideration.

After voting unanimously for old-age pensions for which hundreds of thousands would be eligible, Parliament turned to consider expanding the welfare state in the health sector, but the government was divided on the issue. Unlike the easy agreement on the constitutional amendment that facilitated universal old-age pension legislation, intergovernmental negotiations did not lead to an agreement on a proposed amendment that would have aided provinces in narrowing the gap between their social policy responsibilities and their fiscal resources. Federal by-election losses by the Liberals on the prairies hinted at potentially greater losses by the party. Governing parties were easily re-elected in Newfoundland, Prince Edward Island, and Ontario. In British Columbia, a Liberal-Conservative coalition government continued to show signs of falling apart. Canada continued to turn away from Britain and toward the United States, although Canadian troops in Korea were part of the First (Commonwealth) Division of the UN force. Prime minister St. Laurent praised American leadership on the world stage.

1952

It appears that former Prime Minister Sir Wilfrid Laurier was just about fifty years premature when he prophesied at the beginning of this century: "The Twentieth Century is Canada's."[1]

New York Times

The shift of Canada's population and wealth from east to west continued unabated. The percentage of Canadians living in Quebec and the Maritime provinces fell while the population of British Columbia grew most rapidly. People from the prairie provinces were moving to British Columbia as the agricultural economy, though healthy, was declining, and corporate agribusiness was displacing family farms. Labour shortages abounded but the federal government, concerned with absorbing the post-war immigrants who had already arrived, was reluctant to raise immigration levels.

Parliament passed the first new immigration act since 1910, largely codifying existing practices and not departing significantly from standing legislation. However, new restrictions prohibited homosexuals, drug addicts, and drug traffickers from entering the country.[2] The population grew significantly as, in addition to immigration, there were more than three live births for every death. The birth rate hit a peak of over nineteen per thousand people. Historically, Quebec almost always had the highest birth rate but the Newfoundland and New Brunswick rates, at thirty-four and thirty-two respectively per thousand, surpassed the Quebec rate.[3]

The *New York Times* likened Canada's booming economy to a giant awakening and stretching. The Reserve Bank of New York pronounced that the country stood on the threshold of a new era of economic growth. American corporate executives applauded Ottawa's openness to free enterprise and foreign investment. The federal government, one of the few national governments running a budgetary surplus, was paying down its debt, and the dollar was trading at a premium to the American dollar. Canada was the world's second largest aluminum producer, Ontario's aircraft and automobile industries were flourishing, and every major oil company in the world was drilling in the western provinces. Construction began on the Trans Mountain pipeline to take Alberta oil to tidewater on the Pacific. With three of every five United States newspaper pages printed on Canadian newsprint, the pulp and paper industry ranked first in the value of exports and production, wages paid, and capital invested.[4]

Liberal partisans could boast that 1952 saw the greatest-ever expansion in the economy.[5] The Korean War produced shortages, but it also contributed to the iron and steel fabricating industries recalling laid-off workers. Employment in the tobacco, textile, and furniture industries, however, continued to suffer.[6] To keep more accurate track of the cost of living – inflation had been 11 per cent a year earlier – the Dominion Bureau of Statistics broadened the scope of the index it had been using, renamed it the Consumer Price Index, and publicized it for the first time. The inflation rate for the year fell to less than 3 per cent.[7]

Signalling Canada's changing relationship to Britain, prime minister Louis St. Laurent announced that Vincent Massey would become the first Canadian-born governor general. St. Laurent defended the selection by noting that Canada was the only Commonwealth member besides Ceylon that had not had a governor general ordinarily resident in the country. Some Canadians, however, opposed the selection of Massey, the first governor general to hold the office without a title and the first to have served as a cabinet minister. Conservative leader George Drew regretted that Parliament had not been consulted, declaring, "We are not a party which holds the sceptre of the British Commonwealth as though it burnt our fingers." Massey's appointment was major news, but newspaper editors rated the death of King George VI, within days of the appointment, as the most important story of the year.[8]

In conjunction with his announcement of Massey's appointment, St. Laurent defended replacing the term "Dominion" in statutes as they came up for revision. However, he recognized there was "uneasiness" among some Canadians because they might see it as a desire to weaken links "between the free peoples of the Commonwealth of British Nations." To further avoid controversy, he noted that one of his Liberal backbenchers had withdrawn his private member's bill to change the name of Dominion Day to Confederation Day. Drew retorted that dropping the term Dominion amounted to tampering with the constitution: "To every Canadian who respects the constitution that must remain the name unless it is changed by such procedure as is provided in the constitution itself."[9]

The federal government asserted Canada's cultural independence by mandating CBC television to produce Canadian programs. It also guaranteed the CBC a monopoly on television broadcasting in the major cities, frustrating private radio owners with ambitions to launch their own television stations in the largest markets. Limiting them to owning stations only in smaller centres, they argued, was uneconomic for them, but federal policymakers were concerned that private broadcasters would carry only American programming. CBC's monopoly in the larger markets led a former Conservative MP to compare corporation president Davidson Dunton to Stalin.[10]

With the average weekly wage for a typical worker about $55 ($570 in 2021), television sets sold for between $240 and $430. Thousands of households had been watching American programs beamed from the US when the CBC launched its first television station in Montreal; the first day's programming showed an English film, followed by a cartoon, a French film, a news review, and a bilingual variety show. Two days later, Toronto CBC television, broadcasting four hours a day, debuted with a slide of the CBC logo upside down, a three-puppet sketch, a live performance by Glen Gould, and twenty-five-year-old Norman Jewison as a floor director. The *Globe and Mail* judged the programming, which featured numerous speeches, including ones by the CBC president and St. Laurent, as "cluttered but promising."[11]

The escape of Toronto's most infamous gangsters, the Boyd Gang, was CBC's very first televised news story. The four gang members captured the imagination of the public after they escaped the Don Jail for the second time in less than a year. After the province, the city, and the Canadian Bankers Association offered a $26,000 reward, the gang was captured. The city mayor and the provincial minister of reform institutions visited gang leader Edwin Boyd in his cell. "A year from now," he blustered, he would break out of the Kingston penitentiary.[12]

CBC's radio broadcasts, which included talks by luminaries such as Bertrand Russell and Anna Freud, irked many listeners including some MPs. The Catholic Action Committee of the Montreal diocese asked the corporation to "stop these broadcasts or at least ... have the scripts checked by some responsible person in order that views contrary to our Catholic views not be discussed." The *United Church Observer* wanted church spokesmen to have the opportunity to "answer" the speakers point by point in real time, a broadcasting impracticality.[13]

All the major religious denominations gained members. The abrasive
T.T. Shields, who had once led Canada's largest Baptist congregation,
was the country's most militant and celebrated Christian fundamen-
talist. He was still using his Toronto pulpit to fulminate against French
Canadian popery, his passionate decades-long opposition to Quebec's
Catholic sentiments undiminished.[14] In Quebec, however, the compo-
sition of the Catholic clergy was changing. More of them now hailed
from urban families, and many shifted to supporting the now more independent and vigorously militant trade unionism of the Confédéra-
tion des travailleurs catholiques du Canada, which the Church had
originally sponsored as a conservative bulwark against the radical unionism of "the alien, godless" unions of the American Federation of
Labor and the Congress of Industrial Organizations.[15]

With Canadians fighting in Korea, the Red Army occupying Eastern
Europe, and the Communist regime in China further entrenched, international communism continued to concern the government, the media,
and the public. *Maclean's* magazine identified former United Church
missionary James Endicott as "a favorite instrument and spokesman
for that sworn enemy of both God and his country, the Communist
Party." First-hand accounts reinforced anti-communist sentiments: a
Canadian medical missionary reported being "grilled, browbeaten and
threatened by Communist officials ... forced to kneel before a large
portrait of Mao Tse-tung, China's little Stalin, while a frenzied rabble
shouted taunts and accusations against me," during his eight months
of solitary confinement.[16] After waving aside an earlier Conservative
party proposal to outlaw the activities of Communists, the Liberal government introduced a revised law making it illegal to conspire with the
agent of another state.[17]

The "Petawawa scandal," exposing ill-discipline and irregularities
constituting more than mere misdemeanours, was an embarrassing
contretemps for the army and the government. Among lapses uncovered by military authorities and the RCMP, army officers had stolen
and sold eighteen thousand bags of cement, numerous steel rails, and
tons of scrap metal to private contractors. In addition, the names of
several horses appeared on the army's payroll, and one soldier had
built a summer cabin using army materials and army labour. A scathing
independent report revealing extravagance, lax accounting, and graft
concluded that dozens of army regulations had been honoured more in
the breach than in the observance. The opposition parties then revealed
that the government had altered the report before its release to Parliament, damaging the reputation of defence minister Brooke Claxton and
leading to calls for his resignation.[18]

Federal Politics

St. Laurent and the Liberals boasted about their accomplishments. A flashy forty-three-page party publication, *The Liberal*, cited the appointment of a Canadian-born governor general, Newfoundland's entry into Confederation, the abolition of legal appeals to Britain's Privy Council, federal aid to universities, the universal old-age pension, and a constitutional amendment permitting Ottawa to amend the constitution in federal government matters. *The Liberal* also referred to the initiation of construction of the Trans-Canada Highway, the building of a third of a million new homes, a 40 per cent rise in national and personal incomes, and a revamped foreign policy.[19]

Conservative leader Drew charged the Liberals with adopting "the laissez-faire doctrine [of the] Manchester school of thought," and stated that it was not the philosophy of his own party.[20] Nevertheless, like a classical liberal, Drew regularly blamed the Liberal government for overspending and overtaxing. Some Anglophiles remarked that while St. Laurent was keen in his speeches to talk positively about the Commonwealth and the Crown, he was hesitant to "utter the words Britain, British, England, Empire."[21]

Some party members noted Drew's habit of referring to the Conservative rather than Progressive Conservative party, the label the party had adopted in 1942. Defending himself, he said 'Conservative' was convenient and historically accurate, that "Our principles – the principles upon which our forefathers reared this nation – are unchanged and enduring."[22] Drew used five words beginning with "c" to describe those "unchanging principles" of his party: country, Crown, Commonwealth, Constitution, and the Commons. He argued "not a single word" of the Constitution ought to be changed without unanimous provincial agreement and that Parliament needed to be able to exert more control over public business. He also said that the aged, sick, and disabled deserve to be treated with decency and justice.

If the Conservatives were mainly oriented to the past, the CCF and Social Credit parties were oriented to the future. Minor parties with quite different public policy agendas, they spent more time proposing what the government ought to be doing than did the Conservatives who, as official opposition, spent most of their time criticizing the Liberals for what they had done or were doing. CCF leader M.J. Coldwell delivered speeches stressing that health insurance must be a priority; his amendment to the Speech from the Throne expressed regret "that Your Excellency's advisers have failed to recommend the inauguration of a national health insurance program, with provision for provincial participation."[23]

Soon after the death of Major C.H. Douglas, the formulator of Social Credit theory, former Social Credit MP Orvis Kennedy, a party founder and perennial federal candidate, declared his party was still firmly committed to Douglas's ideas but that the Alberta provincial party had not implemented them because the courts had ruled monetary policy a federal matter. Previously, Douglas had disowned his Canadian acolytes, mystified by their particularly bizarre marriage of Christian fundamentalism and monetary reform.[24] One point of monetary policy on which the Conservatives and Social Credit agreed was that a convertible British pound, or sterling, would contribute to the development of world trade.[25]

Major Douglas's anti-Semitism had attracted some Social Crediters, and in a stirring parliamentary debate, Coldwell quoted a radio broadcast by party leader Solon Low to demonstrate his anti-Semitic beliefs. Low defended his linkage of "international communism," "international finance," and "international political Zionism" because all three "were determined to destroy Britain's strength and to achieve their aims by revolutionary methods." To support his contention, he cited their common determination to end Britain's mandate in Palestine.[26]

The youth wings of the three major parties articulated something of the thinking of their parties at a public discussion of the Universal Declaration of Human Rights. To an audience described by the *Globe and Mail* as having many "colored" in attendance, the Conservatives said, "Progress should be keyed to human values." The individual most concerned the young Liberals: "Our party believes in the development of the complete individual." To the CCFers, "Social progress is ineffectual unless rights are upheld." In an intense debate about Article 18 of the Declaration, the right to leave and return to one's country, the Conservatives attacked the power of the immigration minister to exclude certain immigrant groups, while the Liberals defended the policy on the grounds that without that power, labour problems as well as conflict among racial and religious groups would proliferate. The public, said a young Liberal spokesperson, was simply not ready for such a change: "The Liberal government agrees that racial discrimination exists within Canada, but we must be content with imperfection until we persuade the mass of Canadians that the government must revise its thinking on the matter."[27]

Racial discrimination and immigration attracted only fleeting attention in Parliament. Liberal David Croll attacked South Africa's apartheid policies but received no support from his Liberal colleagues. Conservative John Diefenbaker called, as he had often done in past sessions, for a Canadian bill of rights guaranteeing liberties such as freedom of religion and speech. As a preliminary, he suggested Ottawa ask the Supreme Court in a reference case whether such freedoms would fall under federal or provincial jurisdiction. George Drew cited a *Maclean's* story alleging that corrupt officials and unscrupulous travel agencies were extorting thousands of dollars to smuggle Italian immigrants into Canada.[28]

In eight by-elections, six of which were held on one day in May, the Liberals and Conservatives won four each. The Conservatives gained three seats, one in each of New Brunswick, Ontario, and Quebec. By mid-year Conservative representation in Parliament grew to 49 MPs from 41 a year earlier while Liberal representation shrank from 193 to 185. Despite the Conservative gains, however, a Gallup Poll a month earlier had found 48 per cent of respondents said they would vote Liberal in a general election, a decline of less than 2 per cent from the 1949 election. Brooke Claxton attributed the by-election losses to his party's long hold on power, high taxes, and the public's sense that the Liberals had become remote and lacked a substantive statement of party policy. Thinking that St. Laurent was the party's major asset, Liberal strategists became concerned that if he did not run again – he had not committed to doing so – the party would lose the election expected in 1953.[29]

St. Laurent turned seventy and began collecting the universal monthly old-age pension of forty dollars. Parliament voted to provide MPs with a separate pension despite adverse public opinion; one long-time Liberal wrote to St. Laurent that he "will never vote Liberal again. You in Ottawa are turning people communistic."[30] Parliament also turned to redistributing the seats in the House of Commons based on the 1951 census. Drew accused the Liberals of "gerrymandering" and Coldwell called the proposed distribution of Saskatchewan's seats an "abomination." In the end the House, rejecting Drew's proposal to establish an independent redistribution commission, adopted the proposals of a Liberal-dominated parliamentary committee. The Conservatives, unlike the other parties, insisted that the provinces be consulted before any changes were made to their representation.[31]

With the Korean War still raging, St. Laurent urged young Canadians to enlist. In the western provinces, he told audiences that building up Canada's defence forces and maintaining prosperity required high taxes. Finance minister Douglas Abbott said the same thing to an eastern audience. When a parliamentary committee examining defence expenditures discovered that the military had purchased bayonets for $130,000 and some members opined that the weapon was obsolete, deputy defence minister Brigadier General C.M. Drury, a future minister of defence production, argued that the bayonet had been effective in Korea; he claimed that most soldiers thought of it as a psychological rather than a physical weapon.[32]

Individual petitioners from Quebec and Newfoundland consumed much of Parliament's time because those provinces did not provide for their courts to hear divorce cases. Acting in its capacity as a court, Parliament disposed of about 300 hundred cases. The procedure entailed a private member's bill being introduced in the Senate and, after a Senate committee considered the merits of the case and approved of it, the Senate and the House would pass the bill. The CCF repeatedly tried to have the federal Exchequer Court handle the cases, but St. Laurent's government hesitated to change the procedure. They feared alienating public sentiment in Quebec, which opposed divorce, and may have thought the Exchequer Court would open the floodgates to divorce cases from the province.[33]

Intergovernmental Relations

The major issue in federal-provincial relations during the year, "when federal authority seems to have reached a modern peak,"[34] was the renewal of the five-year tax-rental agreements that had originated in 1942. As a temporary measure, the provinces had surrendered the collection of personal and corporate taxes as well as succession duties, and in return they received federal funds tied to a formula based on their population and the gross domestic product. All the provinces except Ontario and Quebec had renewed the agreements in 1947. Eager to benefit from a modified formula favourable to it, Ontario signed on to a new agreement. Premier Leslie Frost had initially hesitated isolating Quebec after what had been a Quebec-Ontario common front against the agreements. Ontario, however, had lost out by not signing on to an agreement in 1947: Queen's Park would have received $341 million from Ottawa but collected only $318 million on its own. Experts predicted a loss of $40 million if Ontario were to reject the new federal proposal.[35]

Having rejected a tax-rental agreement when he had been Ontario's premier in 1947, it was not easy for George Drew to reject one that his Conservative successor, Frost, had accepted. Nevertheless, Drew did, demanding the restoration of provincial taxation and arguing the "constitution is being threatened by [federal] taxation which leaves provincial governments without the financial resources to meet their constitutional obligations." Although the provinces were responsible for costly social programs, they collected only twelve cents of every tax dollar compared to seventy-two cents by Ottawa and sixteen cents by municipalities. The federal Liberals defended the tax-rental agreements as essential for the redistribution of wealth among the provinces. The

Atlantic provinces were too dependent on the federal funds they received via the tax-rental agreements to spurn them.[36]

Consistent with the Massey Commission's recommendation, Ottawa introduced grants to universities amounting to fifty cents per capita of the population of each province. The money was distributed to universities in proportion to their enrolment. However, Quebec premier Maurice Duplessis instructed his province's universities to refuse the grants because, in his opinion, they trespassed on Quebec's constitutional rights. Quebec preferred losing financial assistance to losing autonomy in taxation. Repeatedly calling for more fiscal independence of Ottawa, Duplessis argued that those spending the money should have the unrestricted power to raise it. He also repeatedly called for including the voices of provincial governments in the selection of Supreme Court justices.[37]

For Manitoba and Saskatchewan, agricultural issues figured in relations with Ottawa while for Nova Scotia, it was infrastructure. Manitoba and Ottawa agreed to jointly fund agricultural research, with the provincial government paying for an addition to the University of Manitoba. Saskatchewan wanted federal relief for flood victims and farmers who had suffered a bad harvest. Regina called on Ottawa to act on the commitment it had made to the South Saskatchewan River dam project. The province also pressed Ottawa to be proactive on health policy; if the federal government did not pursue a public hospital insurance program, said CCF premier T.C. Douglas, his government would extend its own program. In Nova Scotia, joint funding with the federal government allowed tenders to finally go out for the construction of the long-discussed Canso Causeway that would link industrial Cape Breton Island with the mainland.[38]

In the far west, the Alberta government conducted secret negotiations with Ottawa and Ontario during Alberta's provincial election. Alberta was eager to push forward the proposed natural gas project by Trans-Canada Pipelines to serve the Ontario and Quebec markets.[39] In British Columbia, Liberal premier Byron Johnson dismissed his finance minister, Conservative leader Herbert Anscomb, for prematurely revealing the tax-rental terms Ottawa had offered.[40]

The Provinces

Five provincial elections were held during the year. Three governments were re-elected and two new premiers, New Brunswick Conservative Hugh John Flemming and British Columbia Social Crediter W.A.C. Bennett, took office. The election of Flemming, son of a former premier, reflected perhaps his province's traditional political culture; Bennett, formerly a Conservative MLA, was a hardware merchant, a reflection of his province's parvenu political culture.[41] Bennett presciently predicted before the election that the Liberals would lose and "won't come back [to power] for fifty years."[42] They did forty-nine years later.

B.C.'s election, unusual in its method of voting, was surprising in its results. The coalition government of Liberals and Conservatives collapsed with the Conservatives demanding an immediate election, a demand echoed by the CCF.[43] Seeking to foil the CCF, which had won 35 per cent of the vote in the previous election and had been within striking distance of victory, the Liberal government jettisoned the first past-the-post system of voting and introduced a preferential or alternative ballot. The Liberals calculated that Liberal and Conservative voters would opt for candidates of each other's party as their second choice, preventing CCF victories in constituencies where no candidate secured an outright majority vote. However, many voters selected candidates of a new maverick party, Social Credit, as their second choice. Social Credit triumphed, defeating the CCF by one seat, with the Liberals and Conservatives running a distant third and fourth, respectively. Tillie Rolston became the first woman in Canada to hold a cabinet portfolio. One defeated Liberal cabinet minister suggested a four party round table act as another coalition government, but CCF leader Harold Winch shrugged off the idea: "We're a socialist party; we intend to work only for a socialist program."[44]

Montreal's two English newspapers and the English-speaking business community supported Duplessis's Union Nationale in the Quebec election. Duplessis argued that Quebec needed a government free of all ties with federal parties, a slap at the opposition provincial Liberals.[45] He received a boost and was delighted when Laval University conferred an honorary degree on him in the midst of the campaign for "services in the advancement of the French culture and language."[46] English as well as French-speaking voters opted for the UN, which won 50 per cent of the vote and sixty-eight of the ninety-two seats.

New Brunswick's Conservatives prevailed in a landslide that even their most optimistic partisans did not anticipate. They leapfrogged the Liberals, who had governed for seventeen uninterrupted years, to win thirty-six of the fifty-two seats, an impressive gain after having won only five seats in the previous election. Some ridings had multiple seats so that, by convention, both Catholics and Protestants would be elected. The Liberal government tried to make a campaign issue of their refusal to recognize an international union as the bargaining agent for workers at the government-owned Electric Power Commission; they argued that Americans would be directing the union. However, the issue did not resonate with the public and the election results were widely interpreted as a protest vote against the high taxation policies of both the provincial and federal Liberal governments. Premier John McNair, whose Liberals had introduced a 4 per cent tax to pay for social security programs two years earlier, was defeated in his own riding.[47]

In Saskatchewan, the CCF gained 54 per cent of the vote, its highest-ever percentage, while the Liberals were reduced to eleven seats in the fifty-three-seat legislature. Led by future federal minister Alvin Hamilton, the Conservatives fielded only eight candidates and garnered less than 2 per cent of the vote. The results undermined Seymour Martin Lipset's thesis of *Agrarian Socialism*, a book published two years earlier; although Saskatchewan's four largest cities – Regina, Saskatoon, Moose Jaw, and Prince Albert – constituted only 19 per cent of the population, the CCF's urban votes exceeded its rural votes.[48]

Alberta's election produced another crushing Social Credit majority: the party captured 56 per cent of the popular vote, wining fifty-three of the sixty-one seats. A major issue was the construction of the natural gas pipeline to Ontario and Quebec, which both the CCF and the Liberals opposed.[49] The Liberals, with over a fifth of the vote and three seats, displaced the CCF, with two seats, as the official opposition. A reason the Liberal vote increased was that party leader J. Harper Prowse successfully put the government on the defensive, arguing that its healthy balance sheet was a by-product of burdening municipalities. Municipal debt in Alberta had almost tripled since the war while municipal debt nationally had increased by just 2 per cent.[50]

In contrast to the large number of provincial general elections, there were only six provincial by-elections in the country during the year. In Newfoundland, a by-election was called after a series of court battles concluded with a ruling that election officials had improperly marked some ballots.[51] Another Newfoundland by-election returned a Conservative, upping the party's representation from five to six in the twenty-eight-member House of Assembly. In Manitoba, the governing Liberal-Progressives retained one seat, but lost Brandon to the Conservatives. The result paralleled the Liberal federal by-election loss of Brandon to the Conservatives a year earlier. The two British Columbia by-elections were the result of two rookie Social Credit MLAs resigning. Two other rookies replaced them.

Financial and taxation issues were top-of-mind for the political class in economically lagging Atlantic Canada. Newfoundland premier Joey Smallwood confidently predicted that a syndicate headed by a descendant banking firm of the House of Rothschild would open an office to pursue real estate investment possibilities. PEI premier Walter Jones suggested that Islanders would support whichever federal party promised more financial aid for his province, where the average wage was about half of what it was in British Columbia and Ontario.[52]

Labour strife was at the forefront of Quebec politics. After shootings, rioting, and mass arrests marked a nine-month strike by workers in Louiseville, some two thousand workers with just one dissenter at a meeting in Shawinigan Falls voted in favour of a province-wide strike organized by the Canadian Catholic Confederation of Labour (CCCL). Police had acted as de facto agents for the struck company, reading the workers the riot act, imposing a form of martial law, and using tear gas and machine guns in what the CCCL's general secretary, Jean Marchand, a future federal Liberal minister, termed "legalized gangsterism." In solidarity, the mostly English Canadian Congress of Labor endorsed the strike.[53]

In Ontario, Premier Frost appeared to be grooming John Robarts to be his successor, designating him to move adoption of the Speech from the Throne, an honour usually reserved for a favoured son of the governing party.[54] Describing provincial universities as "not only the centre of things cultural, but … also the main spring of scientific and health research which is fundamental to Ontario's progress and betterment," Frost announced in the budget debate that they would receive special capital grants and larger operating funds.[55] New federal grants to universities and a provincial government surplus contributed to the emergence of Carleton University, which had been a non-denominational evening college serving military veterans.

Overall, it was not a good year for provincial or federal Liberals. Provincial Liberal parties lost their hold on British Columbia and New Brunswick, and they proved unable to undo governments in Quebec, Alberta, and Saskatchewan after having been badly beaten in Ontario a year earlier. Federally, the Liberals had lost eight straight by-elections.

Canada in the World

Changes in the Department of External Affairs evidenced Canada's growing role in world affairs. The creation of new posts accelerated: a permanent mission to NATO, a chargé d'affaires in Helsinki, a consulate in New Orleans. Consistent with a policy of exploring trade opportunities in smaller countries, a trade commission office was established in the Dominican Republic for West Indian states not members of the Commonwealth. The department also created a division to meet the material and technical needs of expanding representation abroad and a security unit to protect classified material at foreign posts. It purchased cyber equipment for the secure transmission of cable traffic, and a member of the department was assigned to provide guidance to the CBC's International Service. Ottawa recognized the governments of Vietnam, Laos, and Cambodia and began paying attention to the Middle East, a region it had thus far largely ignored.[56]

Fifty-five-year-old Lester Pearson became Canada's towering figure on the international stage. With lukewarm support from the Americans, opposition by the Soviets, and abstentions by the Arab states, he was elected president of the United Nations General Assembly with the votes of fifty-one of the sixty members.[57] Even before his election, he was being mentioned as a candidate for the Nobel Peace Prize and had been offered the job of NATO's first secretary general; he called it "the biggest job in the world at the moment" but turned it down.[58] St. Laurent hinted that Pearson should succeed him. Of course, when they differed on policy, the prime minister prevailed: Pearson, for example, supported France's request that Canada transfer military equipment to Indo-China under NATO's mutual aid program, but St. Laurent vetoed the idea.[59]

Pearson chaired a NATO meeting in Lisbon which made the unrealistic commitment to field fifty military divisions in Europe by year's end and have ninety to one hundred divisions there by 1954. After the CCF criticized the decision as "irresponsible and disastrous," Pearson retorted that the CCF's position seemed like the Kremlin's view that NATO was an aggressive military alliance. Coldwell termed that retort slanderous, a smear worthy of the rabidly anti-communist American Senator Joe McCarthy.[60] However, Pearson sympathized with the CCF's criticism of NATO that it overvalued its military aspect while downplaying the transatlantic values envisaged in Article 2 of the NATO treaty. Indeed, Pearson spoke of the "spiritual importance of the [North Atlantic] Community," but his audience at the Canadian Institute of International Affairs said that sounded like a reassertion of "the right of Western European nations and their descendants across the Atlantic to run the world in the old 'white man's burden' manner."[61] Knowing that the Americans would not brook it, Pearson hesitated to make the case to them that NATO could be more than a military alliance. He spent time and effort mediating between the United States and India over the Korean issue, but US Secretary of State Dean Acheson saw him not so much as a mediator as a camp follower of the Indians, accusing him later of "sophistries" and a lack of candour.[62]

Economic, defence, and infrastructure issues dominated Canadian-American relations. In violation of the General Agreement on Tariffs and Trade, Congress imposed import quotas on foreign dairy products. Ottawa in turn devised plans for extensive restrictions on American farm imports. One government official said the intention was "to teach the American farm bloc a lesson." However, Ottawa did not follow through on the restrictions.[63] Canada coordinated with Washington and other allies to impose domestic travel curbs on Soviet diplomats after the Soviets had placed similar restrictions on Canadian and other western diplomats based in Moscow.[64] Canada also participated in the largest-ever coordinated air manoeuvres with the US.[65] Demonstrating that they had not been bluffing a year earlier when they had threatened to do so, the government committed to building the twenty-seven-foot deep St. Lawrence Seaway without the US but left the door ajar for American participation.[66]

Months after British prime minister Winston Churchill said in Ottawa that Britain would not seek financial or economic assistance from Canada, an urgent Commonwealth economic conference convened in London to consider the decline and potential collapse of British sterling. All the member states except Canada used the currency. Urging the British to put their economic houses in order, the Canadians thought their strong financial and economic position gave them a certain credibility that the British lacked. Finance minister Douglas Abbott privately thought Britain's problems were largely of her own making – too many subsidies – but he also thought it ungracious of wealthy Canada to read the poor, hard-pressed British a moral lesson. Canada pushed for freer trade and agreed with a proposal to establish a permanent Commonwealth secretariat, but it did not come to realization until 1965.[67]

Canada continued calling for a negotiated settlement to the Korean War as her armed forces doubled, growing from forty-seven thousand personnel before the war began to more than ninety-five thousand. The defence department's budget increased by 23 per cent in the year.[68] Despite her military engagement in Korea, Canada did not consider the Far East economically or culturally significant. Less than 5 per cent of Canada's exports went to Asia, and Asian-Canadians accounted for just one-half of 1 per cent of the population.

Soon after the US ratified a peace treaty with Japan, Parliament followed suit and a Japanese diplomatic envoy arrived. The Conservatives used the resumption of ties with Japan to restate their support for a Pacific Pact along the lines of NATO, but Pearson rejected the idea. The CCF and Social Credit qualified their support for the Japanese peace treaty; Coldwell's concern was that it lacked the backing of Japan's Asian neighbours, India, Burma, and China; Social Credit leader Solon Low suggested American policies had been at least partly responsible for the war and opined that some of the treaty's provisions were "punitive."[69]

An unresolved issue was Germany's pre–Second World War debt: Canada hoped to collect $400 million from the West German government. Parliament approved extending NATO's security provisions to West Germany and the government stationed a brigade there. In addition, air wings were stationed in both England and France.[70]

Canada's booming economy was the envy of the world; the industrial economies of central Canada and the resource economies of western Canada and northern Quebec were thriving. The Atlantic region, however, continued to lag economically and demographically. The federal government ran a surplus and vanquished rampant inflation. With the introduction of television, the world of broadcasting changed. Religious affiliation among Canadians grew but some religious authorities felt threatened by some of CBC's radio broadcasts. As conservatives and Conservatives protested, Louis St. Laurent's Liberal government replaced some symbols of Canada's British heritage.

The Liberals boasted of their accomplishments, the Conservatives criticized the government for overtaxing and overspending, and the CCF carried the brief for a national health insurance scheme. Social Credit spoke of revamping the monetary system. Parliament debated a wide range of issues including the redistribution of House seats, immigration, divorce, and the utility of bayonets. Conservatives made by-election gains, but evidence was sparse that the Liberals would be eclipsed in a general election. Nevertheless, Liberal strategists were nervous if St. Laurent were to decide not to offer himself again.

The terms of the tax-rental agreements between Ottawa and the provinces dominated intergovernmental affairs. Five provinces held elections, with regime changes in British Columbia, where a Social Credit party that was to rule for two decades was victorious, and in New Brunswick, where the Conservatives put an end to seventeen years of Liberal government. The status quo prevailed in Quebec, Saskatchewan, and Alberta. For the first time since the famous Asbestos Strike of 1949 in Quebec, strikers were read the riot act in a labour confrontation.

Canada expanded its presence internationally and was happily anchored in the Commonwealth, the United Nations, and NATO. The defence forces and budget grew as Canada, continuing its military engagement in the Korean War, favoured a diplomatic solution. Elected president of the UN General Assembly, Lester Pearson elevated Canada's international profile.

1953

Ontario threw itself into the arms of Ottawa, but I'll never do that.[1]

Maurice Duplessis

The economy and the federal treasury were sound, more young un-skilled immigrants arrived from Europe, technological advances improved the ability of Canadians to communicate and travel, a new twenty-six-year-old Queen sat on the throne, Lester Pearson served as president of the United Nations General Assembly, and a federal election took place.

An armistice in Korea in late July meant the end of hostilities, but the impact of the war was substantial: Canada had fielded the third largest army in the UN forces, having sent more than 26,000 troops; 516 lives were lost and more than 1,200 wounded. Defence expenditures, which had consumed 16 per cent of the federal budget in 1950, swelled to 45 per cent. Economic growth and burgeoning federal government tax revenues, growing from $2.8 billion in 1950 to $4.3 billion, enabled increased spending. For the fourth consecutive year, the Liberal government ran a modest surplus. With 1953 being an election year, the Liberals announced a reduction of income taxes to 1949 levels.[2]

Various indicators and the completion of the $100 million 1,150-kilometre-long Trans Mountain pipeline from Alberta's oil fields to the west coast offered evidence of a prosperous state of economic affairs. The dollar was trading at a premium to its United States counterpart, imports and exports were roughly in balance, Canada ranked third in the world after the US and the United Kingdom in the value of foreign trade and, for the first time in the post-war period, Canada ranked first in trade on a per capita basis. Labour income in a single month exceeded a billion dollars for the first time, but at mid-year a mild recession set in. Inflation as measured by the Consumer Price Index turned to deflation, prices falling for the first time since the early 1930s. Food costs per week averaged $6.70 ($67.96 in 2021) per person and average hourly wages at $1.36 ($13.80) rose by 5 per cent. However, the average wage rate for men, $1.47 ($14.91), was significantly higher than the average for women, 91 cents ($9.23). Blair Fraser of *Maclean's* magazine observed that Canadians had become "accustomed to high levels of employment and income."[3]

The number of workers in the primary sector – extractive resource industries such as farming, mining, fishing, and logging – declined while the number of workers in the service sector – activities such as teaching and clerical work in which women were more prominent – grew. The percentage of unionized workers also increased, from 30 to 33 per cent of the labour force. Demonstrating the power of organized labour, railway workers received an immediate 12 per cent increase in pay to avert a strike.[4]

A robust economy contributed to changes in lifestyles: north of Toronto in Don Mills, Canada's first large-scale fully planned suburb, land developers marketed affordable ranch-style homes to the growing number of middle-class families. Highway construction and the increasing proliferation of automobiles enabled such development: passenger cars, many more of which now had automatic transmissions and power steering, totalled more than 2.5 million. The Ontario government promised superhighways to accommodate the province's three hundred thousand cars and an expected six hundred thousand American visitors. Canadian Pacific Airlines introduced jet travel with the Comet, although on its maiden transpacific flight, the plane named *Empress of Hawaii* crashed in Karachi, killing all on board and becoming the world's first Comet accident resulting in fatalities.[5]

The complexions of immigrants remained largely the same; all eighteen immigration Canadian offices were in Europe, five in the British Isles. Of the 169,000 immigrants, all but 10,000 were from Europe or the United States. About 11,000 were domestic servants, 10,000 labourers not intending to work in primary industries, and fewer than 9,000 were professionals. Of the 2,400 prospective immigrants refused entry to Canada, 80 per cent were from the US. Of the 47,662 British immigrants, 237 were deported.[6]

Technological advances included Canada's first microwave radio relay system. Stretching from Toronto through Ottawa to Montreal, it made possible more long-distance telephone traffic and direct television transmission between cities. Telegraphs increased as a means of communications; telegraph companies generated $37 million in gross revenues, doubling their revenues from a decade earlier, and telegrams transferred $22 million between customers. Four companies operated submarine cables landing in Canada including one owned by the French Telegraph Cable Company that ran from the North American French islands of St. Pierre and Miquelon to nearby Newfoundland. Telephones became more common – about one for every four people – and telephony research produced new devices, systems, and services. They included the transistor and the ability of long-distance operators to reach distant telephones in North America directly without the assistance of other operators along the route.[7]

The Canadian Sickness Survey confirmed the connection between illness and lower income, contributing to making medical insurance a public policy issue. Families in total spent $374 million on health care with the average family spending $82: $20 for prepaid insurance plans, $45 directly for services, and $16 for drugs and appliances. Hospitals reported over six million patient days, but admission rates and length of stay varied greatly; insured patients were admitted 40 per cent more frequently. Although health and hygiene generally improved, a major polio outbreak occurred. The disabling disease peaked with nearly nine thousand cases and five hundred deaths – the most serious national epidemic since the 1918 influenza pandemic.[8] Inuit were particularly susceptible. To improve their conditions, Jean Lesage, the first minister of the new Department of Northern Affairs and National Resources, announced that he intended "to give the Eskimos the same rights, privileges, opportunities, and responsibilities as all other Canadians, in short to enable them to share fully in the national life of Canada."[9]

Massey's Royal Commission on National Development in the Arts, Letters, and Sciences had noted that Canada might be "the only civilized country in the world lacking a National Library,"[10] so on the Commission's recommendation, the Library was established to acquire and preserve a comprehensive collection of literary and musical works published in and about Canada or written by Canadians. Professor Hilda Neatby, the only woman member of the Commission, argued for sustained support for the arts and letters because "short of some providential intervention we shall not know the extent of our collective artistic capacity."[11]

Hailed as "the most exciting night in the history of the Canadian theatre," an opening night audience for the first Stratford Shakespearean Festival gathered under a big-top tent 150 feet in diameter to see *Richard III*, featuring renowned British actor Alec Guinness. As evidence of a new artistic vocabulary emerging, a group of young artists including Jack Bush, Harold Town, and William Ronald banded together and branded themselves as Painters Eleven with a commitment to exhibiting abstract art. At first, bewilderment and hostility greeted their work; the Group of Seven tradition continued to dominate the aesthetic sensibilities of Canadians.[12]

Excitement grew in English Canada about the coronation of Queen Elizabeth II. Prime minister Louis St. Laurent weighed whether to include "a representative of the Canadian Indian race" in a delegation of four hundred notables scheduled to attend.[13] The coronation brought with it changes in the royal title: St. Laurent said that "defender of the faith," one of the monarch's established subsidiary titles commonly understood as referring to Anglicanism, did not actually allude to any particular faith. He described the Queen's new title, "Head of the Commonwealth," as evidence of "the realistic genius of the British people" for discarding old forms and adapting to new conditions. Conservative leader George Drew termed the Commonwealth an "ancient fellowship" and proposed amending the Citizenship Act to designate the Queen a Canadian citizen.[14] In Quebec, the elevation of Montreal archbishop Paul-Émile Léger to cardinal exhilarated French Canadians; in freezing temperatures, thousands stood roaring a regal welcome when he returned from Rome as a prince of the Roman Catholic Church.[15]

The public was divided on the Canada's flag: 40 per cent of surveyed respondents favoured a new design, a third wanted the Union Jack, and 15 per cent preferred to keep the Red Ensign (which includes the Union Jack). And what was the national anthem? The *Globe and Mail* insisted that it always was and remained *God Save the Queen*; *O Canada* was merely a "patriotic song," despite the government "promoting a bit of covert revolution in anthems." After the death of Queen Mary, the mother of Edward VIII, Duke of Windsor, Canadians were asked for their opinion about permitting the former King and his wife to take up residence once again in Britain. Two-thirds said no.[16]

Attitudes about liquor consumption were evolving. A Roman Catholic priest living on an Ontario First Nation reserve as well as former Ontario Liberal premier Harry Nixon recommended permitting Indigenous people to purchase alcohol at government stores. Alberta extended the hours during which saloons could sell beer. Saskatchewan permitted beer parlours to install radios and television sets. A British Columbia government board of inquiry headed by former federal Conservative finance minister H.H. Stevens and including the rector of Toronto's largest Anglican Church recommended that beer parlours no longer be required to be part of a hotel. To combat bootlegging, the board also proposed permitting a limited number of cocktail lounges in upscale hotels and licensing some all-night liquor stores. The recommendations posed a problem for the teetotalling leaders of the Social Credit government.[17]

Federal Politics

Prime minister St. Laurent pressed the provinces to negotiate a health insurance plan which had been set aside when the Korean War broke out. However, the cabinet continued to be divided on the matter. With an election approaching, it was decided to craft a platform plank that would enhance identifying the Liberals with public health insurance but avoid any time commitment. It would also avoid opening the party to criticism that they intended to impose their priorities on the provinces. The Conservatives, favouring the extension of private insurance plans such as Blue Cross, proposed a conference of provincial health ministers, hospital associations, and doctors to work out a voluntary national plan to cover all Canadians.[18]

The Liberals had good reason to believe they were secure in office as the election approached. Some Liberal supporters and cabinet ministers urged an early election call in case the economy faltered and before the scheduled coronation of the Queen, but St. Laurent thought the public would resent an early election as partisan opportunism.[19] The CBC and the political parties met, when television stations operated only in Toronto, Montreal, and Ottawa, to discuss the use of television by the parties during the election campaign but, unable to agree on the allotment of time and format for political broadcasts, the parties decided to forgo using the new medium.[20]

Shortly before Parliament was dissolved, the Gallup Poll reported that 46 per cent of respondents preferred the Liberals and 31 per cent preferred the Conservatives.[21] Many voters were reassured by St. Laurent's relaxed comportment and patrician bearing; no other politician matched his popular appeal. He and his Liberals represented experience and steadiness and were the only party that could count on substantial support in every region of the country. Well-known author Hugh MacLennan said the Liberals acted like "cautious inhibited trustees," but he would vote for them nonetheless because, "If management were the sole test of a Government, the Liberals have established themselves as one of the finest Governments in the history of the world."[22]

The Liberals, who had won 191 seats in the 1949 election, entered the campaign with 9 fewer seats after having suffered several by-election setbacks. Their platform offered to reduce taxes "as much as possible" and to introduce public health insurance whenever the provinces would willingly join in a national scheme. St. Laurent's keynote campaign speech highlighted that Canada had constructed more housing units per person since the Second World War than any other country. Characterizing his party as reliable guardians of national security, he boasted of his government's "drastic legislation," the 1951 Emergency Powers Act, to protect "our institutions, our defence establishments and essential industries from subversion and sabotage." He said he wanted to pursue a formula for amending the Constitution with the provinces that would safeguard their rights as well as protect the "sacred constitutional rights related to the use of the English and French languages."[23]

The Conservatives promised to cut taxes by half a billion dollars without cutting pensions, family allowances, other social programs, or military spending. They vowed ending "waste and extravagance, increasing efficiency, eliminating duplication and improving accounting methods," without offering specific examples. The party raised the prospect of reforming the Senate, specifically its legislative role, the method of appointing Senators, and their length of tenure. The Conservative platform disparaged "state medicine" and proposed a contributory health insurance scheme that maintained existing private medical insurance plans. An unusual plank, to "put an end to government by secret Orders-in-Council," was inserted after leader George Drew learned of such an order during a debate on renewing the Emergency Powers Act.[24]

Titled "Humanity First," the CCF platform had a social democratic orientation, while Social Credit railed against "state socialism," declaring itself in favour of "free competitive individual enterprise." The CCF called for economic planning, progressive taxation including taxes on "excessive" profits and capital gains, and "nation-wide health insurance ... regardless of income ... [for] full hospital, medical, dental, optical and other health care." Drawing on the monetary theory of Major C.H. Douglas, the Social Credit party led by Solon Low vowed to maintain "effective consumer purchasing power to make financially possible the distribution of all wanted production." Low spoke of Social Credit as a "crusade," framing Douglas's secular theories as the tailoring of Biblical teachings to political action; he promised to apply "the highest standard of Christian morality in politics and government."[25]

The Liberals and Conservatives threw charges back and forth during the election campaign. St. Laurent ridiculed the Conservative promise of tax cuts, pointing out that the Republican party in the United States had won the 1952 election by proposing similar tax cuts which proved to be nothing but "hot air."[26] Drew repeatedly referenced the Petawawa scandal, referring to horses on the army's payroll.[27] Conservative MP John Diefenbaker proved to be a particularly effective campaigner. External affairs minister Lester Pearson and Diefenbaker spoke at party rallies in Moncton on the same night that a circus was performing. The next day the Moncton *Transcript* rated their performances: "Circus first, Diefenbaker second, Pearson third."[28]

In Toronto, Conservative MP George Hees attacked St. Laurent's failure to appoint a cabinet minister from southern Ontario as an "appalling injustice." His Conservative colleague Albany Robichaud, an Acadian MP, criticized the "linguistic apartheid" of the Liberals for issuing bilingual federal cheques in Quebec but unilingual cheques in the rest of Canada. Conservatives also protested a letter the Liberal National Federation sent to all servicemen in Korea that warned a Conservative government would eliminate their amenities such as gymnasiums.[29]

The tax-rental agreements between Ottawa and the provinces, not due to expire for another four years, nevertheless drew attention during the campaign. Drew criticized the use of such agreements during peace time as a violation of provincial autonomy and repeated the point in every speech he made in Quebec. St. Laurent, implicitly criticized Drew's outreach to Quebec, countering that Drew proposed to undo the arrangements of the British North America Act while the Liberals had "no separate appeal for one section or one class." To Drew's charge that the Liberals were irresponsible, wasteful, and arrogant, St. Laurent retorted that Canada's impressive economic gains could not have been the product of bad government.[30]

Knowing the Conservatives could not win, Quebec premier Maurice Duplessis, though conservative by heritage and training and a former Conservative MLA, avoided identifying himself with Drew. Nevertheless, Quebec's federal Conservatives sought to leverage Duplessis's popularity to their advantage; one party organizer announced that the "two great patriots ... will save the pact of Confederation." The party's candidate in Îles de la Madeleine attacked the Liberals for bringing in immigrants with "revolutionary ideas" who were taking jobs "while our boys are in Korea, or ... in that military hospital without arms and without legs."[31]

Voter response to the campaign was apathetic; a month before the vote, *Globe and Mail* reporter George Bain observed, "Nobody's talking election yet except the people actually working it."[32] Turnout at the polls was the lowest since 1925. The Liberals emerged with 169 seats, a very comfortable majority. Even though their popular vote increased by only 1 per cent, the Conservatives gained 10 seats, to 51, in a House of Commons that grew from 262 to 265 seats. The party doubled its seats in Quebec, from 2 to 4, but the province had 75 seats and most Quebecers voted, as in the past, for a party leader who was a fellow Quebecer. For the Conservatives, the election marked their fifth consecutive loss in 18 years. A marked change was the election of 4 women as compared with none in 1949, and the number of women in the Senate rose to a record 5 by year's end.

No party nominated candidates in every riding, but the Liberals came close with 262; the Conservatives fielded 248, the CCF 170. Social Credit contested just 71 constituencies, fewer than the 100 contested by the communist Labor-Progressive Party. Adrien Arcand, who had once described himself as a Canadian führer, saying he would march on Ottawa to take control of the country in the style of Italy's Benito Mussolini, captured 39 per cent of the vote as a "Nationalist" candidate in a Quebec constituency.[33] LPP leader Tim Buck, who like Arcand had been imprisoned during the Second World War, received less than 9 per cent of the vote in his Ontario riding.

Troubling the Liberals in western Canada was their promised irrigation and power project for the South Saskatchewan River. The pledge had been made by federal agriculture minister and former Saskatchewan premier Jimmy Gardiner. Dealing a blow to Gardiner and to farmers in Saskatchewan and Alberta, a royal commission deemed the planned quarter billion-dollar project uneconomic. This left the Liberals, hesitant to admit their promise might not be kept, saying they would determine the project's fate after the election.[34] That proved unsatisfactory to voters; the Liberals lost votes and seats in both provinces, dropping from 14 to 5 seats in Saskatchewan, their biggest setback in any province.

After the election, St. Laurent did not conceal his desire to retire as soon as possible.[35] He also appointed future Quebec premier Jean Lesage to the cabinet as minister of Northern Affairs and National Resources. As a backbencher, Lesage had bluntly warned St. Laurent that if a distinctive Canadian flag were introduced with a Union Jack anywhere on it, he and other Quebec MPs would vote against it even if it meant defeating the government.[36]

Intergovernmental Relations

The three Maritime premiers and a Newfoundland cabinet minister met to discuss several matters including a potential uniform highway code, a joint tourism-promotion program, and regional education. Most of their time, however, was devoted to discussing the creation of a council like the council of six New England states, which included business leaders along with the state governors.[37]

Newfoundland premier Joey Smallwood lured Jack Pickersgill, who had served at the apex of the federal civil service as Clerk of the Privy Council, to contest a Newfoundland seat in Parliament. Smallwood hoped his province would receive favourable treatment from Ottawa if it improved its access to the levers of federal power. Some MPs had charged that Pickersgill had become too closely connected with St. Laurent's political activities to serve as clerk. Pickersgill's stature was such that St. Laurent appointed him to the cabinet even before his election.[38]

During the federal election, the Liberals offered to renegotiate the tax-rental agreements with the provinces in the future. The Conservatives promised to convene a Dominion-Provincial conference immediately with the aim of reducing various forms of taxation.[39] Quebec, the only province that had not signed a tax-rental agreement, had an acrimonious relationship with Ottawa regarding the very existence of tax-rental agreements and other fiscal matters, including Ottawa's direct grants to universities. Duplessis said that Ottawa was "trying to pit Quebec against Ontario," that Ontario was "forced" to sign a tax-rental agreement, but "we will not abdicate."[40] Saskatchewan premier T.C. Douglas claimed Ottawa had "welshed" on its agreement with his province regarding social benefits that had been negotiated but were not forthcoming.[41] British Columbia complained of being short-changed by the formula on which the tax-rental agreements were based. Uncomplaining Manitoba, which greatly benefitted from its agreement, transferred much of the federal money it received from Ottawa to its municipalities.[42]

Ottawa influenced provincial spending by introducing three new health grants, two of which required matching provincial funds. These conditional grants required provincial health authorities to submit proposed projects to Ottawa that would be part of an overall plan to improve health services. However, provinces could also influence Ottawa's spending: a Saskatchewan CCF cabinet minister claimed the health grants came about only because his government had "shamed" the Liberals into providing them.[43]

After having "tolerated" federal grants to Quebec universities at their request a year earlier, Duplessis now rejected them, saying that they would allow Ottawa to pressure the universities in certain directions. If Ottawa had money for education, he contended, it should be transferred directly to provincial governments. To pursue his brief that Ottawa was overbearing, his government created a Royal Commission of Inquiry on Constitutional Problems, to inquire, among other things, into "encroachments by the central power in the field of direct taxation." He described the Commission as another step in the fight against "invasion of provincial rights by Ottawa."[44]

British Columbia and Alberta disagreed about the 718-mile Trans Mountain pipeline that crossed their border. Alberta supported and

British Columbia opposed Ottawa's approval for construction of a pipeline spur in B.C. that would divert Alberta oil to Washington State. Victoria complained that the spur would deprive Vancouver of shipping business.[45]

The Provinces

Nova Scotia, Manitoba, and British Columbia held provincial elections. Nova Scotians re-elected a long-serving Liberal regime, Manitobans re-elected a longer serving Liberal-Progressive government no longer in a coalition cabinet with Conservatives, and British Columbians converted a short-lived Social Credit minority government into a majority.

Conservative strategist Dalton Camp assessed Liberal Nova Scotia as "a formidable fortress." Angus Macdonald, the premier in the 1930s who reclaimed the position in 1945 after serving in the federal cabinet during the war, was in Camp's estimation "a living legend" who "had the Gaelic" and "a reputation for integrity remarkably unsullied" despite his Liberals "seething with corruption."[46] Labelled "The Last Pre-Modern Premier" by political scientist Peter Clancy, Macdonald was already in the pantheon of Nova Scotian politicians.[47] The Liberals ran on their record while the Conservatives ran daily newspaper advertisements written by Camp that used the slogan "Twenty's Plenty."[48] The Liberals were re-elected with a reduced majority. Robert Stanfield's Conservatives scored some success in linking the government with some corrupt practices; winning 43 per cent of the vote, they had their strongest showing since 1933. After the election, Macdonald announced he would not attend the Queen's coronation and instead would go to a Gaelic mòd festival in Scotland.[49]

Social Credit's success in both Alberta and British Columbia energized Manitoba's Social Credit party. After not having contested the previous election, the leaderless party fielded more candidates than either the Conservatives or the CCF. Douglas Campbell's Liberal-Progressives, a coalition party of Liberals and Progressives formed in the early 1930s, won the same number of seats as they had in the 1949 election but with a smaller government caucus because the party's coalition with the Conservatives had collapsed. A six-point program issued by the Conservatives nearly a year before the election focussed on taxes: no to a provincial sales tax, yes to reducing land taxes, and yes to more clearly defined municipal taxation powers.[50] The CCF promised hospital insurance while Social Credit did not offer a platform, declaring that the application of Christian principles would "purify Manitoba's political bloodstream."[51]

Indigenous Peoples in Manitoba, who had gained the right to vote in 1952, were the majority in the far-flung Rupertsland constituency where voting was set for a later date because extra time was required to enumerate voters in the riding's scattered small communities. Campbell's government took a major plunge into the power business on the eve of the election campaign, purchasing the privately owned Winnipeg Electric Co.[52] It was an uncharacteristic act for the frugally minded government. Manitoba historian W.L. Morton wittily interpreted the re-election of Campbell's government as demonstrating that "the dominant rural constituencies, still [approved] the political changes of 1922" when the United Farmers of Manitoba had swept into office with Campbell as an MLA.[53]

British Columbians went to the polls the day after Manitoba's election. Support for W.A.C. Bennett's Social Credit party increased by more than 10 per cent while the opposition CCF held its own. The biggest change was the further decimation of the Liberals and Conservatives; the Liberals were reduced to four seats and the Conservatives, who received less than 6 per cent of the vote, to one. A polarized contest between the anti-socialist Social Credit and the socialist CCF was to become the political norm for the next four decades.

Disarray in the CCF camp and Conservative weakness benefitted Social Credit. After Bennett's government had been defeated in a no confidence vote, the lieutenant governor rejected CCF leader Harold Winch's request to form a government, and the election was held.[54] Winch resigned as MLA and party leader and then won a seat in the House of Commons in the federal election. Tillie Rolston, the Conservative-cum-Social Crediter, was defeated by Liberal leader Arthur Laing, who later served in the cabinets of Lester Pearson and Pierre Trudeau. Conservative leader Deane Finlayson won only 979 votes of the over 20,000 cast in a Victoria by-election, his third reversal at the polls in six months. A Liberal took the seat, defeating Finlayson and Social Credit finance minister Einar Gunderson, who had continued as a cabinet member after having lost his seat in the general election.[55]

As in the 1952 election, British Columbia used a transferrable ballot, also known as the alternative vote; if no candidate received a majority of the ballots cast, the candidate with the fewest votes was dropped and his or her second choices were allocated among the remaining candidates, a procedure repeated until a candidate receives a majority. Another feature of the election was that Doukhobors, who had been disenfranchised in 1931, regained the right to vote. The "politics of localism" had driven earlier elections, but this election, following the pattern begun in 1952, accentuated the "politics of provincialism"; local candidates and local networks were less important.[56]

Atlantic Canada's chronic problem was high unemployment. Economic development bedevilled Newfoundland's Liberal government. Premier Smallwood attempted to mitigate unemployment by replacing senior economic advisor and Latvian émigré Alfred Valdmanis, whom he had previously hailed as "the savior for Newfoundland," with a former *TIME* magazine editor who had worked under Valdmanis in the province's economic development research unit. Smallwood's efforts also led to the creation of a consortium of British companies (Brinco) to act as a catalyst for the development of Newfoundland's natural resources. New Brunswick's Council of Labour asked the Conservative government to increase taxes to finance power development so that mining and processing companies could be attracted and create jobs. Nova Scotia had only a limited market for its coal, producing less of it than it had before the First World War. Prince Edward Island's "Farmer Premier" J. Walter Jones, who had sought to cultivate trade with Newfoundland, stepped down to sit in the Senate. The Liberal caucus selected health minister Alex Matheson as his successor.[57]

Quebec's Georges-Émile Lapalme, who had led the Liberals from outside the legislature, finally won a seat in a by-election. However, the governing Union Nationale's grip on power remained firm: they easily retained wealthy, heavily Anglophone Outremont and two rural, largely Francophone ridings in three other by-elections. Duplessis's government remained an unyielding foe of an increasingly discontented labour movement. As a strike by textile workers entered its tenth month, Duplessis characterized the threat of a general strike by the Canadian Catholic Confederation of Labour as "a call to generalized crime."[58]

Ontario's government estimated that its population, 4.5 million in 1951, might increase to 6 million by 1958. However, a buoyant economy did not shelter the Conservative government from criticism by the growing labour union movement; the secretary-treasurer of the Federation of Labour called Conservative premier Leslie Frost an "utter hypocrite" for not intervening in a long-running strike, branding him as "more reactionary and opposed to labor than people like [former premiers Mitchell] Hepburn and Drew. We knew where we stood with them."[59] A legislative committee unanimously recommended enfranchising the province's twenty-three thousand Indigenous people although two bands the committee visited opposed the idea. They said that based on their experience with federal government trickery and treaty breaking in the past they did not trust that the province could give them the vote without any loss to them.[60]

Healthy provincial economies led all four western provincial governments to introduce record spending budgets, highlighting highway construction and education. Saskatchewan planned to blacktop the Trans-Canada Highway for all but eighty miles between Manitoba and Alberta, and British Columbia asked Ottawa to contribute more than $150 million over five years for roads and railways to access the province's forest wealth. Oil revenues contributed to expanding Alberta's expenditure budget by $50 million to $174 million, almost identical to B.C.'s $175 million budget. Their budgets were more than triple the size of Manitoba's, while Saskatchewan, with a budget of $110 million, ran a significant deficit. In contrast to Saskatchewan, which had public hospital insurance, Alberta proposed to subsidize private insurance companies that offered policies covering hospital "extras." By-products of Alberta's fast-growing economy included shortages of skilled labour, a significant rise in hourly wages, and rising inequality as the gap between the average wage and the minimum wage increased greatly over what it had been before the discovery of oil at Leduc.[61]

Canada in the World

The Korean War ended, and 32 Canadian soldiers were released from Chinese prison camps along the Yalu River. The Cold War, however, continued. The number of Canadian troops in Korea diminished rapidly, but some remained as part of the Commonwealth Division. Britain floated the idea of a joint Commonwealth military presence in Hong Kong or Malaya, but Ottawa was unwelcoming of the idea.[62] Aside from the Korean conflict, most of Canada's defence spending went toward meeting NATO obligations: an infantry brigade, twelve jet fighter squadrons, and forty-two vessels. In addition, more than 900 pilots and 1,600 navigators from various NATO countries were training in Canada.[63]

A series of articles in the Soviet media described Canada as an "American military base," hinted that the United States was planning to annex it, and that "diabolical" experiments with robots and bacteriological weapons were taking place on Canadian soil. Canada's Communists, in turn, wrote of Ottawa sheltering "fascist war criminals."[64] When the government asked Parliament to extend the Emergency Powers Act because "an emergency of apprehended war" threatened Canada, some Conservative MPs asked that the wider arbitrary powers of the War Measures Act be invoked.[65] The Conservatives did not attack the Americans or the government for their Korean War policies, but criticized the Liberals for using an obsolescent aircraft carrier loaned by the Royal Navy and leaving Canada unguarded. The CCF favoured recognition of the Peking government, denounced the sale of arms to the Formosa government, criticized the US for having pushed past the pre-war Korean boundaries without UN authorization, and called for UN police action against South Korea if it became an aggressor. For its part, Social Credit wanted a blockade of Red China.

External affairs minister Lester Pearson did double duty as president of the UN General Assembly. He also campaigned actively during the election, hoping "that never again will there be a year" so challenging.[66] Canada's isolationism of the inter-war period was impossible in a world of nuclear weapons, and critical for such weapons were Canada's newly discovered uranium reserves near Elliot Lake, in Pearson's Algoma East constituency. Canada became a storehouse of one of the world's largest uranium deposits.[67]

The United States and its European allies differed on how to confront communism in Asia, with Canada's position closer to that of the Europeans. With McCarthyism at high tide in the US, Pearson boldly told an American audience that he did not see Asian communism as an "implacable foe bound hand and foot to Moscow." For Pearson, "the only justification for direct western intervention is when Communism expresses itself in military aggression." Intervention "would be stigmatized in Asia as western and colonial." He opposed interpreting the UN's objectives in Korea as including "unification by force."[68] Otherwise, Canada's role in Asia was limited to providing $77 million in economic and social development aid to South and Southeast Asian governments as part of Ottawa's contribution to the Colombo Plan. Canada took a complete "hands-off" approach to the Middle East, lacking diplomatic representation and the capacity to track developments in the region.[69]

Ottawa established consulates in Los Angeles and Seattle to cultivate friendly relations, increase trade, and assist Canadian citizens in the United States. Despite continued disappointment that Congress had not yet approved the estimated $750 million deep-water St. Lawrence Seaway project, St. Laurent acceded to the American ambassador's request to delay going ahead with it as an all-Canadian project; by year's end he was more hopeful that the legislation Congress had shelved would proceed.[70] Ottawa also accommodated other American requests: American officials were once again given permission to question Soviet defector and now Canadian citizen Igor Gouzenko in Canada after he issued a statement that he would not testify in the US, and trade minister C.D. Howe unhappily agreed to limit shipments of oats to the US after an American tariff commission recommended to President Eisenhower restrictions on their importation.[71]

Canadian diplomats were stationed in nineteen countries and thirty-four countries had representation in Ottawa. Canada expanded its presence abroad, notably in Latin America; the ambassador to Argentina also became accredited to Uruguay, and embassies were established in Venezuela and Colombia. Their primary purpose was to enhance commercial relations. At the UN, Canada expressed concern about human rights in South Africa but abstained – an abstention the *Globe and Mail* endorsed – on an Indian motion denouncing apartheid. Few MPs spoke to the issue although one Liberal defended the government's inaction. John Diefenbaker expressed regret that certain countries, including South Africa, ignored UN resolutions. Ontario Communist MLA Joseph Salsberg flatly condemned "that vile racist scourge of South Africa" as well as the "racist immigration policy" of the Liberals.[72]

The predictions of American observers a year earlier that Canada stood on the brink of a new era of economic growth and development proved prescient. There were some bitter rivalries in Parliament and on the hustings, but the differences between the Liberals and Conservatives were largely matters of tone. The federal election and three provincial elections produced no upsets. The CCF increased its representation in Parliament, but its popular vote declined.

The tax-rental agreements continued as a source of contention in federal-provincial relations. The Atlantic provinces considered a regional response to their common economic challenges while Ontario and the western provinces were thriving. Quebec escalated its castigation of Ottawa, launching a commission to investigate federal "encroachments" on Quebec's constitutional powers. Despite the end of hostilities in Korea and the continuing intensity of the Cold War, foreign policy was not a major issue in domestic politics. Canada's diplomatic engagement beyond the North Atlantic world was growing but limited. Meeting Canada's NATO commitments required a large increase in defence spending.

1954

Moving pictures were taken of the opening of Parliament in 1949 and 1952. With the development of television, it seems to me appropriate that advantage should be taken of this latest medium to carry the significance of the event to the Canadian people as a whole.[1]

Senate Speaker Wishart M. Robertson

The economic recession that began in the latter half of 1953 continued in the first half of the year, and the value of commodities produced decreased for the first time since 1945. Some pundits warned that Canada might spiral downward "toward a depression such as the country went through in the '30s."[2] With the United States economy in recession, Canada could not avoid its own slowdown. Construction and manufacturing, as well as the agricultural, forestry, and fishing sectors underperformed.

Unemployment hit a record post-war high in March; six months later the seasonally adjusted unemployment numbers leapt to 289,000 from 190,000 a year earlier. Although the economy was in recession, it was not a severe slump; a record level of planned investment of nearly six billion dollars suggested brighter prospects. Capital expenditures by governments and investments in housing, utilities, hospitals, mining, oil wells, and services increased.[3] Fears of an economic crash turned out to be overblown; the recession ended in the latter half of the year.

Technological developments affected Canada's regions and economic sectors differently. Alberta's oil and gas production and the proliferation of diesel engines, for example, reduced the operating costs of railways, made some railway labour redundant, and led to the retirement of equipment that made steam locomotives. This, however, struck a blow at Nova Scotia's coal industry. Alberta's piped natural gas to central Canada, and a partnership between Atomic Energy of Canada and Ontario's Hydro-Electric Power Commission to develop atomic energy for electrical power, promised to reduce costs to existing industries and foster new ones. In response to a request from a labour deputation for assistance to laid-off workers in Ontario's struggling farm implement industry, acting prime minister C.D. Howe bluntly told the farm implement workers to "shift to another industry."[4]

The rival Trades and Labor Congress (TLC) and the Canadian Congress of Labor (CCL), together representing nearly a million workers, decided to merge some of their efforts. They created a joint committee to explore greater cooperation and agreed not to raid each other's members. They also launched a joint campaign to lobby the federal government to tackle unemployment.[5] The CCL, politically more radical than the TLC, expressed concern about the behaviour of Canadian firms abroad; they singled out Noranda Mines for exploiting South America and demanded that Ottawa support South American democratic movements. The annual CCL convention, however, overwhelmingly rejected a proposal by some delegates that workers insist on wage increases even when their particular industry is in decline: "We would be stupid ... and held up to a thousand times more ridicule," said CCL secretary-treasurer and Ontario CCF leader Donald MacDonald, "if we did not take cognizance ... that some industry cannot conform to our basic policy of wage increases." The CCL's proposed corrective for economic recession was to have Ottawa run deficits instead of budgetary surpluses.[6]

A public opinion survey found just 45 per cent of Canadians were favourable to immigration. However, there was no outburst of xenophobia. Indeed, the conservative *Globe and Mail* editorialized that "the current unemployment is not in any way due to immigrants, and without immigrants would be worse."[7] The TLC asked for curbs on immigration, but the CCL did not, calling instead for an advisory committee of labour, management, farmers, welfare agencies, and government officials "to assure that immigration is planned and attuned to national needs."[8]

The national population topped 15 million. Of the 154,000 immigrant arrivals, one in six was a displaced person or a refugee.[9] The immigrant intake exceeded the annual average of 101,000 since 1910 but was the lowest number since 1950. Striking was the decline from countries behind the Iron Curtain: only 75 immigrants in total from Poland, Czechoslovakia, and the Soviet Union, a drop from nearly 28,000 in 1951. In contrast, the number of American immigrants rose by more than 25 per cent from a year earlier, and fewer Americans returned to the United States than in any year since the Second World War. Asia produced 2,700 immigrants, South America 600, and Africa (other than British subjects) 186. Constant in each year since 1950 was the ethnicity of immigrants: one-third British and two-thirds continental European.[10] Ontario absorbed more than half of all immigrants, Quebec less than a fifth. Immigrants were no longer required to provide a year's notice of their intent to apply for citizenship. Only 429 of the 27,000 unilingual citizenship certificates issued were in French. A new bilingual citizenship application form was drafted for future use.[11]

Television became a major source of news as the number of television sets increased from 146,000 in 1952 to 800,000. New stations in Halifax, Winnipeg, and Vancouver complemented established stations in Montreal, Toronto, and Ottawa (the latter offering bilingual programming). Prime minister Louis St. Laurent habitually watched CBC's televised news programs at both the supper hour and before retiring in the evening.[12] The political parties opposed televising parliamentary debates, arguing that it could lead to stage acting and turn important national deliberations into a form of entertainment. However, it was decided that the pomp surrounding the opening of Parliament and the Speech from the Throne could be televised after the CBC assured the Speaker of the Senate and the governor general that it would be handled "with dignity and clarity and with a minimum of inconvenience to the Governor-General."[13]

Legal and illegal drugs were becoming significant issues. Estimating that there were about three thousand drug addicts nationally, federal health minister Paul Martin announced that the government would ban the legal importation of heroin after doctors said they could get by without it. A week later, however, a bill making opium available for medical purposes received royal assent.[14] Ontario's pharmacists wanted Queen's Park to order that headache pills be sold exclusively by pharmacies and not, as one pharmacist put it, at "pool halls and grocery stores."[15] A more serious medical concern was polio: 8,500 cases, over 400 deaths, and no proven way of preventing the infectious disease, which weakened muscles and could paralyze. However, doctors predicted that polio would soon be eliminated.[16]

The worst riot in Canadian history broke out at the Kingston penitentiary. After a fire broke out, ostensibly cooperative prisoners handed firefighters coffee containers with drugs that had been stolen or otherwise obtained. Many of the fireman fall ill or felt sluggish, but no prisoners escaped. After a second deliberately set fire, firemen called on the assistance of the provincial police and troops carrying fixed bayonets to fight it. With two-thirds of the penitentiary a smouldering ruin, and the commissioner of penitentiaries describing the ringleaders as psychopaths and arsonists, damage was set at two million dollars.[17]

Toronto was planning for an expressway along Lake Ontario and, as an example of the optimism and growth of the post-war age, the city opened Canada's first subway: the 7.4-kilometre journey took twelve minutes. A few months later, the most famous hurricane in Canadian history pummelled the city with more than two hundred millimetres of rain in less than twenty-four hours and 110 km/hr winds. Thousands were left homeless, and eighty-one people died. Hazel washed out bridges and streets and some homes and trailers were washed into Lake Ontario.[18]

Mores and tastes continued to change but not without complaint or anxiety. American magazines accounted for 80 per cent of the magazine market.[19] A new American publication, *Playboy*, contributed to continuing concerns about the circulation of sex and crime comics, gambling, and the impact of television. Ontario's printing trades unions debated whether to boycott publications displaying sex and crime because, as one union member said, they represent the "prostitution of our industry." A member of the Anglican Church's religious education board described television as "the greatest temptation to mass mediocrity the Devil has yet devised." Another board member lamented "the new forces of visual education which we have singularly failed to control or indeed, understand."[20]

The Canadian Welfare Association called for more Criminal Code restrictions on gambling and lotteries. Details of a mink-coated madam driving a Cadillac and city councillors feigning ignorance of corrupt police officers who protected gambling dens emerged in a judicial probe into corruption and organized vice in Montreal. The police chief and nineteen other officers of Canada's largest police force were dismissed, and fines levied. The Gallup organization found that Quebecers, unlike residents elsewhere in the country, supported the whipping of young criminals, while Quebec's esteemed Abbé Lionel Groulx wrote that his "sweetest and most valuable" joys came from saving youth "who seemed corrupted and depraved."[21]

Parliament passed a potpourri of laws. Among them, the Criminal Code was completely revised and consolidated, the post office gained authorization to increase the price of postage, and a new housing act introduced a system of insured mortgage loans and extended the life of mortgage loans from twenty to twenty-five years. Salaries for politicians were also raised; the prime minister's salary went from $15,000 to $25,000 ($251,785 in 2021), ministers' salaries from $10,000 to $15,000, and the sessional allowance for MPs doubled from $4,000 to $8,000.[22]

Federal Politics

Ten by-elections were held but only one seat changed hands – the Liberals lost a Manitoba riding to the CCF. The results suggested that public opinion had not changed much since the general election the previous year. Nevertheless, the Conservatives had high hopes in Quebec where the Liberals "admit quite openly that George Drew has made real progress [with] prolix sermons on provincial autonomy. Some Quebeckers think him the only man in Ottawa who cares about this (to them) vital issue."[23] Conservatives were particularly optimistic about capturing St. Antoine-Westmount, but their candidate, Egan Chambers, brother-in-law of philosopher and future NDP vice president Charles Taylor, lost after having failed in the 1953 election.

A major reconstruction of the cabinet came at mid-year; considered by many to be St. Laurent's successor, finance minister Douglas Abbott requested appointment to the Supreme Court. Replacing Abbott, Walter Harris became the first Ontarian to hold the finance portfolio since 1926. Associate defence minister Ralph Campney replaced long-serving defence minister Brooke Claxton, who left government to become an insurance company vice president, and transport minister Lionel Chevrier left to head the St. Lawrence Seaway Authority after the United States finally agreed to joint construction of the Seaway.[24] Former senior civil servant and master tactician Jack Pickersgill was elevated from the junior portfolio of secretary of state to become the minister of citizenship and immigration as well as the government's house leader in the Commons.

Abbott's appointment to the Supreme Court upset the court's traditional English-French, Catholic-Protestant balance in favour of English Protestants, stirring controversy. St. Laurent broke with another tradition by elevating a Catholic to succeed another Catholic to chief justice. To compensate for the departures of Abbott and Claxton and to avoid breaking the tradition that the cabinet include an English Protestant from Quebec, St. Laurent appointed former Quebec Liberal leader George Marler.[25] These manoeuvres did not engage the public: a majority of respondents in a Gallup survey after the shuffle could not recall or state the name of any cabinet minister. The best known was C.D. Howe (9 per cent), followed by Walter Harris and Lester Pearson (6 per cent each).[26]

Toronto had more ridings than seven of the ten provinces, but the city was unrepresented in the cabinet. Indeed, Toronto had not been represented in cabinet since the Liberal victory of 1935 and no Torontonian had served as a parliamentary assistant since the creation of the position in 1945. Given his military and long parliamentary experience, Colonel David Croll was a logical choice to replace Campney as associate defence minister, but St. Laurent left the position vacant. Some speculated that Croll was excluded because he was too outspoken, too independent, and too left wing. Others thought it was because he was Jewish; no Jew had served in cabinet, a tradition that survived until 1969.

The governing Liberals and the labour movement had frosty relations. To avoid a strike by 135,000 railroad workers, St. Laurent prepared to recall Parliament and impose compulsory arbitration, leading chief labour negotiator Frank Hall to resign his position; he charged the government with "repression and discrimination."[27] Catcalls and booing greeted labour minister Milton Gregg when he delivered his annual address to the CCL convention. After boasting that the economy had turned the corner on the recession, which was true, he sat tight-lipped as the convention passed its annual resolution identifying the CCF as the political arm of the labour movement.[28]

Some Conservatives grumbled about party leader George Drew; the Conservative-inclined *Toronto Telegram* and *Winnipeg Tribune* called for a leadership convention. However, the Conservative student federation and the national party association reaffirmed their faith in him. The association elected George Hees as its president, which was the first time since its formation in 1926 that there was a vote for the position. Drew contended that the tax-rental agreements Ottawa had signed with the provinces "threaten the very survival of our federal system." He also condemned the government's centralization of authority under the Emergency Powers Act, which Conservative John Diefenbaker denounced as "a monster of democratic dictatorship."[29]

Parliament renewed the act annually, but it steadily lost support among Liberal MPs, leading the government to announce that it would lapse. From the day of its introduction in 1951, the Conservatives had questioned its purpose. They and the Social Credit party argued that the act impaired the supremacy of Parliament, and that the government had the more drastic and comprehensive War Measures Act at its disposal if need be. The CCF supported the act initially with the hope it would be used to effect price controls, but they now turned against it.[30]

Exposing a difference of opinion within the Conservative caucus, the party's finance critic, MP J.M. Macdonnell, publicly dissociated himself from the view of Toronto Conservative MP Rodney Adamson that "all the people who formed the international monetary fund and its officers, or at least a large number of the original executive, were Communists." Social Credit's former parliamentary leader, MP John Blackmore, endorsing Adamson's opinion that the IMF was a communist concoction, moved to create a parliamentary committee that would seek out Communists and their sympathizers in the civil service, industry, and elsewhere. An ardent admirer of American Senator Joe McCarthy, Blackmore came under criticism for using his free mailing privileges as an MP to send out anti-Communist literature containing anti-Semitic content.[31]

The CCF diverged sharply from the other parties in its foreign policy prescriptions. Party leader M.J. Coldwell called for more trade in non-strategic goods with the Soviet Union and China. The party also opposed West Germany's rearmament, called on the United Nations Security Council to determine whether the activities of the United States in Guatemala had violated the UN Charter, and condemned South Korean president Syngman Rhee's proposal to invade China. CCF MP Colin Cameron condemned the Liberal government for acceding to the request of the US to question Soviet defector Igor Gouzenko once again years after his defection: it was "stupid and distressingly silly," a case of "being pushed around" by the Americans. CCF MP Hazen Argue called on the government to increase economic aid to Asia from 25 million to 1 billion dollars. Characterizing the government's immigration policies as "dominated by racism and political opportunism," the biennial CCF convention resolved that these policies were "dictated by the desire for cheap labor for the industrial interests [the Liberal government] represents."[32]

Donald MacDonald personified the partnership of the industrial unions and the CCF: he served as both the secretary-treasurer of the CCL and leader of the Ontario CCF. The Ontario Federation of Labor (OFL), the umbrella organization for the Ontario craft unions in the Trades and Labor Congress, considered endorsing the CCF but decided against it. The Federation president insisted that the OFL was required to conform to the TLC's non-partisan policy.[33]

Intent on expanding nationally, Social Credit transferred its headquarters and its two organizers from Edmonton to Toronto. In Parliament and on CBC's free-time radio broadcasts, "The Nation's Business," the party kept its focus on monetary policy. Party leader Solon Low, criticizing the government for having permitted a "financial Frankenstein" to grow, called for boosting the purchasing power of consumers by increasing pension payments and allowances for families and veterans. Countering accusations that the party practised discrimination, the Ontario Social Credit president insisted they welcomed all with "no barrier to any race, class, color, or creed."[34]

Parliament's most verbose MP, the polite and colourful Jean-Francois Pouliot, engaged in much non-stop oratory, speaking more in the

Commons in any one year than York East Conservative MP Robert McGregor spoke in all the years since McGregor's election in 1926. Originally elected in 1924, Pouliot was descended from forebears who had served continuously in Canadian parliaments since the 1830s. Despite being described by a columnist as a buffoon and a "vocalamity,"[35] St. Laurent accommodated Pouliot's ambition to round out his career by appointing him a Senator.

Intergovernmental Relations

Composed of business leaders, the Atlantic Provinces Economic Council, a non-statutory interprovincial administrative body, was created. The council's purpose was to explore opportunities for regional economic cooperation and development. Provincial government officials from New Brunswick and Newfoundland and a Conservative MP assisted in founding the council, the executive vice president of the six states in the New England Council served as an adviser to it, and all four Atlantic provincial governments pledged to support its work.[36]

The three Maritime governments wanted Ottawa to address problems that affected them caused by the construction of the St. Lawrence Seaway. Struggling with deficit financing, Newfoundland's government saw Term 29 of its Terms of Union with Canada as a fiscal lifeline. With Ottawa constitutionally obligated under Term 29 to appoint a royal commission to review Newfoundland's financial position by 1957, Smallwood decided to prepare his province's case by appointing his own royal commission headed by a former Liberal MHA and advised by well-known Montreal Liberal and labour lawyer Carl Goldenberg.[37]

Most intergovernmental relations were bilateral, between Ottawa and individual provinces, but sometimes there were bilateral relations between individual provinces. Ontario attorney general Dana Porter, for example, travelled to Edmonton to discuss with Alberta premier Ernest Manning the proposal to construct a natural gas pipeline from Alberta to Ontario, while Alberta's representative in the federal cabinet, George Prudham, took it upon himself to raise the pipeline project with Queen's Park.[38] British Columbia wanted Ottawa to bear 40 per cent of the cost of relief payments to B.C.'s "unemployed employables," but the federal government said it would not. B.C. and Ottawa also disagreed about a project to construct a storage dam on the Columbia River to facilitate power generation in the United States; Ottawa quashed the deal the province had made with a private American company.[39]

The most contentious intergovernmental relations were between Quebec City and Ottawa. Quebec was the only province that did not sign a tax-rental agreement with Ottawa or agree to share with Ottawa the cost of constructing the Trans-Canada Highway of which little more than a quarter had been completed. Quebec continued to spar with the federal government over their respective taxation powers. Premier Maurice Duplessis's Union Nationale government introduced a provincial income tax bill, which had the support of two dissimilar men: conservative cleric Lionel Groulx and liberal Pierre Trudeau. The bill asserted that the province had constitutional "priority" in levying income tax. Duplessis also demanded, and Ottawa rejected, that Ottawa permit Quebecers to deduct the provincial tax they paid from their federal tax payment. He declared that "the power to tax cannot be replaced by subsidies," and "independence cannot be replaced by tutelage." Colourfully, he accused the federal government of trying to change the federal system to one of "trusteeship," making Quebec an "auxiliary government," a situation appropriate for "drunks, imbeciles, and people incapable of looking after themselves."[40]

The deadlock between St. Laurent and Duplessis was only broken when Duplessis agreed to amend his income tax legislation by deleting the claim to constitutional priority in taxation. St. Laurent in turn agreed to provide a larger share of the taxes collected by Ottawa to the provinces, with a possible additional "special deal" for Quebec. The two agreed that the issue of taxation could be revisited at a federal-provincial conference dealing with fiscal issues, the type of conference Drew's Conservatives had been proposing and to which Ottawa and all the provinces agreed. What St. Laurent ruled out was a conference leading to a constitutional amendment. Nevertheless, he said he was confident that a method of amending the Constitution without reference to the United Kingdom Parliament would eventually be found.[41]

Ontario generated a much larger budgetary surplus than it had forecast because the government benefitted much more than it had anticipated from its tax-rental agreement. Premier Leslie Frost and St. Laurent jointly requested chartered accountant Walter Gordon, who had worked at the Bank of Canada, the federal finance department, and chaired a royal commission in 1946, to devise a new fiscal arrangement between Ottawa and Queen's Park. To combat unemployment, Frost proposed that Ottawa increase its share of the costs for all approved capital projects in Ontario from 20 to 50 per cent; if that was unacceptably high, he was prepared to negotiate and "play ball on this issue."[42]

The *Globe and Mail* urged the prairie premiers to press Ottawa to direct more immigrants to their provinces after official data showed that more immigrants were settling in Quebec than in the three prairie provinces combined.[43] The Ontario-Manitoba Boundary Act 1953 was given royal assent, confirming the boundary line between the two provinces as "surveyed and marked on the ground" by various commissioners between 1897 and 1931. Passed by Parliament and the legislatures of the affected provinces, this procedure for constitutional amendment came to be entrenched as Section 43 in the Constitution Act, 1982.[44]

The Provinces

It was an unusual year: there were no provincial elections. However, there was a new premier: after Nova Scotia's Angus Macdonald died, Oxford-educated Henry Hicks defeated five other candidates at a Liberal Party convention of 547 delegates. After five ballots, he became Canada's youngest first minister. At thirty-nine, he was the same age as Macdonald had been when he became the premier.[45] A vigorous campaign by Nova Scotia's black community for equal access to education led the government to end 150 years of school segregation. Nevertheless, some segregated schools continued to operate, and the integrated schools continued to teach a Eurocentric education with no acknowledgement of the role of the black community in Canada's or Nova Scotia's history.[46]

Shortly after premier Joey Smallwood exclaimed that "Newfoundland will one day erect a statue to Dr. Alfred Valdmanis," the recently dismissed head of Newfoundland's economic development program was arrested on a warrant issued on Smallwood's personal order. After testimony by Smallwood and others, Valdmanis pleaded guilty to defrauding the government of hundreds of thousands of dollars. The editors of the *Montreal Gazette* opined that "the resignation of the whole Smallwood Liberal cabinet must automatically follow a conviction," but resign they did not.[47]

New Brunswick's government considered acting on a report by the International Joint Commission proposing a $200 million hydropower development in the Saint John River basin involving rivers running through New Brunswick and Maine. The New Brunswick Electric Power Commission became more autonomous of its political masters with control of the Commission transferred to a committee that included bureaucrats and engineers as well as politicians. In a major policy shift, the government changed the focus of its economic development strategy from pulp and paper to mining.[48]

At the annual meeting of Quebec's de facto Social Credit movement, L'Union des électeurs, which claimed one hundred thousand members, five thousand delegates responded to the Quebec government's imposition of its own income tax by calling for the abolition of provincial taxes and the doubling of family allowances. A book by Laval

University economist and future federal Liberal minister Maurice Lamontagne supported Ottawa's position on federal-provincial fiscal relations, contending that Quebec was "waging a losing battle already lost" by "trying to bring back federalism to what it was before 1940." Infuriated, Duplessis forced the university rector to dissociate himself from the book's contents.[49]

Three Ontario by-elections took place as a committee of the legislature was investigating highway contracts and legal charges were pending of malpractice by contractors and government employees. The by-election results strengthened Leslie Frost's Conservative government, which won all three contests with larger majorities than they had scored in the general election.[50] The official opposition CCF proposed a scheme of hospital insurance modelled on that of Saskatchewan. The party also called for an investigation of secret contributions to political parties and public ownership of warehouses and brewers' retail stores so that their profits could be directed to rehabilitation programs for alcoholics.[51] Farquhar Oliver, originally elected to the legislature in 1926 as a United Farmers of Ontario candidate, became the Liberal leader for the second time in six years. He noted that "our inability to stick to one leader has hampered the party" and identified his party's obfuscations: "We need a clear-cut policy – our hands have been tied because we have been trying to interpret Liberal policy without knowing what it is."[52] Oliver's point highlighted the contrast between the ideological orientation of the social democratic CCF with its specific policy proposals and the Liberal party's lack of both explicit ideology and program.

Talk of a farmers' revolt circulated on the prairies. The Saskatchewan Farmers Union claimed 112,000 members in 1,045 locals and its leader, former CCF MLA Joe Phelps, called for a national farmers union. Future CCF MP Jake Schulz, who wanted governments to rein in the lending policies of banks, declared that his upstart Manitoba Farmers Union, more militant than its rival Manitoba Federation of Agriculture, had 40,000 members. In Alberta, a Farmers Union with 60,000 members emerged out of two older organizations, its president Henry Young calling on Ottawa to set a floor price for wheat, barley, and oats. The *Globe and Mail* predicted that the "Road to Depression" was assured if a radical national farmers union were to join forces with radical trade union leaders.[53]

The *Winnipeg Tribune* reported that only two caucus members firmly supported Errick Willis, the Manitoba Conservative party leader since 1936, and that Duff Roblin, a future premier, and another MLA planned to contest his leadership.[54] After Winnipeg mayoralty candidate Stephen Juba was almost elected on a liquor reform platform, Liberal-Progressive premier Douglas Campbell recruited former federal Conservative leader John Bracken to recommend changes to the liquor laws that had been in place since 1928 when Bracken was Manitoba's Progressive premier. The laws, which barred women from beer parlours, also prohibited restaurants from serving alcohol with meals and forbade cocktail lounges.[55]

Cash income per farm in Saskatchewan was above the national average, but an anxious premier T.C. Douglas feared that farm incomes would decline 20 per cent during the year. Nevertheless, after citing Wilfrid Laurier's forecast that the twentieth century would belong to Canada, Douglas presciently predicted that "the second half of the 20th century belongs to Western Canada, and more particularly to the northwestern section."[56] That northwestern section was prospering because its oil and gas riches allowed Alberta's provincial budget to grow to three times the size of the Saskatchewan budget. Even so, thirty thousand Albertans, mainly in the cities, were unemployed. The opposition parties charged that Social Credit cabinet ministers had abused the public's trust in the procurement and tendering of land and materials and that the provincial Treasury Branch was giving favourable loans to government MLAs.[57]

British Columbia's Social Credit government did away with the transferrable ballot voting system that had brought it to power. In a libel suit filed by B.C.'s former attorney general, the Supreme Court of Canada upheld two B.C. court decisions that Blair Fraser of *Maclean's* would be held in contempt of court if he failed to reveal his sources of information for a story titled "B.C. Coalition Commits Suicide."[58]

Canada in the World

Canada's diplomatic presence in the world expanded: embassies were opened in Egypt and Israel in response to regional tensions and pressure from Arab and Israeli governments anxious to enlist Ottawa's support. Canadian officials, however, were aware of their analytical shortcomings and not inclined to take sides. "Our information is not always free from bias and doubt," they cautioned external affairs minister Lester Pearson. "Any assessment must be hedged with reservations."[59] Ambassadors were also appointed to the Dominican Republic and Haiti, and a plenipotentiary minister was assigned to Lebanon.

St. Laurent raised Canada's international profile during his six-week world tour, the first by a Canadian prime minister. Visiting a dozen countries, his longest stay was a week in India; repeated invitations by Jawaharlal Nehru had sparked the trip. However, St. Laurent, with no specific diplomatic goals in mind, resolved not to engage with Nehru about the Kashmir dispute between his country and Pakistan.

St. Laurent and Nehru differed about the role of the United States in the world, with St. Laurent describing the US as "the most unselfish country ... with no other ambition than to live and let others live in mutually helpful intercourse." His attitude led a Canadian diplomat to observe privately that St. Laurent and Nehru "haven't got anything to say to each other after all." St. Laurent's most controversial comment regarded the Peking government, which India had recognized in 1950 – the first non-Communist country to do so. Determined not to be offside with the US, he told the Indians that Canada was not prepared to follow suit, even though recognition was "the common-sense realistic approach."[60] Meanwhile, external affairs minister Lester Pearson, addressing the National Council of the Churches of Christ in America in a talk titled "Christian Foundations for World Order," underscored the cultural cleavage between Asia and the West.[61]

The armed forces grew to a total of 114,000. Hostilities had ended in Korea, but a brigade of 6,000 Canadians remained. Two-thirds were to be home by year's end when the last Canadian prisoner, a fighter-pilot, was to be released.[62] A few months after Canadian troops cheered St. Laurent during his stop in West Germany, the murder of a Canadian soldier there raised the issue of whether the accused, a Toronto-born German citizen, would be tried under Allied law or German law. The High Commissioner of the British Zone of occupied Germany was charged with deciding whether Canada's troops shared the status of the British, American, and French troops as an occupying force or whether they were a security force.[63]

Ottawa refused to sign two international draft Covenants on Human Rights at the United Nations because, the government said, "Canada could not become a party to the Covenants owing to the nature of its Constitution which divides legislative powers concerning human rights between the national parliament and the provincial legislatures."[64] Canada's delegate to a UN committee, Liberal MP George Weaver, said Canada had no sympathy for policies of racial discrimination, but he voted against a proposal to create a commission to study "race conflict in South Africa resulting from the policies of apartheid." Weaver, questioning the "competence" and "utility" of such a commission, observed "there is no quick and easy solution" to the South Africa issue.[65] Similarly, despite its officially favourable disposition toward the UN, Canada refrained from contributing to a UN Fund for Economic Development; representing Canada, Liberal Senator Charles B. Howard said it had to "balance" its "sympathy for the needs and aspirations of developing countries ... against the requirements of its own economy and defense."[66]

Canada was one of the big four western powers. Backed by the United States, Britain, and France, Canada presented a plan at the UN Security Council to narrow differences between the big four and the Soviet Union on issues of disarmament and the prohibition of atomic weapons. Health minister Paul Martin served as the spokesperson for the western powers.[67] On most international issues, Ottawa and Washington took common positions and Canada accommodated many American requests. Pressured by the US, Ottawa reluctantly agreed to serve with India and Poland on the Indo-China Supervisory Commission.[68] Parliament amended the Radio Act to permit Americans to operate US government radio stations for American troops stationed in Canada. The government also supported President Eisenhower's proposal for an international atomic agency. The two American senators who came to interview former Soviet cipher clerk Igor Gouzenko learned nothing new.[69]

Ottawa's support for Washington's positions was not absolute: after secretary of state John Foster Dulles announced a new US defence policy of using his government's "great capacity to retaliate instantly, by means and places of our own choosing," Pearson warned an American audience that the US would have to consult its allies before striking back if it expected their support in an emergency. He also made it clear that excessive economic nationalism on the part of the US could weaken the unity of the West. In its position of leadership, Pearson said, the US had "a special obligation to cultivate the self-denying qualities of patience, restraint, and forbearance."[70]

Many Canadians were suspicious of the anti-Communist crusade in the US, and a majority in all the provinces except Quebec favoured expanding trade with the Soviet Union.[71] Even before the US Senate censured Joe McCarthy at year's end, University of Toronto economist B.S. Keirstead wrote of Canadians' "dismay and distrust of American leadership and a troubled sense that our closest and most trusted friends had been attacked by a spiritual illness that left us baffled as to how we were to conduct our affairs with them."[72]

The economy went in and out of recession, immigration receded as unemployment rose, ownership of television sets surged, and cultural mores continued to evolve. Parliament completely revised and consolidated the Criminal Code, passed a law encouraging home ownership, and provided pay raises for MPs. The prime minister reconstructed his cabinet, in which the absence of Torontonians persisted. Conservative hopes were dashed once again in a Quebec by-election, and the Liberal government's relationship with the labour movement cooled. The CCF was the only party proposing an alternative foreign policy while Social Credit advocated boosting the purchasing power of consumers.

Quebec's assertiveness on taxation and premier Duplessis's continuing fight with Ottawa led Ottawa and all the provinces to agree to hold a federal-provincial conference on fiscal issues. Atypically, no provincial elections were held. The most dramatic development in Atlantic Canada was the criminal conviction of an émigré government economist once hailed as Newfoundland's saviour. In Ontario, a former Liberal leader returned to face the province's popular Conservative government. There was talk of a farmers' revolt on the prairies, and British Columbia's Social Credit party did away with the transferrable ballot that had brought it to power. Atlantic business leaders formed an economic council to promote regional economic development. Parliament and the provinces of Manitoba and Ontario amended the Constitution confirming the boundary between the two provinces.

Prime Minister St. Laurent embarked on a world tour, Canadian diplomatic representation abroad grew, and the foreign policies of Canada and the United States generally corresponded. Although support for the United Nations was a cornerstone of Canadian policy, Ottawa did not endorse UN initiatives to foster economic development in the developing world or to investigate South Africa's apartheid policies.

1955

I've more to do than spend my time amusing Parliament.[1]

C.D. Howe

Montrealers were passionate about their first place *Canadiens* hockey team. Following the suspension of star player Maurice Richard for the balance of the season and the playoffs by National Hockey League president Clarence Campbell, a major riot broke out in the city; during the game following the suspension a tear gas bomb was set off, Campbell was pelted with eggs, peanuts, and tomatoes, a furious mob looted thirty stores, and seventy people were arrested. Almost forty people were injured, including a dozen police officers. The main shopping district was compared to "the aftermath of a wartime blitz in London."[2] In another violent disturbance a few months later, described by Montreal police as "appearing worse" than the hockey riot and unequalled for its "prolonged activity" since the anti-conscription riots of 1917, hoodlums took over a peaceful student protest against higher streetcar fares; streetcars were set on fire and the police made 150 arrests.[3]

The Dominion Bureau of Statistics noted that immigration, a rising birth rate, and a declining death rate had contributed to population growth of almost 30 per cent since 1945. Insurance company statisticians predicted a record high number of births, a new low in maternal mortality, and a drop in the death rate from twelve per thousand in the late 1940s to eight per thousand.[4] The increase in the birth rate heartened the *Ottawa Citizen* while the less impressionable *Montreal Gazette* editorialized that the "population gain is really ... not at all encouraging." The paper accurately predicted it would take "at least 30 years" for Canada's population of 15.6 million to double (it rose to 25.8 million in 1985).[5] A McMaster University professor, more concerned with the implications of an overpopulated world, speculated that the global population would reach 3.25 billion in 2000 (it grew to 6.1 billion); he told the Royal Society of Canada that he foresaw "hungry nations equipped with modern weapons seeking by conquest to expand their food capacity."[6]

Various modes of transportation provided faster, farther, and more convenient travel. Canadian National and Canadian Pacific railways reduced their Montreal to Vancouver runs by fourteen to sixteen hours. Canadian Pacific Airlines, created thirteen years earlier from an amalgam of ten bush lines, became the world's sixth largest air carrier. It was the world's only airline with routes that crossed the Equator (to Peru), the international date line (to Australia), and the Arctic Circle (to Amsterdam) after it introduced a 4,825 mile over-the-roof-of-the-world polar route from Vancouver.[7] To facilitate coast-to-coast automobile travel by the end of the decade, Ottawa offered to increase spending to complete construction of a hard-surfaced Trans-Canada Highway. Off Canada's northern coast, government scientists completed a survey of the Arctic Archipelago.[8]

While nuclear weapons continued to be a source of international tensions, nuclear power was being promoted as potentially fuelling domestic prosperity. Ontario Hydro announced it would build a demonstration nuclear power plant at a cost of $13 to $15 million ($130 to $150 million in 2021), with the cost shared among Hydro, the federal government, and the company building the plant. Although the experimental plant would be uneconomic, the Hydro chairman predicted it would lead to the development of nuclear fuel at costs competitive with other fuels and allow commercial consumption by 1958.[9]

Rapidly expanding capital investment and relatively stable prices produced an exceptionally large increase of almost 10 per cent in the gross domestic product, the largest of any post-war year. Corporate profits, personal incomes, and imports of machinery and equipment rose sharply. Higher personal incomes and the ready availability of mortgage funds had boosted the per capita consumption of durable goods since 1949 by 40 per cent and much of the increase occurred between 1954 and 1955.[10]

Major changes were stirring in the trade union movement. Hoping to advance their influence in national affairs, the ranking officers of the six hundred thousand-member Trades and Labor Congress and the four hundred thousand-member Canadian Congress of Labor announced their intention to end their inter-union disputes by asking their conventions to ratify the amalgamation of their organizations to form a new Canadian Labor Congress. This posed a vexed question for Quebec's

hundred thousand-member Canadian Catholic Confederation of Labor, commonly known as the "national syndicates": what would the
CCCL's relationship be vis-à-vis the CLC given that that the Quebec
union was based on the social doctrines of the Roman Catholic Church,
the only Roman Catholic trade union movement in the Commonwealth? Although the CCCL's membership included non-Catholics, the
union's religious character was of major importance in Quebec. Many
felt that any formal association with the CLC would have to allow for
the CCCL's autonomy and special character.[11]

Two exceptionally long strikes by the United Auto Workers came to
an end. A 109-day labour disruption in which 163,000 workdays were
lost by autoworkers in three Ontario cities ended with a commitment
to raise wages in twenty weeks' time. The agreement led the conservative *Globe and Mail* to opine, "Striking is utterly obsolete; and in any
case, utterly futile since the losses always and inevitably far outweigh
the gains." Union officials presented the outcome of the strike differently: "we have not given up anything ... We have taught the Canadian
Manufactures Association ... they have taken on someone a little too
big." An even longer strike by Toronto aircraft workers resulted in a
settlement that gave workers more gains in pay and benefits than the
autoworkers had received.[12]

A severe shortage of clerical workers in the federal civil service led
Ottawa to lift all restrictions barring married women from employment, and marriage no longer resulted in dismissal, demotion, or a
salary ceiling.[13] Despite a low unemployment rate, there was public
anxiety about unemployment. More Gallup poll respondents than ever
thought that unemployment would increase and was the most serious
problem faced by Canada; two of three respondents said all three levels
of government were responding inadequately.[14]

Greater Montreal and Toronto had populations exceeding 1 million.
The third and fourth largest metropolitan centres were Vancouver and
Winnipeg. Edmonton ranked eighth and Calgary, with 139,105 people,
tenth. Only in Ontario did the population surpass five million. It had
663,000 more residents than Quebec, but Ontario's increase of 137,000
people during the year barely exceeded Quebec's increase of 132,000.
Six provinces had fewer than 1 million people and Alberta had scarcely
more than a million. British Columbia was the fastest growing province, and no province lost population.[15]

The federal government grew modestly, from 138,000 to 143,000
full-time employees. The external affairs department with 1,107 personnel had 139 fewer employees than the fisheries department. The
combined salaries of the four foreign service officers assigned to NATO

headquarters was $37,000 ($370,000 in 2021). Defence, the largest department, had 33,000 people, labour 7,000, agriculture 6,000, finance
5,000, and health and welfare 3,000. The Chief Electoral Office had 20
employees, the Auditor General 141, the Privy Council Office 106, the
governor general's office 24, and 7 civil servants attended to the prime
minister's residence.[16]

CBC, reporting that sixty-nine residential boarding schools had
11,000 students, visited the Anglican school in Moose Factory where
every school day began with a religious service. The glowing broadcast
stated that the schools offered Indigenous children a "chance at a new
future" because students were given a "free and equal chance to the
children in urban areas," leaving behind "the neglect and isolation of
the past." A Liberal MP asked citizenship minister Jack Pickersgill to
build another residential school in his constituency to accommodate
the "nomad Indians [who] leave for the hunt in the fall and return only
the following spring depriving their school age children of education."
Pickersgill, however, favoured abolishing residential schools and inte-
grating their students in the public school system.[17]

Federal Politics

In the parliamentary session which began in January, the Progressive
Conservatives were handicapped by the absence of leader George
Drew, convalescing after a severe illness. Nevertheless, before the session ended in July, the Conservatives had their best session since the
1930s. They benefitted from fissures in the Liberal government; trade
and defence production minister C.D. Howe, the cabinet's most senior
minister, suffered two major setbacks, leading him to talk of resigning.

First, Howe had given his word to TransCanada Pipelines Limited that Ottawa would underwrite the company's bonds for an all-
Canadian pipeline route. Many, including finance minister Walter
Harris, observed that the government would be taking most of the financial risk while only the company would gain any eventual profit.
The pro-Liberal *Winnipeg Free Press* described the arrangement as "irresponsible finance, bad economics, and worse government." According
to Blair Fraser of *Maclean's*, Harris prevailed in cabinet over Howe in a
"Homeric contest."[18]

Second, the Conservatives humiliated the Liberals in the debate regarding the sweeping emergency powers in the Defence Production
Act. Passed in 1951 when it seemed that the Korean War might become
a third world war, the act was due to expire in 1956. When the act was
first passed, Howe had objected to making its duration three years

instead of five, as the opposition had proposed, because "That would mean coming back to Parliament again in three years and I've more to do than spend my time amusing Parliament."[19] Howe's attitude exemplified the arrogance of Liberal ministers that was becoming habitual in parliamentary debate. His new Defence Production Act proposed to make permanent the emergency powers, which he as minister could exercise at will. Howe described the bill as a "model Act," to which Conservative Donald Fleming retorted that it would "be better regarded as a model decree of a Caesar" and an assault on the rights of Parliament.[20] The CCF initially opposed the bill but soon decided to support it on the grounds that Parliament could check misuse of the emergency powers during the annual consideration of the spending estimates for Howe's department. The press opposed the bill: the *Winnipeg Free Press*, for example, condemned it as an indefensible violation of Liberal principles and demanded that it be withdrawn.[21] Prime minister Louis St. Laurent and the Liberal caucus, succumbing to the protests, undercut Howe once again.

The issue of Senate reform, where seventy-three Liberals outnumbered a rump of seven Conservatives, received an unusual amount of attention. St. Laurent, who had allowed Senate vacancies to accumulate, raised the idea of filling some of the twenty-three vacancies in the upper house with opposition party members and others who had distinguished themselves in various walks of life. MP George Hees, president of the national Progressive Conservative Association agreed, calling for the appointment of outstanding citizens, "a group of the best minds in the country." The CCF and Social Credit parties supported a Conservative proposal to establish a commission to study Senate reform, but in the end partisan Liberals dissuaded St. Laurent from his idea and voted down the Conservative proposal. For their part, the Liberals in the Senate rejected a Conservative bill requiring Senate vacancies be filled within six months of their occurrence.[22]

Several interest groups also weighed in on the issue of Senate reform. The CCCL proposed replacing the chamber with a body of federal and provincial representatives and eliminating the Senate's veto power on constitutional matters. The CCCL also proposed constitutionalizing a bill of rights and the Supreme Court, both of which would eventually occur in 1982. Speaking to Quota International, an American-headquartered organization dedicated to empowering women, the daughter of one of Canada's first woman judges urged that St. Laurent appoint women to fill all the Senate vacancies. To continue the tradition of including English Canadians among Quebec's Senators, St. Laurent appointed Hartland Molson, scion of the wealthy brewing company. He was one of thirteen appointed on one day, along with a dozen Liberals and one Conservative who was a lifelong friend. The appointees included, for the first time, a Jew and a Ukrainian Catholic. St. Laurent said he hoped and believed David Croll would consider himself a spokesman for all Canadians of Jewish origin.[23]

Conservative Senator Walter Aseltine of Saskatchewan, who had been appointed by R.B. Bennett in 1933, sponsored a bill to liberalize Canada's archaic divorce laws, proposing desertion for three years, cruelty, and incurable insanity to be added to adultery as causes for divorce. Aseltine's bill, which he described as "the only cure for the cancer of broken marriages" and a remedy for perjury in many divorce petitions, would have applied in all the provinces except Newfoundland and Quebec, where the civil code made no provision for divorce. The bill did not reach the House as Catholic Liberal Senators mobilized some of their Protestant colleagues to assist them to reject the bill.[24]

The anonymous Canadian correspondent for the British journal *The Round Table* judged CCF leader M.J. Coldwell as the best parliamentarian in the Commons and the twenty-four-member CCF caucus as having "a higher average ability than any other party."[25] However, outside the halls of Parliament, CCF leaders were taking stock because the party appeared in the doldrums intellectually and electorally. Party chairman David Lewis, party secretary from 1936 to 1950 and future leader of the New Democratic Party (NDP) in the 1970s, argued that the party's fortunes might improve if it dropped the strident Depression-era phraseology about eradicating capitalism in the party's 1933 Regina Manifesto.[26] CCF MP Ross Thatcher, a successful hardware merchant long out of step with his colleagues, produced the biggest surprise of the parliamentary session by resigning from the party, explaining "that left wing elements have gained dangerous and unwarranted recognition within the councils of the party ... [which] has taken a line on foreign affairs that in my opinion, no matter how honestly taken, can only give comfort to communist nations."[27] An example he cited was the admission of a rearmed West Germany to NATO on which the caucus divided in a Commons vote; some MPs including Coldwell were in favour, others opposed, and some abstained.[28]

Social Credit, taking a more right-wing posture on most issues than the Conservatives, spent much of its time attacking the CCF. Despite being the smallest and an inconsequential party in Parliament, Social Credit was attacked by the major parties as hopelessly divided internally, a claim voiced by George Hees, whom leader Social Credit Solon Low termed a "meddlesome playboy." Liberal mines minister George Prudham said Social Credit's doctrines could only be implemented in a rigid dictatorship. Low termed Social Credit "the greatest movement ever conceived outside of Christianity" and proposed that Canada adopt British sterling, "instead of us tying ourselves to the United States." Soon after, Low suffered a heart attack, throwing the party's leadership into doubt.[29]

The Liberal government's Speech from the Throne outlined a broad legislative agenda, but the bills that were introduced were largely amendments to existing legislation rather than new initiatives. The government's budget, which Harris referred to as a "plain ordinary Liberal budget," included reduced income taxes for 85 per cent of taxpayers, reduced corporate taxes for large companies, a reduced excise tax on new automobiles, and made permanent the temporary tax concessions enjoyed by oil, gas, and mining industries. The budget speech also announced the creation of a Royal Commission on Canada's Economic Prospects to be chaired by successful accountant and business executive Walter Gordon.[30] A forecast deficit of $160 million in an expenditure budget of over $4.3 billion turned out to be a substantial surplus. It reduced inflationary pressures, helped pay down debt, and supported the operations of crown corporations such as the Central Mortgage and Housing Corporation, whose activities contributed to stable housing prices, easier financing terms, and a record construction year.[31]

A revised Unemployment Insurance Act, originally enacted in 1941, provided for increased benefits. Another bill gave the Chief Electoral Officer full status as a deputy minister and increased the allowance for the campaign expenses of federal candidates. Yet another bill implemented a convention with the United States to establish a joint commission to study the decline of Great Lakes fisheries and formulate a conservation program.[32]

Intergovernmental Relations

Two federal-provincial first ministers' conferences were held, the first since 1950. The first conference was to deal with unemployment insurance but since many premiers wanted to discuss other subjects as well, it was decided that the second conference, originally intended to address intergovernmental fiscal relations, would also deal with natural resources, health and welfare, and the establishment of a federal-provincial continuing committee. In between the conferences, the Supreme Court unanimously rejected a challenge by Alberta, Ontario, and Quebec to the federal labour code regulating labour relations in federal industries such as railways, maritime shipping, communications, and aviation.[33]

At the first conference, St. Laurent proposed gearing Ottawa's contributions to unemployment relief payments to increases in the jobless numbers in the individual provinces. The provinces however wanted Ottawa to pay the full cost of relief. Ontario's Leslie Frost was the conference's major player, arguing that Ottawa had reneged on the proposals for unemployment relief it had made at the 1945 federal-provincial conference. St. Laurent retorted that the provinces had rejected the proposals at the time and were no longer on offer. Frost also insisted that the conference address health insurance, which St. Laurent rejected.[34]

Ottawa's position prior to the conferences was that any permanent reallocation of taxation powers between Ottawa and the provinces would be unlikely to meet all contingencies and that medium term arrangements like the tax-rental agreements, while imperfect, had the benefit of periodic reconsideration and renewal.[35] At the conferences, which served as preliminaries to renegotiating the tax-rental agreements set to expire in 1957, it became increasingly clear to Ottawa that the fiscal needs of the provinces could not be linked to the surrender of provincial taxing authority because the provinces would not stand for it. Fiscal aid to the provinces had been an incidental element of the original tax-rental agreements of 1942, but the steady growth of provincial power and capacity in the post-war era meant the link was increasingly unsustainable.[36]

Most of the provinces wanted to continue the five-year tax-rental agreements but with adjustments. The Maritime premiers pressed for modifications that would consider their specific circumstances. New Brunswick's Hugh John Flemming insisted on adjustment grants over and above those provided in his province's tax-rental agreement. British Columbia's W.A.C. Bennett criticized his province's tax-rental agreement, which had been negotiated by the previous provincial Liberal-Conservative government, as short-changing his province. Several premiers asked that Ottawa transfer more money to support education. Newfoundland's Joey Smallwood wanted federal scientific aid in identifying Newfoundland's natural resources.[37]

At the second conference, which ran for an unusually long four days, St. Laurent offered to help fund a national health insurance program if "a substantial majority of provincial governments, representing a substantial majority of the Canadian people" supported such a program.[38] Quebec's Maurice Duplessis rejected that idea. Unusually reticent, he refused to answer reporters' questions after his opening statement in which he called for clarifying the taxation powers of the federal and provincial governments, simplifying tax collection, and reducing taxes. Manitoba's Douglas Campbell suggested convening a constitutional conference to consider daylight savings time and a uniform voting age for all jurisdictions. His rationale was that agreement on such minor issues would encourage further cooperation on major issues. Saskatch-ewan's T.C. Douglas wanted Ottawa to enter fields of provincial ju-risdiction that had national significance. Again, Ontario's Frost was particularly outspoken at this conference, arguing that in calculating federal fiscal transfers, a province ought not to be judged a "have" province based on its concentration of industry.[39]

The conference established a "technical and advisory committee" of federal and provincial officials to collect data, liaise, and prepare the ground for future meetings of political leaders. Another committee, consisting of federal and provincial ministers, was created to study health insurance.[40] St. Laurent termed the conference a success, Frost said it would eventually prove to have been successful, and B.C.'s Ben-nett called it a "fiasco": "Nothing has been accomplished which could not have been by letter or by sending a clerk from Victoria down to Ot-tawa."[41] The size of the various delegations may have indicated some-thing of the significance the provinces attached to the conferences: of the 90 delegates at the first conference, Ottawa had 17, Ontario 28, Que-bec 4, and Alberta 3. The larger second conference had 169 delegates. Ontario again had the largest number, 37. Ottawa had 23, Quebec and Saskatchewan 15 each, and New Brunswick, which had 8 at the first conference, 23.[42]

After the second conference, Ottawa offered to increase its share of the cost of completing the Trans-Canada Highway from 50 per cent and up to 90 per cent in some cases. All the provinces except Prince Edward Island dismissed the offer as insufficient. Quebec persisted in refusing to accept a federal grant for highway construction in the province on the grounds that its autonomy would be prejudiced.[43]

The Provinces

Provincial elections returned incumbent governments in Prince Ed-ward Island, Ontario, and Alberta. The PEI Liberals swept to their sixth consecutive victory, winning twenty-seven of thirty seats and result-ing in the resignation of the Conservative leader. In Ontario, Frost's Conservatives captured nearly half the vote while the share of votes cast for both the Liberals and the CCF declined. In Alberta, the Liberals surged from three to sixteen seats and the popular vote for Social Credit dropped by 10 per cent. Nevertheless, the party won a comfortable ma-jority in its sixth consecutive victory.

Every provincial government raised and spent a record amount of money.[44] However, this did not solve all their challenges, particularly in the Atlantic region. Economic development continued to bedevil

Newfoundland's government. Herbert Pottle, who had once termed Joey Smallwood a "prophet of the average 'Joe'" and had been a cabinet minister since Newfoundland had entered Confederation, resigned suddenly on the eve of the first federal-provincial conference, saying Smallwood's economic policies were not in the public interest. Embarrassed, Smallwood deplored the abrupt manner of the resignation and said Pottle had failed to understand the policies.[45] Smallwood later told the commissioners studying Canada's economic prospects that "have-not" provinces needed a Canadian version of the massive Colombo Plan designed to aid south Asian states.[46]

American multinational mining corporations in New Brunswick warned Premier Flemming that unless they were provided with inexpensive, plentiful, publicly generated electric power, they would not develop the province's substantial lead and zinc deposits. This led Flemming to tell the commission on Canada's economic prospects that if Ottawa failed to assist New Brunswick in power development in the same way that it was assisting the Alberta-to-central Canada pipeline and St. Lawrence Seaway projects, his province would remain no more than an ore digger.[47] PEI's Alex Matheson noted that many people educated in his province moved to other provinces because his province's small economy could not support them; Ottawa should therefore help "to repay the debt owed by other provinces to PEI."[48]

The Canso Causeway, the two-kilometre ribbon of granite linking Cape Breton Island with the Nova Scotia mainland, opened; approximately thirty-five thousand people lined the roads and nearby hills as one hundred bagpipers crossed the 4,300-foot-long road, which had taken three years and ten million tons of rocks to complete. The deepest causeway in the world, it became part of the Trans-Canada Highway. A major employer on the island, the Dominion Coal Co., laid off eight thousand workers, leading the company to lobby the provincial government which in turn pressed a reluctant Ottawa to subsidize the export of one hundred thousand tons of coal to England.[49]

Opposition to Quebec's Union Nationale government was growing. Le Devoir exposed the generous arrangement Duplessis had made with an American corporation which paid a royalty of just one cent for every ton of iron ore extracted in the province's far northern region while Newfoundland collected 33 cents per ton extracted in Labrador. Attracting 1,200 delegates to their first convention since 1950, the Liberals hoped provincial autonomy would fade as an issue so that they could fight the anticipated 1956 election on the administrative record of the Union Nationale. Leaders of the right-wing L'Union des électeurs agreed to support the Liberals in the election in exchange for the inclusion of a tenet of social credit doctrine in the Liberal platform. Quebec's CCFers, thinking it would help their cause, changed the party's name to Parti social démocratique du Québec because of "the impossibility of translating CCF."[50]

Ontario enfranchised Indigenous people after twenty-two of twenty-five bands signalled approval in a plebiscite. Nevertheless, many Six Nations people boycotted the election.[51] Liberal leader Farquhar Oliver issued a twenty-five-point manifesto, recruited federal cabinet ministers Lester Pearson, Paul Martin, and Walter Harris to campaign on his party's behalf, and said it had its best chance of forming a government since 1937. However, the Liberals gained just three seats in the election to hold eleven. The CCF gained a seat after it expelled fourteen party members on the grounds that they were members of the Communist Party.[52] The lone Communist MPP, J.B. Salsberg, lost his seat.

Under their new leader, thirty-eight-year-old Duff Roblin, Manitoba's Conservatives defeated the governing Liberal-Progressives in two by-elections, giving rise to a degree of optimism unknown in the party's ranks since the 1930s. Fought on the issue of the government's pay-as-you-go road construction policy, the disappointing by-elections results led the government to rethink and partially abandon the policy. Former premier John Bracken's examination of the provincial liquor laws concluded that competition among the breweries was "dead and buried"; they fixed prices, received 20 to 25 per cent more than eastern Canadian breweries, and profited at the expense of the provincial treasury. The disclosures led the opposition parties to charge the government with neglecting roads, welfare, and education while permitting the breweries to profit unfairly.[53]

The Saskatchewan association representing three hundred rural municipalities challenged the CCF government to build more market roads to accommodate farmers. The province had passed labour legislation more "advanced" than that of other provinces but because farmers were anxious to have their grain transported as cheaply as possible, Premier Douglas disagreed with the TLC and CCL's proposal to aid shipyard workers by restricting foreign vessels from carrying Canadian goods. To inspire a higher quality of medical practice, Douglas's government created a full-term medical school and opened a "magnificent" five-hundred-bed university hospital.[54]

Alberta's Social Credit government cautioned in its election campaign literature, "Don't be Misled by False Propaganda," a reaction to the *Calgary Herald*'s claim that at least eleven government MLAs were sitting in the legislature illegally because they had received preferential treatment in their dealings with the government-owned provincial bank. Unsurprisingly, the main plank of the official opposition Liberals called for prohibiting MLAs from dealing with the bank. Campaigning for the provincial CCF, federal leader Coldwell criticized the government for failing to exploit the province's resources for the people's benefit. However, Alberta's substantial fiscal capacity – per capita receipts were nearly double the average for all provincial governments – had allowed the government to garner working class support by establishing an array of health, education, and social programs.[55]

Deane Finlayson, the leader of British Columbia's small Conservative party, was expelled from the national executive of the federal Conservative party, censured for alleging that British Columbia's three Conservative MPs and other supporters of federal party leader George Drew had made a deal with the provincial Social Credit government. Finlayson responded that his party, which was unrepresented in the legislature, was composed of "simon-pure Tories." The Social Credit government opposed foreign-registered ships carrying Canadian goods because, unlike Saskatchewan's farmers, B.C.'s forestry industry could use the Panama Canal to get its products to eastern seaboard markets whenever Canada's railways were uncompetitive.[56]

Canada in the World

Although 1955 was the first year since the end of the Second World War that Canada did not open any new diplomatic missions abroad, changes were afoot in the external affairs department: all five women of the sixteen qualified applicants in the competition to serve as foreign service officers were offered positions.[57]

Canada, which had provided the third largest contingent of UN troops in Korea, still had five hundred soldiers on the peninsula.[58] Canadians also continued to play a part in NATO's deterrence and containment project: in addition to the infantry brigade and a dozen jet fighter squadrons in West Germany, the navy assigned forty ships for the protection of Atlantic convoys.[59] Canada had been instrumental in the adding of Article 2 to the NATO charter, which called for the "development of peaceful and friendly international relations [among NATO members] by strengthening their free institutions," and external affairs minister Lester Pearson gave an encouraging assessment of Article 2 to Parliament. However, in private he had become doubtful that it would amount to anything.[60]

Canadian concerns about Chinese and Soviet aggression subsided despite the creation of the Warsaw Pact by the Soviet Union and seven satellite states; the external affairs department concluded that the Soviets were "prepared to accept the present division of the world for some years."[61] Fisheries minister James Sinclair, the future father-in-law of Pierre Trudeau, became the first NATO cabinet minister to go behind the Iron Curtain; after visiting China and the Soviet Union, he described the considerate treatment he had received and said he favoured exchange visits between Canadian and Soviet parliamentarians.[62]

Soon after Sinclair's trip, Pearson embarked on a twelve-country tour that included the Far East, the Soviet Union, and Egypt. The first NATO foreign minister to be invited to Moscow, Pearson received the "red carpet" treatment, spent a weekend with Nikita Khrushchev at his Black Sea "palace," and took the first step in securing Canada's first agreement to sell wheat to the USSR. The two countries also resumed parcel service. On his return to Canada, Pearson predicted that revolutionary developments in Asia would have more far-reaching consequences than the Russian Revolution.[63]

Pearson, who enjoyed a particularly warm relationship with Anthony Eden, was delighted that he succeeded Winston Churchill as the United Kingdom's prime minister. Neither Pearson nor Eden cared much for American secretary of state John Foster Dulles; together they hoped to correct what they considered his erratic policy vis-à-vis China.[64] The Americans, in turn, considered Canadian policy erratic; although Ottawa closely cooperated with Washington in North America's defence, Pearson upset them by telling Parliament that Canada had made "no commitment to share in the defence of either Formosa or the coastal islands, or to intervene in any struggle between the two Chinese governments for possession of these offshore islands." Canada, unlike the US, favoured negotiations between the Communists and Nationalists to settle the status of Formosa.[65]

As Pearson travelled abroad, health minister Paul Martin led the Canadian delegation in ongoing disarmament and other negotiations at the UN. Martin's success in breaking a deadlock over the admission of twenty-one new applicants for membership heightened Canada's stature in the organization. John Holmes, assistant undersecretary of state for external affairs, credited Martin with "one of the most remarkable feats in the history of the General Assembly," earning him a standing ovation at the Assembly.[66]

Relations between Canada and the US were at times bruised. In the debate over the admission of new UN members, Washington was so upset with Ottawa that it threatened to cancel Canada's exemption from American restrictions on oil imports. Some Canadian officials, whose objective was finding practical solutions to world problems, suspected that the US wanted to employ the UN only to extend its own version of democracy.[67] Pearson continued to intimate that Canada preferred to recognize Red China, as Britain had done years earlier, but that Ottawa would not do so if Washington was opposed.[68]

The Commonwealth conference of prime ministers convened in London with no agenda. St. Laurent spoke supportively of the Commonwealth but his statement in the House of Commons underlined that the conference exercised no powers and that the informal meeting could make no decisions; it was only "an opportunity for a full and frank exchange of views about the many events of great importance in the international field." This led the *Globe and Mail* to opine that the conference was fruitless, amounting to "plenty of nothing."[69] Because of the Commonwealth connection, however, Canadian foreign aid focussed on the organization's Asian states. As the third largest contributor (after the US and the UK) to the Colombo Plan, Canada purchased steam locomotives for India, donated wheat that indirectly contributed to the construction of a "Canada Dam" in West Bengal, and helped build a cement plant and expand electric power capacity in Pakistan.[70]

Africa, to which Ottawa had devoted little attention, gained increasing notice. A trade commission office was opened in Rhodesia and after the UK announced plans for African decolonization, a memorandum prepared for the external affairs department recommended opening a mission in the independent Gold Coast (Ghana). Their department was concerned that the USSR would use decolonization as an opportunity to "propagandize, meddle and generally make trouble in Africa."[71]

Major-General E.L.M. Burns continued as Chief of Staff of the UN's Truce Supervision Organization in the Middle East. As tensions between Egypt and Israel escalated, Pearson was one of several international figures who served as a channel for dialogue between them. The external affairs department assessed relations with Israel as "on a sound footing" – less so with the Arab states.[72] Social Credit leader Solon Low made the far-fetched charge that Pearson's visit to Egypt and not to Israel could set off a third world war.[73] Canada maintained its historic ties with the Caribbean but admitted few immigrants from the region because of Ottawa's discriminatory race-based immigration policy. However, a shortage of European housekeepers, together with persistent lobbying by the Negro Citizenship Association, led to a limited number of "coloured" domestics from Jamaica and Barbados being welcomed as immigrants.[74]

The birth rate was up, the death rate down, the gross domestic product increased more than in any of the post-war years. Travel became more convenient, and Canada's competing national trade union federations, representing a million workers, moved toward a merger. Montreal experienced two riots and Ontario planned to deploy nuclear power to drive its growing economy.

The Liberal government reduced taxes, ran a sizeable budgetary surplus after forecasting a deficit, created a Royal Commission to study Canada's economic prospects, and revised the Unemployment Insurance Act because of pressure by provincial governments to carry more of the burden. The Conservatives benefitted from a couple of major policy pratfalls by cabinet minister C.D. Howe. The CCF caucus suffered a major defection, Ross Thatcher, who a few years later became the leader of the Saskatchewan Liberals and defeated the long-governing Saskatchewan CCF-NDP. An unusually high number of vacancies in the Senate brought attention to the issue of Senate reform.

The first of two first ministers' conferences dealt with unemployment insurance, the second addressed a host of issues including intergovernmental fiscal relations and health insurance. Ontario's Leslie Frost was the most active leader at both conferences. Three provincial elections returned three incumbent governments: Liberal in Prince Edward Island, Conservative in Ontario, and Social Credit in Alberta. All ten provincial governments tabled budgets with record high revenues and expenditures.

Canada was active in world affairs. External affairs minister Lester Pearson travelled widely, Canada broke a deadlock at the UN over the admission of new member states, concerns about Soviet expansionism receded, and Canada's relationship with the US deteriorated somewhat as their policies differed vis-à-vis China and at the UN. Canadian foreign aid to Asia's Commonwealth states began to bear some fruit. Largely ignored by Ottawa in the past, Africa and the Middle East gained more attention as African decolonization was on the horizon and fears emerged of war between Egypt and Israel.

1956

The guillotine![1]

Stanley Knowles

Tranquilizers and new household products were introduced, including the air freshener Glade, scouring powder Comet, and the toxic insecticide Raid. Commercial aviation entered its golden age; passengers dressed up to fly and an airline flight was seen not just as a means of getting to a vacation but as a vacation itself. Ottawa issued 92,000 passports, almost 30,000 more than in 1950. The first transatlantic coaxial cable connecting Canada with Britain replaced the relay of telephone calls by radio waves, and in the first twenty-four hours of the cable's operation there were 119 calls between Canada and London.[2]

Governor General Vincent Massey, whose term of office had been extended for a year, went on a ten-thousand-mile aerial tour of the Far North that included a flight over the North Pole. The Northwest Territories Council, most of whose members were federal civil servants, met above the Arctic Circle for the first time.[3] For maritime reconnaissance, the Royal Canadian Air Force (RCAF) selected Montreal-based Canadair to produce the largest aircraft ever manufactured domestically.[4]

Trading on the Toronto Stock Exchange was buoyant, imports surged, and corporate profits and business inventories reached peaks. Consumer prices rose by less than 2 per cent, purchases of durable goods increased, and outstanding consumer credit swelled by 26 per cent.[5] Home builders complained of a shortage of money available for construction, which the government attributed to competition for credit in Canada's expanding economy.[6] Britain, Canada's largest export market before the Second World War, bought only a third of what the United States bought. About 60 per cent of Canada's exports went to the US and the US exported more to Canada than it did to all of Europe. Trade minister C.D. Howe predicted that Japan would eventually replace Britain as the leading customer for Canadian wheat.[7]

A growing number of Canadians moved to the United States and the flow of immigrants slackened. However, after the Soviet Union crushed an uprising in Hungary, immigration minister Jack Pickersgill, predicting a severe labour shortage, said that Canada was willing to provide free passage for an almost unlimited number of Hungarian refugees. Thousands of visas were issued.[8] The overwhelming majority of the eighty thousand new citizens lived in urban centres. Only 1 per cent of them lived in the Atlantic provinces while 17 per cent resided in Quebec and 60 per cent in Ontario. The municipality of Metropolitan Toronto was North America's fastest growing city, outstripping the rate of growth of Houston and Los Angeles. Metropolitan Toronto chairman Fred Gardiner predicted the city's population would grow to 2.8 million in 1981.[9] (It grew to 2.1 million that year, and the Toronto census metropolitan area reached three million.)

While Canada was a net importer of beef and poultry, an extraordinary surplus of wheat spoiling for lack of elevator storage space and a shortage of railway cars disgruntled farmers. An early freeze also halted grain shipments at Port Arthur. Cash income from the sale of farm products was up, but total receipts were less than they had been in 1952. Few farmers took advantage of new legislation that allowed their stored grain to be used as security to access bank loans. Trade minister Howe's impolitic response to the plight of farmers was to shrug off the glut in wheat and butter as a positive development.[10]

The Canadian Federation of Agriculture voiced support for the sale of agricultural products to Iron Curtain countries at prices lower than domestic prices.[11] Within days, the Crown-owned Export Credit Insurance Corporation guaranteed a loan to facilitate a major sale of wheat to Poland, and a Russian delegation arrived to negotiate another sale.[12] (Demonstrations like those that had upset earlier Soviet delegations and embarrassed the government did not take place.) Noting an international trend away from controls in marketing grains, the Globe and Mail editorialized that the Canadian Wheat Board monopoly on grain sales ought to be discarded in favour of open, free competition.[13]

The Trades and Labor Congress and the Canadian Congress of Labor merged to become the Canadian Labor Congress as the number of union members continued to increase. After 148 days the unionized employees of General Motors ended the costliest strike in Canadian history. The growth of the service sector meant more non-union workers as well as more working women, who constituted about a quarter of the labour force. About one hundred thousand women worked in each of retail sales and factories, fifty thousand as waitresses, and forty thousand as telephone operators. Passage of the Female Employees Equal Pay Act required businesses within federal jurisdiction to pay women as much as men for identical work but they numbered only seventy-three thousand, leaving the vast majority of the working women uncovered.[14] The pay gap between men and women in all businesses remained, as did differences in earnings by city: average hourly earnings in Windsor were $1.81 for men and $1.25 for women ($18.10 and $12.50 respectively in 2021) while in Winnipeg they were $1.48 and 88 cents.[15]

Various industries submitted briefs to the Royal Commission on Canada's Economic Prospects, whose hearings stirred a great deal of public interest. It was the first time that a country had attempted such a comprehensive undertaking. The Montreal Dress and Sportswear Manufacturers' Guild, needing more workers for their industry, called for increased immigration, particularly of women. Two major automobile manufacturers urged tax relief and investment in better roads. The president of Ford, noting that one dollar of every five in retail spending was for the purchase or use of a motor vehicle, was "appalled by … the traffic congestion, bad roads, and limited parking space." The Canadian Electrical Manufacturers' Association and Canadian Westinghouse complained that protectionist policies had virtually shut them out of the US and British markets. They contended that government policy gave preference to the export of raw resources rather than manufactured goods and that adherence to the General Agreement on Tariffs and Trade harmed Canada.[16]

Ontario Hydro chairman Richard Hearn told the Royal Commission that "We are going to need all the power we are able to get from every available source," and Premier Leslie Frost accurately predicted that Ontario's population would be eight and possibly ten million in 1975 (It rose to 8.2 million). Frost once again insisted, as he had a year earlier, that Ontario was "prosperous" but not "wealthy"; indeed, in his estimation Ontario belonged in the ranks of the "have-not" provinces, and to demonstrate, he invited the commissioners to a "frugal luncheon."[17] Quebec was the only provincial government that boycotted the Commission's hearings. Chairman Walter Gordon's preliminary report reflected his primary concern: the sale of Canada's natural resources and businesses to foreign, mostly American, interests.[18]

After vacillating for five years, the Liberal government introduced legislation to create the Canada Council, whose purpose was to develop Canada's home-grown cultural and intellectual life as the 1951 Massey Commission had recommended. Prime minster Louis St. Laurent said the public supported such an organization, although he acknowledged there was some concern that it could intrude into provincial jurisdiction in education. St. Laurent told Parliament it was difficult to recruit personnel to serve on the council: many "Canadian personalities that would make it a really influential body … are all very busy."[19] In addition to an endowment of $50 million for the council, the government earmarked another $50 million for university construction over a ten-year period. Annual federal grants to universities were also doubled to help address what St. Laurent termed a crisis in higher education with enrolments expected to double in a decade.[20]

Alcohol consumption continued to arouse public concern. Although the number of drinkers in the US had declined since 1945, from 67 per cent to 60 per cent of the adult population, it had increased in Canada from 59 per cent to 72 per cent. Drinkers were also imbibing greater quantities: per capita consumption in Ontario had jumped by more than 50 per cent in eight years. The Alcoholism Research Foundation told Queen's Park that the number of alcoholics in the province had doubled since 1945. Others also rang an alarm bell: "The greatest threat to Western civilization today is not communism but alcoholism," the vice president of the University of Illinois told a meeting of the West Toronto Inter-Church Temperance Federation. He predicted prohibition would be reinstituted between 1965 and 1970.[21]

Federal Politics

Ann Shipley became the first woman to move acceptance of the Speech from the Throne in a parliamentary session that lasted 152 days, the longest since 1903. However, it was a debate regarding a pipeline that made it one of the most memorable sessions in Canadian history.

Ontario's Frost, who had been conspicuously neutral in federal politics, denounced federal Liberal policy in increasingly strong language. Pundits speculated that he would campaign for the federal Conservatives in the expected 1957 election after he held a widely reported meeting in Ottawa with a number of leading Conservatives, including federal party leader George Drew.[22] However, Frost's position on the construction of an Alberta-to-Montreal natural gas pipeline deviated from that of his federal Conservative counterparts; he was keen to have it completed as soon as possible while they insisted it be built only if Canadians owned it.

Solon Low's impaired health raised doubts that he would lead his Social Credit party in the election. He announced that a party convention would decide but no convention was held, and he declared himself fit to continue. To avoid his having to travel back and forth, the party moved its national headquarters once again, this time from Toronto to Ottawa.[23] The CCF convention adopted the Winnipeg Declaration, which modified the party's position on nationalization. While not disavowing public ownership, particularly of natural resources, the party explicitly recognized the "need for private enterprise which can make a useful contribution to the development of our economy" and recommitted itself to social planning.[24]

C.D. Howe and finance minister Walter Harris, who also served as the government's House leader, were the two most influential cabinet members. Howe prevailed in cabinet in opposing cash advances to farmers. He also rejected the proposal of future Quebec premier Jean Lesage, the minister of natural resources, that Ottawa share the cost of provincial hydro-electric projects. Howe's attitude was that junior ministers like Lesage ought to wait their turn before making such proposals.[25] Harris claimed that for the first time since the 1920s with the exception of the war years, inflation had become a concern, and he cautioned against excessive government spending.[26] Inflation rendered his budget, nominally larger than it had been in 1955, effectively smaller; it was "In every sense but the political ... a conservative budget," according to Blair Fraser of *Maclean's*.[27] It announced the replacement of the tax-rental agreements with the provinces with what became known as equalization payments. Intended to reduce the differences in the capacities of provincial governments to generate revenue, equalization payments became entrenched in the Constitution Act, 1982.[28] The formula for the payments, which Harris initially described as "grants," was based on the amount of personal and corporate income taxes and succession duties (i.e., inheritance taxes) collected in the two wealthiest provinces, Ontario and British Columbia.[29]

The 1955 parliamentary session had been the best for the Conservatives in over two decades, and the 1956 session proved even better. The public, generally uninterested in the complexities of pipeline finance, became transfixed by the wild, bitter, and tense debate regarding the planned pipeline. To help finance the part of it that was to run through northern Ontario, Ottawa partnered with Queen's Park, which badly wanted natural gas, to create a Northern Ontario Pipeline Crown Corporation. However, the company building the pipeline, TransCanada Pipelines, which began as a private syndicate of Canadian and American businessmen, then learned that it could not get financing to construct the line from Alberta to Winnipeg. This led the Liberals to transfer $80 million from the Crown Corporation for that section of the line.[30]

The government was divided; some cabinet members agreed with Ontario's Frost that the pipeline ought to be publicly owned and jointly financed by Ottawa and the affected provinces.[31] Howe though, supported by Social Credit, most of whose MPs were Albertans, was determined that the pipeline be privately owned, and that construction begin before the end of the summer. The government announced that they would limit debate on the bill to underwrite the project before the debate had started by invoking closure, a parliamentary procedure aimed at bringing debate to a quick end.

Closure was used four times during the debate, the opposition parties crying "shame" each time. Conservative leader Drew spoke of "the threat of dictatorship," the CCF's Stanley Knowles exclaimed, "The guillotine!" and Conservative Davie Fulton termed the bill "a treaty of surrender" to US interests because Americans held most of TransCanada's shares. Drew said it was "an invitation to investors in the United States to come to Canada and be financed to the extent of 90 cents of every dollar, and still retain control over the investment." CCF leader M.J. Coldwell called for public ownership: "a Canadian undertaking, under Canadian auspices, with Canadian ownership, with Canadian guidance [to] serve the Canadian people without building enormous profits for private United States economic buccaneers." Howe argued that if Canadians did not step up to purchase a majority of TransCanada's shares and "If public ownership is what the [Conservatives] want when they demand Canadian control, let them stand up and be counted with the party to their left, who at least advocate public ownership out of intellectual conviction, not out of intellectual confusion."[32]

Using procedural tactics, the Conservatives and the CCF succeeded in damaging the public's image of the government. Coldwell spoke of the government's attempt to short circuit debate as "a travesty on democratic procedure, an abomination, an outrageous thing." CCF MP George Castleden called the government "a gang of dictators." Seeking to reverse procedural mistakes he had made by nullifying part of the previous day's debate, Speaker René Beaudoin lost control of the House on what became known as "Black Friday." Conservative Donald Fleming claimed that Beaudoin's refusal to recognize a member on a point of privilege marked "the lowest moment in Canadian parliamentary history." His colleague Robert Mitchell spoke of "the pipeline that runs from the desk of the leader of the House to the Chair." Amidst opposition cries of protest and catcalls from the government benches, a furious Drew moved to censure the Speaker after he ruled a motion out of order. Shaken, Beaudoin retired to his office, attended by a nurse. In a tumultuous scene upon his return, angry MPs stormed the aisle separating the two sides of the House, gathered around the mace, and called Beaudoin a "dictator" and "puppet." Charging the opposition with obstruction, the Liberals sang "Onward Christian Soldiers."[33]

To political scientist Hugh Thorburn, Parliament's problem stemmed from two facts: it was not well adapted to represent local opinion and fuse it into a consensus, and the perception that the Speaker was not impartial. Some observers noted ironically that two years earlier the Conservatives and the CCF had suggested Beaudoin would make a good non-partisan permanent Speaker.[34]

Canadians were keenly aware of the debate; nearly nine in ten said they heard of it. The weight of public opinion favoured a pipeline built and run by private Canadian investors, while nearly three in ten wanted the pipeline built, financed, and administered by the government.[35] As the atmosphere in Parliament deteriorated, the opposition succeeded in turning the debate into a fight over the rights of Parliament. Closure led to the widespread perception that the Liberals were arrogant, behaving as if they had a divine right to govern arbitrarily. In persisting with their bill, the Liberals misread the temper of the public. The stature of the Speaker, the government, and the prime minister suffered. The Liberal party was "a badly battered fortress, with its principle [sic] defences, the images of 'Uncle Louis' and 'C.D.' torn away."[36]

The row over the Speaker's actions revealed a gulf between Quebec and the rest of Canada. In Quebec, where the provincial Speaker dutifully obeyed premier Maurice Duplessis's open instructions to rule opposition members out of order, the Speaker was seen as a servant of the government. The dominant view in English Canada was that the Speaker presides impartially in parliamentary debate. Thus, while most English Canadian media criticized Beaudoin's actions, Quebec City's *L'Événement-Journal* denounced the opposition parties as "agitators having lost all respect for parliamentary authority."[37]

Two months after the pipeline imbroglio, Drew retired. Saskatchewan MP John Diefenbaker, who had been defeated four times in federal and provincial elections and twice in contests for the Conservative party's leadership, finally won the leadership by defeating Donald Fleming and Davie Fulton. Tall, eloquent, and colourful, Diefenbaker had the support of all but a handful the party's Ontario MPs, who constituted two-thirds of the fifty-two-member caucus. Diefenbaker was very much in tune with western agrarian sensibilities but there were few farmers among the Conservative MPs and none from west of the Great Lakes.

At the leadership convention, Nova Scotia premier Robert Stanfield gave the keynote address and New Brunswick premier Hugh John Flemming nominated Diefenbaker, indicating the intimate links between the federal and provincial Conservative parties.[38] MP Leon Balcer, the party's national president and a future Diefenbaker cabinet member, criticized Diefenbaker for not appointing a Quebecer to move or second his nomination. Quebec's three-hundred-plus delegates, whose preferred candidate was Fleming, considered a unanimous push against Diefenbaker. Many remained seated or walked out while other delegates stood and cheered during his acceptance speech. An influential Quebec delegate opined that Diefenbaker would "be out in two years." A Liberal organizer concluded, "This means we don't even have a fight on our hands in Quebec."[39]

Intergovernmental Relations

At a federal-provincial conference of health ministers, Ottawa offered to pay half the cost of a national hospital insurance program contingent on the agreement of six provinces representing most of the national population. The Canadian Medical Association and the Manitoba government were opposed to such a program, but Manitoba recognized that they would have to accept the federal proposal eventually because Ontario, Saskatchewan, Alberta, British Columbia, Nova Scotia, and Newfoundland had signalled they would take up the offer. The program, to be introduced in 1957, dimmed prospects of a tax cut in that year's federal budget.[40]

A federal-provincial first ministers conference on taxation resumed the conference that had adjourned a few months earlier. Held two weeks before the federal budget came down, Ontario's Frost spoke for all the premiers at the four-hour meeting. He claimed that the provinces should receive more of the direct taxes collected in their province and proposed that Ottawa transfer an additional quarter billion dollars to them. St. Laurent and Walter Harris responded that Ottawa's position on the new equalization payments was non-negotiable; although the provinces would receive a smaller percentage of the personal, corporate, and inheritance taxes than they wanted, the new unconditional equalization payments would guarantee higher revenues to the provinces than the old tax-rental agreements. St. Laurent's position was that federal payments for the benefit of individual Canadians should be made equally for the benefit of Canadians regardless of the province in which they live because taxes imposed by Ottawa are applied equally to all Canadians regardless of their province of residence. Newfoundland's Joey Smallwood was the only premier who had no criticism of the federal proposal.[41] Soon after the meeting, Frost charged that the federal government had ordered the Bank of Canada to raise interest rates, a concern because higher interest rates made it more expensive for Ontario to borrow the money it needed to fund infrastructure programs.[42]

Quebec's Maurice Duplessis denounced the proposed equalization payments as inadequate and demanded that provincial autonomy be "rightly understood." However, he added that he would accept whatever amount was to be transferred to Quebec as a form of restitution for previous encroachments on provincial taxation rights. Quebec could accept equalization payments, Duplessis said, because unlike the tax-rental agreements, its agreement was not required. These payments would end the fiscal isolation of Quebec, which had refused to enter the 1947 and 1952 tax-rental agreements, forfeiting $150 million in federal transfers. Though Ontario's Frost spoke of Ottawa's new payments as a "tax pact" no actual pact was involved: Ottawa alone administered and funded the equalization program through general tax revenues.[43]

At a conference of Atlantic premiers, Prince Edward Island's Alex Matheson rejected any consideration of Maritime union, which the premiers thought St. Laurent had been encouraging.[44] The Atlantic premiers also held a joint conference with New England's governors with a view to expanding trade between their regions.[45] Matheson was furious with Ottawa for demanding repayment of over a million dollars mistakenly paid out to his government. Nova Scotia's Robert Stanfield immediately set out after he took office as premier to obtain federal aid for the coal industry and health services in his province.[46]

Quebec's Royal Commission of Inquiry on Constitutional Problems (Tremblay Report) condemned the federal government's grants-in-aid programs such as those for post-secondary education as unwarranted interventions in fields of provincial jurisdiction. The Commission proposed that the provinces have full control of personal, corporate, and succession taxes and that Ottawa control most sales and service taxes. However, Duplessis, who had established the Commission, was reportedly "too weary" to read the Report and did not use it in his party's bid for re-election.[47]

The Provinces

Six provincial elections – in Saskatchewan, Quebec, New Brunswick, Newfoundland, British Columbia, and Nova Scotia – took place. Not since 1890 had so many provinces held elections in a single year. The Saskatchewan, Quebec, and New Brunswick contests happened within three days in June. All three easily returned incumbent governments and in all three Social Credit played a more significant role than it had in the past. The Saskatchewan CCF scored its fourth consecutive victory, but they and the official opposition Liberals dropped 9 percentage points each in the popular vote as Social Credit, running a full slate of candidates for the first time, won three seats and increased their vote share from 4 to 22 per cent. Premiers W.A.C. Bennett of British Columbia and Ernest Manning of Alberta, as well as a dozen of their cabinet ministers, campaigned for Saskatchewan's Social Crediters. They generated high hopes, as did the party's recruitment as candidates the mayor of Regina and the president of the city's Canadian Legion. Led by future federal cabinet minister Alvin Hamilton, the Conservatives put up only nine candidates, received less than 2 per cent of the vote, and lost the sole seat they had held.[48]

Duplessis's Union Nationale recorded its fifth consecutive victory, gaining seats and doing surprisingly well in Montreal and Quebec City. Pierre Trudeau's essay in *La grève de l'amiante* (*The Asbestos Strike*) and the emergence of Rassemblement, an organization dedicated to political education and the promotion of democratic values, caused a stir in intellectual circles but had little impact electorally: every cabinet minister was re-elected, and Liberal leader Georges-Émile Lapalme was defeated. The alliance struck by the Liberals with Quebec's former Social Crediters, L'Union des électeurs, led four of the latter to run as Liberals, but this repelled some voters. Some federal Social Crediters, embarrassed by the Union's anti-Semitic utterings, were pleased to see their former Quebec colleagues rejected: "We were glad to see the defeat of the so-called Liberal candidates who claimed to be Social Crediters," said one Social Credit MP.[49]

A stridently anti-Enlightenment conservative prayer aired on CBC's Radio Canada on the morning of the election contributed to the Union Nationale's success:

> Sovereign authority, by whatever government it is exercised, is derived solely from God, the supreme and eternal principle of all power … It is therefore an absolute error to believe that authority comes from the multitudes, from the masses, from the people, to pretend that authority does not properly belong to those who exercise it, but that they have only a simple mandate revocable at any time by the people. This error, which dates from the Reformation, rests on the false principle that man has no other master than his own reason … All this explanation about the origin, the basis, and the composition of this alleged sovereignty of the people is purely arbitrary. Moreover, if it is admitted, it will have as a consequence the weakening of authority, making it a myth, giving it an unstable and changeable basis, stimulating popular passions and encouraging sedition.[50]

Duplessis's Bill 34 also assisted the Union Nationale victory in urban areas by providing for a single enumerator, always or almost always a Union Nationale partisan. As a result, the voters list excluded many Liberal supporters and included the names of fictitious and deceased people. Strong-arm tactics by some Union Nationale supporters included smashed Liberal committee rooms, intimidation, and stuffed ballot boxes. Bill 34 also required that any challenges to the conduct of the election be heard by Magistrates Court judges appointed by the Duplessis government, rather than the federally appointed judges on the Superior Court.[51]

Hugh John Flemming's Conservatives gained a seat and increased their popular vote in New Brunswick. Both the Liberals and Conservatives campaigned in favour of hydro-electric development, rendering it a non-issue. The Conservatives benefitted from rising personal incomes, an increase in construction, a record value of retail trade, and the support of the electrical workers union. The Liberals accused the government of corruption, charging that the premier, a lumber businessman, was associated with companies that sold materials to the government. Making its first significant bid in the Atlantic provinces, Social Credit put up eighteen candidates, but all were soundly defeated. According to federal party leader Solon Low, who had hoped to field up to forty candidates, potential candidates "were frightened away by employers and political bosses who told them they would lose their jobs if they accepted the Social Credit nomination."[52]

Joey Smallwood, a formidable campaigner, scarcely bothered to campaign in Newfoundland's election yet his Liberals won thirty-two of the thirty-six seats and two-thirds of the vote. The government's popularity rested on the family allowances, unemployment insurance, and old-age pensions Smallwood had secured for Newfoundlanders by joining Confederation. The landslide bested his party's performances in the 1949 and 1951 elections. The Liberals boasted that they had brought Newfoundlanders "the best eight years yet" while the Conservatives, who did not offer candidates in every riding, built their campaign around charges of Liberal "wastefulness" and "incompetence."[53] Smallwood gave the Conservative leader a free pass to his election by not putting up a candidate against him. Running in a Newfoundland election for the first time, the CCF lost its one seat, originally held by a Liberal who had defected.

British Columbia's third election in four years resulted in a gain of eleven seats for Social Credit to a slightly enlarged legislature. However, the popular vote for the parties remained virtually identical to that of 1953. This election was different in that the alternative voting system used in 1952 and 1953 was scrapped. Nineteen-year-olds were enfranchised, and two women were elected. Premier Bennett emphasized the "new two-party" situation in the province and the need to keep the "socialists" at bay. He repeatedly spoke of the individual as God's greatest creation and made clear that he was not an adherent of Social Credit monetary theory.[54] The opposition parties tried to make an issue of the government's suppression of a police report regarding a former minister and much name-calling took place: CCF leader Robert Strachan described Bennett as a "pussy-footing political schemer" and his government as the "most slippery, ingenious collection of political heelers ever to grace the political scene in British Columbia"; Liberal leader Arthur Laing accused Bennett's cabinet of being "the most immoral government in Canadian history."[55]

Only in Nova Scotia did an election produce a change in government. Robert Stanfield, the son of a former lieutenant governor and a member of the Stanfield textile family, led the Conservatives to their first win since 1928 and only their fourth since Confederation. Labour unrest, driven by the decline in the coal mining industry, contributed to the defeat of the Liberal government; Conservatives won five of industrial Cape Breton's six seats. Henry Hicks's Liberal government had passed legislation requiring equal pay for equal work by women, but it was not enforced.[56] Stanfield used to great effect a report that concluded Nova Scotia lagged behind New Brunswick and Newfoundland in developing its mineral resources.[57] After the election, he told his party's convention that he would not make wholesale changes in the civil service, as had been the case when governments changed hands in the past, because he refused to "allow the claims of any individual seeking reward to jeopardize the future" of his government.[58]

Government officials in the Maritime provinces sometimes spoke of harmonizing their policies, but liquor legislation demonstrated how dramatically provincial policies and practices varied. Only Nova Scotia granted licences to taverns and only if approved by a majority of municipal residents. PEI's Temperance Act permitted clubs with permits to serve alcohol but prohibited customers from taking it home. In New Brunswick, liquor was legally available only at government stores, yet hundreds of clubs served alcohol illegally, and cabinet ministers and officials of the liquor control board were often seen drinking in them.[59]

There was speculation of a snap election in Manitoba because the government had not proclaimed legislation based on the report of Canada's first independent boundaries commission. A hurting farm economy hurt the Liberal-Progressive government whose electoral base of support was rural. Nevertheless, the party had reason to be optimistic; although not the bonanza it was in Alberta, newly discovered oil was pouring millions of dollars into the provincial economy with twenty-two oil companies and fifty-four trucking, pipeline, and other oil service industries operating out of the town of Virden. The mining industry was also looking to grow: the International Nickel Company announced plans to build a $175 million mining and smelter complex that would include a refinery, power plant, railroad facilities, and a new town named after the INCO chairman, John Thompson.[60]

Canada in the World

An unprecedented number of heads of government – from Pakistan, India, Ceylon, Indonesia, Italy, the United Kingdom, Australia, and New Zealand – visited as guests of the federal government. The budget of the external affairs department had nearly tripled since 1951, and the government reversed its policy of not sending female officers to difficult posts. The government succeeded in defeating an attempt to relocate the Montreal headquarters of the International Civil Aviation Organization (ICAO) and the General Assembly chose Canada to sit on the UN Economic and Social Council.[61] C.D. Howe explored expanding trade with Japan, meeting with the Emperor, the prime minister, and his cabinet.[62] Ottawa recognized the newly independent states of Tunisia and Morocco, leading many of their French residents to inquire about immigrating to Canada. Ontario, which had a trade representative in Chicago, appointed another to New York City. Immigration minister Jack Pickersgill welcomed Hungarian refugees, for whom Ottawa provided free passage after the Soviet invasion of their country, as ideal immigrants: "They are way above the average as employables."[63]

Defence expenditures accounted for almost 40 per cent of the federal budget. Defence planning shifted from placing more divisions in Europe to air defence, distant early warning radar systems, and submarines capable of launching missiles. A retired army adjunct-general challenged the changes, comparing the three radar chains Canada was building with the US to the Maginot Line, which the Germans easily bypassed in their invasion of France. He ridiculed spending eight times as much on air force equipment as on army equipment and fifty times as much for aircraft as for tanks; it was "an air-power concept gone wild."[64] Canada and West Germany signed an air training agreement, arranging to train 360 German aircrew in Canada. Canada also signed a tripartite atomic energy agreement with the UK and the US, allowing the governments and industries of the three countries to make use of each other's inventions and discoveries.[65]

In addition to renewing the income tax convention originally signed with the US in 1944, Canada ratified income tax agreements with Denmark and West Germany.[66]

St. Laurent met with US president Dwight Eisenhower and Mexican president Adolfo Ruiz Cortines in West Virginia for informal talks in the first-ever meeting of North America's three heads of government. Puzzled and disappointed by Eisenhower's invitation to the Mexicans, Canadian officials feared the meeting would sideline their bilateral issues with the US. St. Laurent and external affairs minister Lester Pearson wanted to know what the Americans thought of inviting the Soviet Union to participate in talks to settle the Arab-Israeli dispute. The Americans wanted Canada and Mexico to reach out to neutral states like India and Ceylon to aid them in the development of democratic institutions. After the Mexican president left the meeting, the Canadians and Americans discussed power development on the Columbia River, Ottawa's excise tax on the advertising revenues of Canadian editions of *TIME* magazine and *Reader's Digest*, and their differences over Communist China's admission to the UN.[67]

At the Commonwealth conference of heads of government, St. Laurent rejected Britain's proposal for a Canadian initiative to help settle the Kashmir dispute between India and Pakistan. Like earlier Commonwealth conferences, this meeting exposed the varied views of member states on issues such as the Middle East. St. Laurent told Parliament, "The situation there is dangerous, but the danger has become a little less acute."[68]

Two weeks later, Egypt's seizure of the Suez Canal gave the lie to St. Laurent's assessment. Britain, deciding on military intervention, assumed that Canada, like Australia and New Zealand, would be supportive. Conservative external affairs critic Diefenbaker wanted Canada to back Britain, called Egyptian president Nasser a "dictator," and compared him with Hitler and Mussolini.[69] However, the cabinet and public opinion were divided on the issue, which threatened the unity of the Commonwealth and the Western alliance. The government took the same position as the US: no support for the use of force, although Ottawa had unknowingly contributed to the crisis by having exported arms to Egypt and fighter jets to Israel.[70] Canadian policymakers were blindsided and confused when Britain, France, and Israel acted on their secret plan to attack Egypt. Canada's ambassador to France, Jean Désy, thought that the French, scarred by their defeat in Vietnam two years earlier, were "sort of blind hitting out at the 20th century and all the calamities it has brought to France."[71] Pearson tested support at the UN for an international police force to separate the parties and successfully proposed a UN Emergency Force under the command of Canadian General E.L.M. Burns to which Canada contributed the largest contingent.

Pearson's role in the Suez Crisis and his participation in a group of three NATO foreign ministers tasked to report on methods of implementing NATO's non-military objectives raised his stature with Washington. American officials supported his selection as secretary general of NATO, thinking he could help remedy its "sickness" and shakiness which Britain and France had caused by ignoring the interests of their NATO partners in the Suez Crisis. However, Pearson, who had rejected the NATO position twice before, did so once again. His decision to stay in Ottawa fuelled speculation that he would be the heir to the seventy-five-year-old St. Laurent.[72]

The creation of the Canada Council and the preliminary report of the Royal Commission on Canada's Economic Prospects indicated a rising nationalist impulse. The trade union movement was reconfigured, Canada experienced its costliest-ever labour strike, and farmers urged the government to sell their surplus wheat to countries behind the Iron Curtain. Legislation advanced the position of women in federally regulated workplaces but significant gaps in pay between men and women in the private sector persisted. Premier Leslie Frost of prosperous Ontario, whose capital Toronto was reportedly North America's fastest growing city, insisted his province was not "wealthy." Nevertheless, the profits of large corporations, many of which were headquartered in Ontario, reached a new peak.

The House of Commons witnessed chaotic scenes as a debate about a trans-Canada pipeline shook and weakened the Liberal government. The federal government announced that equalization payments would replace the tax-rental agreements with the provinces, and Ontario's Frost overshadowed Quebec's Duplessis as the foremost provincial protagonist in federal-provincial relations. Prospects for a national hospital insurance program improved as most provinces warmed to Ottawa's offer to pay half the cost. Conservative leader George Drew retired, succeeded by John Diefenbaker, a westerner and the first Conservative leader without an English surname. The CCF's Winnipeg Declaration officially moderated the anti-capitalist stance of the party's 1933 Regina Manifesto.

Six provinces held elections, returning winning parties with five different names: Liberal, Conservative, Union Nationale, CCF, and Social Credit, but only in Nova Scotia did government change hands. Social Credit's attempted breakthroughs in Saskatchewan and New

Brunswick failed. Some supporters of the Duplessis government re-
sorted to unsavoury and unlawful tactics in the Quebec election.

Canada's international standing and Lester Pearson's status in world
affairs reached new heights. A record eight heads of government came
to Canada and Prime Minister St. Laurent participated in the very first
meeting of the leaders of the three North American states. The government's defence priorities shifted from tanks and soldiers to air defence and air power. Conservatives criticized the Liberal government
for breaking with Britain and France by opposing their use of force in
the Suez Crisis. Canada's initiative regarding a UN peacekeeping force
helped defuse the crisis and forged Canada's reputation as a peace-
maker in world affairs.

1957

A lot of men in our universities would be happier if they took a coal shovel and shovelled coal.[1]

Senator Ralph Horner

On the same day that the man-made satellite Sputnik launched into orbit, the Canadian designed and built supersonic Avro Arrow was unveiled. Sputnik put the Soviet Union ahead of the United States in the space race; the Arrow was among the world's most advanced high-altitude interceptors. Sputnik and the Ford Edsel, introduced a few days before the satellite's lift-off, could be seen as symbols of East and West. As Sputnik streaked over Canada seven times daily, the tail-finned Edsel with its push-button automatic transmission was being marketed to North Americans. While the Soviets hailed their satellite as an achievement of "the new socialist society," the unattractive, over-priced Edsel dashed the sales expectations of its promoters.[2]

The United States established a scientific research station at the South Pole while at the opposite end of the globe, Canadian scientists uncovered evidence that Inuit had once penetrated the Arctic near the tip of Ellesmere Island, a few hundred miles from the North Pole. The newly formed Canadian Seafood Workers Union called on Ottawa to establish a twelve-mile exclusion zone for foreign fishing vessels, and the first completed lock of the long planned and long delayed St. Lawrence Seaway opened for the first vessel. Nova Scotia hosted the first Pugwash Conference on Science and World Affairs, promoted by philosopher Bertrand Russell; it brought together scientists and public figures from ten countries including Canadian psychiatrist Brock Chisholm, the first director general of the World Health Organization. Chief preoccupation of participants at the "thinkers' retreat" was the danger of nuclear war.[3]

The Asian flu arrived. Believed to have originated in northern China, the *Toronto Daily Star*'s front page headlined, "Flu in Ontario Is Asian: Ottawa." Scrambling to head off a devastating epidemic, public health officials forced the closure of schools and public gathering places. Sudbury reported 4,300 cases. North of the city, in Capreol, half of the population was confined to bed; east of the city, in Sturgeon Falls, the Notre Dame Convent school closed when 150 students got the flu. Almost half the 1,700 boy scouts scheduled to attend a camping event north of Toronto were stricken.[4]

A sharp economic recession set in, corporate profits declined, and the dollar traded at a premium of 5 per cent to its United States counterpart. Farmers' incomes and crop production fell; slumping grain production alone lowered the gross national product by 1 per cent. The unemployment rate rose from 3 per cent the previous year to 4.3 per cent, and prices rose by 3.7 per cent.[5] After a railway strike was averted early in the year, a four-month strike by 6,500 employees at Quebec's Aluminum Company of Canada led the president of Quebec's powerful Canadian Catholic Confederation of Labour to wire US president Eisenhower, urging him to prohibit the company's American parent Alcoa from shipping stock to its Canadian subsidiary.[6]

Air travel became more direct and convenient; Trans-Canada Airlines began non-stop flights from Toronto to Vancouver, skipping the former refuelling stop in Winnipeg and completing the journey in eight and a half hours.[7] In Canada's worst aircraft accident to date, seventy-seven people perished near Quebec City.[8] Party leaders increased their use of airplanes during the 1957 election campaign, but most of their campaigning was still done by train and automobile. The Liberals dropped the idea of launching their re-election campaign in the Arctic, deciding that it was too expensive and too tiring for prime minister Louis St. Laurent, only the second prime minister to reach the age of seventy-five in office. They settled on a two-day train trip to Winnipeg. Fond of political train tours, Conservative leader John Diefenbaker and his wife were "at their best at a whistle stop."[9]

The Royal Commission on Canada's Economic Prospects, expressing concern about excessive reliance on natural resources to drive economic growth, concluded that Canada was in danger of economic domination by American corporations. Most Canadians were unconcerned: only one in five in a survey agreed that the "Canadian way of life is being too much influenced by the United States." Indeed, most respondents thought American investment had been a good thing and wished for more.[10] The Commission's recommendation that the government establish a national energy board to regulate energy exports delighted the opposition Conservative and CCF parties; columnist Peter Stursberg described it and some other recommendations as "taken holus bolus [all at once] out of a speech" by former Conservative leader George Drew.[11]

The Royal Commission forecast a national population of 26,650,000 in 1980 (it grew to 24,520,000) with 80 per cent of Canadians living in urban centres compared to 62 per cent in 1951. The Commission's other forecasts for 1980 included a tripling of the gross national product, an increasing percentage of women in the labour force, shortages of skilled labour, and an agricultural labour force more than halved.[12] The Dominion Bureau of Statistics underscored the latter prediction, reporting that farm-based Saskatchewan was the only province to lose population during the year.[13] Only one in ten Canadians thought Canada's economic conditions would deteriorate during the year, although prairie residents were somewhat less optimistic. Similarly, only 10 per cent of Canadians thought a war would break out in contrast to the belief earlier in the decade when over 50 per cent thought the Soviet Union was bent on "world domination, power, [and] supremacy." University-educated Canadians were somewhat more distrustful than others of the USSR.[14]

Indigenous Peoples and Inuit had the highest rate of population increase. Of the 476 schools for Indigenous children, 66 were residential schools. Enrolment in all schools totalled 10,599, of which 2,210 were receiving secondary or higher education. More than half of the two million dollars spent on building new houses on reserves came from band funds, Veterans' Land Act grants, and personal contributions. A majority of the 155,000 Indigenous people living on 2,200 reserves were Roman Catholics, while 3,760 listed Aboriginal beliefs as their religion. Decreasing supplies of game and a precarious fur market altered the long-established cultural patterns of Inuit, all 11,000. Many turned to wage employment with mining companies and the Mid-Canada and Distant Early Warning (DEW) radar lines, some working in transportation, communications, and government construction projects. Wage employment raised Inuit living standards but the shift from trapping and hunting was disruptive of traditional ways of life.[15]

Reading the Speech from the Throne for the first time, the Queen opened the twenty-third Parliament. Ellen Fairclough became the first woman to hold a federal cabinet portfolio and the second in the history of the Commonwealth. Nevertheless, according to the secretary of the International Council of Social Democratic Women, Canadian women were not as active in politics and party councils as were women in Britain and Europe. Only 9 of the 868 federal candidates in the 1957 election were women: 5 CCFers and 1 standing for each of the Liberal, Conservative, Social Credit, and communist Labor-Progressive parties.[16]

The permanent structure which replaced the tent at the Stratford Shakespearean Festival impressed *Globe and Mail* theatre critic Herbert Whittaker, but he was not so enthused with Christopher Plummer's opening night performance in *Hamlet* as he had been with Alec Guinness's opening night in *Richard III* four years earlier, the festival's first year. Social Crediter George McLeod, the only MP voting against the creation of the Canada Council, objected to St. Laurent's statement that it would play a role in the "spiritual development" of Canada and contribute to "intellectual world brotherhood." "We see in this a method," protested McLeod, "for promoting state culture." For their part, the Conservatives and the CCF wanted Parliament to maintain scrutiny of the Council's operations. Conservative Senator Ralph Horner, a Saskatchewan farmer, thought "a lot of men in our universities would be happier if they took a coal shovel and shovelled coal."[17]

Canada's teen idol, Ottawa's Paul Anka, had fan clubs on both sides of the Canadian-American border. "Diana," his number one song on the hit parade, sold three million copies, but a song by Toronto vocal quartet The Diamonds, "Little Darlin'," reached number three, ahead of Anka's song on *Billboard* magazine's top 50 singles of the year. CBC TV's "Country Hoedown" became one of the network's most popular programs. In addition to presenting country singers including Johnny Cash and Tommy Hunter, it introduced Macedonian, Estonian, and Lithuanian dance groups to the broader Canadian audience. King Ganam, the program's fiddler, had taught Arabic at Edmonton's first mosque and was one of the first Muslims to star on Canadian television.[18] Like the Christian Anka, Ganam was the son of Lebanese immigrants.

Rock and roll sensation Elvis Presley, whom critics considered vulgar for his hip-shaking singing, played two sold-out shows at Toronto's Maple Leaf Gardens followed by another sold-out performance at the Ottawa Auditorium. Many MPs attended the show; the next day the House of Commons was notably empty with only thirty-seven members present. Protesting Presley's appearance, students of the local Notre Dame Convent had signed a pledge not to attend.[19]

Federal Politics

The outlooks of the governing Liberals and Ottawa's senior civil servants had fused during the twenty-two uninterrupted years of the prime ministerships of Mackenzie King and St. Laurent. The bureaucratic state-and-party had become "an instrument for the depoliticization" of political life.[20] Conservative MP Roland Michener, who would later become Speaker of the Commons and subsequently governor general, lambasted the Liberals for building "a monolithic state where the government runs everything." Anticipating an economic slowdown, trade minister C.D. Howe, a cabinet minister since 1935, urged finance minister Walter Harris to introduce an expansionary pre-election budget. However, St. Laurent sided with Harris, the only minister who rivalled Howe in status, and he introduced a balanced budget. Cabinet members also differed on whether to act on Bank of Canada governor James Coyne's suggested changes to the regulation of banks after bankers protested that his proposal would represent a socialization of their assets by requiring banks to stabilize the market for federal, provincial, and municipal bonds. Diefenbaker said the changes would reduce banks to "sycophants answerable to the government."[21]

The opposition parties criticized the government for having run a series of budget surpluses while failing to increase old-age pensions and family allowances. Suggesting that the government was giving directions to the Bank of Canada, Diefenbaker and Conservative MP Donald Fleming decried its "tight money" policy. Social Credit MPs also condemned the "ill-conceived tight money policy" and proposed cutting income taxes by 30 per cent, instituting a monthly old-age pension of $100 ($959 in 2021), and expanding the national housing program. The CCF wanted to tax undistributed corporate profits and to channel chartered bank deposits into investments in housing, schools, and hospitals.[22]

Shortly before the election campaign began, St. Laurent elevated thirty-three-year-old Paul Hellyer to cabinet; he had entered Parliament in 1949 as the youngest-ever MP. The Liberals felt confident about retaining power and were therefore content to run on their record. To a young party strategist's suggestion that the party needed an election platform, a senior strategist countered, "St. Laurent will be seventy per cent of the campaign. What do we need a program for if we have him?" St. Laurent considered any ordinary election promise a "mere puff of a thing, with more air than substance." Liberal MPs laughed at Conservative MP Earl Rowe's comment that the government could be defeated and perhaps someone other than St. Laurent would be attending the Commonwealth conference scheduled for soon after the election. Even before election day, the Liberals secured a seat when one of their Newfoundland candidates was acclaimed, winning by being the only candidate, the first federal acclamation since 1930.[23]

The Liberals had good reason to feel secure: the Gallup organization reported three weeks before the election that they led the Conservatives by 14 per cent. A week before the vote, the *Toronto Daily Star* projected an "absolute minimum" of 140 Liberal seats in the 265-seat House of

Commons. Weighing in again five days before election day, Gallup reported that a change in government was unlikely because the voting preferences of farmers and workers "remains much the same as it did before the last federal election."[24] What Gallup did not report was that these data drew on the same three-week-old survey that had shown the Liberals with a commanding lead.

Evidence accumulated of Conservative momentum and trouble for the Liberals. A disappointing crowd of three hundred greeted St. Laurent at Winnipeg's train station, and Liberal-Progressive premier Douglas Campbell and members of his cabinet were noticeably absent on stage as St. Laurent launched his campaign. Diefenbaker, who had honed his reputation as a small-town lawyer, was quite unlike the straight-laced Conservative leaders who had preceded him. He attracted a boisterous crowd of 3,800 to the Victoria arena where St. Laurent had attracted less than half that number in the 1953 election. In Vancouver, 5,000 people tried to get into an auditorium to hear him; St. Laurent attracted 3,000 to the same auditorium and Social Credit leader Solon Low drew 2,500. Police had to clear a path for Diefenbaker through a cheering crowd; in contrast, police were called to expel numerous hecklers who greeted St. Laurent.[25]

Diefenbaker used television effectively, St. Laurent did not. Conservative strategist Dalton Camp understood that television was best used to make a personal impression, not to win a debate. Refusing to wear make-up in his free-time broadcasts, St. Laurent looked older than his years; declining to use a teleprompter, he stared downward to read his written text rather than look at the camera. "I will be more interested in seeing people," he told a reporter, "than talking to a camera."[26]

Diefenbaker demonstrated an orator's understanding of crowds. Thunderous and humorous, he had "a kind of manic grandeur."[27] Political scientist John Meisel wrote of his "electrifying performance."[28] The Liberals misjudged the mood of the electorate. They won a plurality of votes but lost 64 seats, reduced to 105 while the Conservatives won 112. Diefenbaker spoke excruciatingly bad French and his party had consciously abandoned making inroads in Quebec, focussing its efforts on the other provinces. Nevertheless, the Conservatives won nine Quebec seats, five more than in 1953. In Atlantic Canada, where the Liberals promised to spend $200 million for power development and Conservatives had not won more than seven seats since the 1935 election, the latter increased their representation from five to twenty-one. The gains came partly because the regional press had highlighted the "Atlantic Resolutions," a manifesto authored by Camp, the Conservative campaign organizer in the Maritimes.[29] The Liberals were reduced from 50 to 21 seats in Ontario. In the West, where the Liberals had held 24 seats to the Conservatives 8, the Conservatives won 21 seats and the Liberals retained just 7.

Joined by premiers Ernest Manning of Alberta and W.A.C. Bennett of British Columbia, Social Credit leader Low started his party's campaign in Toronto with two messages: "Where there's Social Credit [as in Alberta and B.C.] there's prosperity," and "We believe government was instituted by God for the benefit of man."[30] All 19 Social Credit seats were won in Alberta and British Columbia. The CCF, led by M.J. Coldwell, won less than 11 per cent of the popular vote. The party's strongest showing was in Saskatchewan, and all but 3 of the party's 25 seats were west of Ontario.

In winning the election, Diefenbaker, the vindicator of Parliament in the pipeline and other debates, was like a David vanquishing Goliath. St. Laurent stepped down as Liberal leader three months later. For the first time, the cabinet had more ministers from the Atlantic and western provinces than from Ontario and Quebec. Diefenbaker's government promptly transferred the federal travel bureau's advertising account from a Liberal-friendly agency to three other firms and designated Camp as account executive. The new prime minister demonstrated great energy, travelling over thirty thousand miles in his first six months, meeting as many as fifty people daily in his office, and attracting so much mail that one of his secretaries described it as "*beaucoup depressing.*" His generous policy agenda included enriching pensions for seniors, the blind, and disabled, increasing veterans' allowances, and providing farmers with cash advances. The Liberals had promised to increase monthly old-age pensions by six dollars; the Conservatives increased them by a further nine dollars and expanded the rolls of those eligible for other pensions. They also promised tax cuts and announced $150 million in loans for low-cost housing.[31]

Defeated Liberal cabinet ministers tried to expose the inexperience and ignorance of neophyte Conservative ministers in the House of Commons, but the neophytes were impressive, relying on briefings by civil servants. The Conservatives hoped that their government would be quickly defeated so that they could capitalize on the post-election disarray in the other parties, converting their minority to a majority in a fresh election. Signalling Conservative strength, the Ottawa West riding association, which had had difficulty recruiting a candidate in April, was swamped by eleven people angling for the nomination by October, including newly elected Ottawa mayor George Nelms. In Quebec as well the Conservatives had no shortage of prospective candidates.[32]

Intergovernmental Relations

From the beginning of the decade, Ottawa's percentage of all taxes collected by Canada's governments slowly declined, as did its percentage
of all government spending. While the total net revenues of provincial
governments rose by 112 per cent to over $2 billion, Ottawa's total net
revenues increased more modestly, by 77 per cent. However, provincial
premiers clamoured for more federal transfers as Ottawa's total net revenues of $5.4 billion still exceeded theirs.[33]

The equalization payments to the provinces that finance minister
Walter Harris had announced in 1956 began, bringing the per capita yield of personal, corporate, and succession taxes collected in the
"have-not" provinces up to the level of the average per capita yield
of the taxes collected in Ontario and British Columbia. The Hospital
Insurance and Diagnostic Services Act, which Parliament had passed
before its dissolution, also provided for federal contributions to participating provinces once six provinces with at least half the national
population entered into agreements.

To enable the provinces to present a common front in dealing with
Ottawa, the Montreal Chambre de commerce urged the establishment
of a permanent federal-provincial body and a council of provinces
before Diefenbaker convened his first federal-provincial conference.
Conference participants included forty-six federal and provincial cabinet ministers, over ninety aides and advisors, eighteen representatives of municipalities, and four women of whom two were research
economists and two secretaries. Before the meeting, Diefenbaker had
promised a revised fiscal system to put "an end to this centralization
complex" of the Liberals.[34]

Diefenbaker's appointment of four cabinet ministers from the Atlantic region, the largest number since the Second World War, encouraged
the two Liberal and two Conservative Atlantic premiers at the conference to think their requests would be looked upon favourably. They
presented a jointly formulated wish list asking that the federal government compensate them for the northern territories it had transferred to
other provinces, and that Ottawa fund a causeway to Prince Edward
Island. Both British Columbia's W.A.C. Bennett and Ontario's Leslie
Frost proposed tax-sharing formulas that would be of greater benefit
to their provinces. Quebec's Maurice Duplessis and Alberta's Manning
contended that the provinces should have priority in taxation powers
to fund programs falling under provincial jurisdiction.[35]

In addition to the new equalization payments, Diefenbaker proposed
to introduce the hospital insurance program earlier than planned,

waive the requirement that six provinces sign on, and extend coverage for mental health and tuberculosis patients. He also announced special grants-in-aid to the Atlantic provinces, an increase in the previously announced $150 million for low-cost housing loans, and removal of the threshold for unemployment insurance payments that applied to some but not all the provinces. As a result, Ottawa would share the costs of relief for an additional twenty thousand jobless Ontarians.[36]

Except for extending coverage for mental health and tuberculosis patients, the premiers accepted Diefenbaker's proposals for the hospital insurance program. British Columbia, Alberta, and Saskatchewan benefitted from the earlier start of the program because they already operated their own hospital insurance programs. Not keen on the program but joining it nonetheless, Manitoba's delegation thought Diefenbaker's proposals detracted from the main business of the conference, revising the tax-sharing formula.[37]

The Provinces

It was an atypical year: no provincial elections were held.

Before its defeat, the federal Liberal government appointed a royal commission headed by New Brunswick's chief justice, former Liberal premier John McNair, to review Newfoundland's terms of union with Canada. Newfoundland premier Joey Smallwood described his deeply indebted province as "a poor, bald rock bathed mostly in poverty ... as far behind Nova Scotia in the levels of our public services as Nova Scotia is behind Ontario."[38] Efforts by J.W. Pickersgill, the former senior federal civil servant whom Smallwood had lured to represent Newfoundland as an MP, contributed to broadening Ottawa's unemployment insurance program, providing additional benefits to Newfoundland's fishermen. After premiers Robert Stanfield of Nova Scotia and Hugh John Flemming of New Brunswick actively supported Diefenbaker in the election campaign, he announced millions in loans at favourable rates to build power facilities in their provinces. He also offered subsidies, which St. Laurent had refused to do, for coal mined in their provinces to be used by the power plants.[39]

All four Atlantic provinces faced difficulties in attracting, training, and maintaining qualified teachers. Nova Scotia needed a thousand new teachers but fewer than five hundred candidates had proper training. Of Newfoundland's teachers, 30 per cent did not meet minimum teaching requirements. The demand for qualified teachers led New Brunswick's government to create a Bachelor of Education program at the provincial university. Prince Edward Island's Conservative leader,

R.R. Bell, cited low salaries for teachers as "the whole root and evil" plaguing the education system.[40]

Maintaining its record of winning every by-election in ridings won in the previous general election, Quebec's Union Nationale increased its majority in all four by-elections held during the year. They gained a seat from the Liberals, outnumbering them seventy-three to seventeen in the legislature. The Liberals had hoped to elect party secretary Paul Gérin-Lajoie, a constitutional authority and future cabinet minister, and hoped he could succeed ailing party leader Georges-Émile Lapalme, who lacked a seat in the legislature, but he lost.[41]

Nevertheless, there were signs of faltering support for the Union Nationale. With the apparent blessing of Quebec historian Abbé Lionel Groulx, who had described Duplessis as a "man of the robe encrusted in legality," a new school of nationalist thought was emerging. Adherents called themselves "social nationalists." Drawn largely from the intelligentsia, they included Le Devoir editor-in-chief André Laurendeau. He agreed with Duplessis that Ottawa had invaded provincial jurisdiction in social policy but felt that Quebec's pressing challenge was to gain control of its natural resources, largely controlled by American corporations, and Quebec's wealth, largely in the hands of the English community.[42]

Canada's Supreme Court overturned Duplessis's Padlock Law in an 8–1 decision. The law had given the attorney general the power, without a warrant or court order, to search and padlock any premise that he believed was propagating communism. The court determined that this encroached on Parliament's exclusive right to legislate in the field of criminal law. Justice Ivan Rand opined more broadly: freedom of expression and communication, he wrote, "is little less vital to man's mind and spirit than breathing is to his physical existence." Duplessis responded that Quebec's late Cardinal Villeneuve had requested the law and that his government remained opposed to communism.[43]

With assistance from American unions, the Fédération provinciale du travail and the Fédération des unions industrielles merged to form the Fédération des travailleurs et travailleuses du Québec (FTQ: Quebec Federation of Labour). The federation supported the thousand miners at Murdochville who were striking to form a union. In solidarity, the ladies' auxiliary of English Canada's Communist-influenced Mine, Mill and Smelter Workers Union sent the strikers hundreds of pounds of clothing.[44] Duplessis's government dispatched the provincial police to subdue the strikers, and the company, a subsidiary of giant Noranda Inc., employed strike-breakers.

Ontario premier Leslie Frost, who had hitherto avoided engaging in federal politics, enthusiastically endorsed Diefenbaker at the launch of the Conservative campaign. Telling an audience "I always back a winner," he promised to put the whole weight of his provincial party, cabinet, and MPPs behind the federal party. Frost intimated that a Conservative government would look more favourably than the Liberals at sharing Ottawa's financial resources with Ontario. He was prescient in predicting that the Conservatives would win most of the province's eighty-five seats: they won sixty-one and almost half the popular vote.[45]

Queen's Park passed its largest-ever budget and announced that Ontario's hospital insurance program would begin in 1959. Claiming it would be the most comprehensive program in Canada and indeed the continent, Frost could not, however, say what the cost of the premiums would be.[46] Liberal leader Farquhar Oliver charged to little effect that Frost was a "cleverly camouflaged autocrat." The Conservatives prevailed easily in three by-elections and held eighty-four of the legislature's ninety-eight seats.[47] Oliver resigned as Liberal leader before year's end. The Conservative *Globe and Mail*, dismissing the Liberals as having "gone to seed," was "sorry" that the Conservative majority was "top-heavy," because a stronger opposition would have "obliged the government to do some hard thinking."[48] The provincial CCF held just three seats, while the communist Labor-Progressive Party, which had two seats when the decade began, now had none. Former LPP MPP J.B. Salsberg lamented that his party had become possibly the most backward Communist party in the world after its Albanian counterpart.[49]

Manitoba premier Douglas Campbell's thrifty approach to governing continued; the province had the lowest expenditures, measured as a percentage of total personal income, of any province. Campbell's Liberal-Progressives had a budgetary surplus as they had every year since 1950.[50] The federal Conservatives had won all the province's rural ridings, which were the support base for the Liberal-Progressives, and this encouraged Duff Roblin's provincial Conservatives. There was speculation that Diefenbaker would ask Roblin to join his cabinet because of his fluency in French, and the two went fishing together, but "Nothing was offered. Even if it had been," said Roblin, "I wouldn't have accepted because I must finish the job in Manitoba."[51]

Saskatchewan's most noteworthy political event was the "debate of the century" between former CCF MP-cum-Liberal Ross Thatcher and CCF premier T.C. Douglas. Over two thousand people came to Mossbank, a town of six hundred, where radio and television crews recorded the debate, which centred on the CCF's stable of crown corporations. The Liberal Regina *Leader-Post* editorialized that Thatcher easily won the debate.[52] However, the Liberals suffered from former premier Jimmy Gardiner's inability to convince his federal Liberal cabinet colleagues to proceed with the South Saskatchewan River Dam, a blow to both the provincial and federal Liberals.[53]

Christian evangelicalism infused politics in Alberta, where a vaguely worded plebiscite on liberalizing the liquor laws passed overwhelmingly.[54] Calgary, Edmonton, Lethbridge, and Red Deer also held plebiscites on water fluoridation; only Red Deer voters approved it. A majority of Edmontonians voted in favour but the bar for approval had been set at two-thirds of votes cast. Residents of Lethbridge also voted on their system of electing the mayor.[55] Vancouver held a plebiscite on permitting commercial sporting events on Sunday; the provincial government refused to accept the positive result but relented after a second plebiscite. In another plebiscite, Vancouverites voted in favour of fluoridation.[56]

Canada in the World

Canada's thirty-three remaining combat soldiers in Korea returned home, and a Japanese shipping line resumed service between Vancouver and China. Canada turned over to India a four million dollar hydro-electric project built under the Colombo Plan and appointed a high commissioner to Malaya.[57] A consulate was opened in Hamburg, and West Germany was provided with 225 Sabre jets under a mutual aid program.[58] Ottawa negotiated tax agreements with the Netherlands and South Africa, increasing to ten the number of bilateral agreements to prevent double taxation and tax avoidance.[59] New Brunswick premier Flemming, Halifax mayor Leonard Kitz, and a group of Canadian academics visited Jamaica to discuss immigration and trade between Canada and the newly created West Indies Federation.[60]

Prime Minister St. Laurent and external affairs minister Lester Pearson told British prime minister Harold Macmillan, who had soured on the UN because of its role in the Suez Crisis, that the organization was a cornerstone of Canadian foreign policy. They expressed concern about the UK's plan to cut back its contribution to NATO and reduce British forces in Europe and voiced uneasiness about potential high tariffs if Britain were to join a proposed European common market. Trade minister C.D. Howe urged Macmillan to make Britain a steady customer for Canadian uranium. To help address Britain's financial difficulties, Ottawa agreed to defer annual instalments of principal and interest on the fifty-five-year loan it had made in 1946.[61]

Canada's ambassador to Egypt, Herbert Norman, committed suicide after US Senate investigators made unsubstantiated allegations that he was a Communist. Shock and dismay were expressed in Britain,

Australia, and New Zealand. The London *Times* condemned the Senate's "reckless persecution," and CCF MP Alistair Stewart termed the suicide "murder by slander."[62] Although Norman's death tainted Canadian attitudes to the US, Ottawa maintained close military and diplomatic cooperation with Washington; as one example the two nations agreed to regulate and divide equally "so far as practicable" the catch of Pacific pink salmon fisheries.[63]

The DEW radar line, a joint US-Canada defence project, officially began operation, and the Canada-United States Continental Air Defence Command (later, NORAD) was formed, with a Canadian as deputy commander. Diefenbaker assured Parliament that stationing RCAF personnel at NORAD's Colorado headquarters did not really violate his principle that Canadian troops would not be posted abroad without Parliament's approval.[64] Canada continued as one of the four western powers, along with the US, Britain, and France, to engage in disarmament talks with the Soviet Union at the UN.[65]

Under the command of Canadian Major-General E.L.M. Burns, the United Nations Emergency Force (UNEF) took control of the Gaza Strip, using tear gas to quell Arab demonstrators who insisted the Strip belonged to Egypt; street banners termed UNEF as "Nasser's guests." Pearson received the Nobel Peace Prize not long after leaving office for defusing the Suez Crisis with the creation of UNEF. In response to the Nobel committee chairman's introduction at the award ceremony, the self-deprecating Pearson, whom the *New York Times* described as an "unstuffy diplomat" and a "superb conciliator," offered a typically Canadian apology for not being able to understand the chairman's Norwegian.[66]

Diefenbaker left for the Commonwealth conference in London a day after his cabinet convened for the first time. Britons found him intriguing: the *Sunday Express* headlined, "Watch the Man with the Burning Eyes (one day he may lead the Empire)." His priorities at the conference were to sell Canadian wheat and offer Ottawa as the venue for a Commonwealth trade conference, which the Conservatives had repeatedly proposed when in opposition. On his return, he announced his government's intention to shift 15 per cent of Canada's imports from US to British suppliers.[67] At a conference of Commonwealth finance ministers in Mont Tremblant, finance minister Donald Fleming was unreceptive to a British proposal for an eventual free trade agreement with Canada. Canadian-born London publisher Lord Beaverbrook called the proposal "a trick ... the British government will say that the rejection of empire free trade leaves no alternative [for Britain] but European free trade."[68]

In addressing the General Assembly, which had elected Canada to the Security Council, Diefenbaker declared that the UN remained "the cornerstone of Canadian foreign policy."[69] Canada, he said, opposed an international system of power blocs and counter-blocs and would withdraw from the UN's disarmament subcommittee if this would speed an agreement with the Soviets. Diefenbaker also said that Ottawa had no solution for the Middle East problem and although he favoured a permanent UN police force, he acknowledged there was no realistic prospect of such a force. He stressed that Canadian foreign policy remained unchanged, including refusal to recognize the Peking government: "The attitude of this government is unchanged," Diefenbaker told the House of Commons, "until such time as the ... communist government of China expiates its wrongdoing under international law there certainly will be no justification for the granting of recognition."[70]

Another sign of continuity in Canadian foreign policy came at the first meeting of the fifteen NATO heads of government. Canada had no specific proposals beyond the general objective of increasing economic and political cooperation among member states. Diefenbaker expressed his sensitivity to the feelings of Canada's Eastern Europeans and his hostility to the Soviet Union by meeting with a delegation of the Assembly of Captive European Nations, a coalition of exiles from the Soviet bloc. He asked that a paragraph supporting the Assembly's position be inserted into NATO's final communique.[71]

Canada unveiled the supersonic Avro Arrow, an economic recession began, air travel became more convenient, a Royal Commission expressed anxiety about American domination of Canada's natural resource industries, and Inuit were adjusting to a new way of life: wage labour. For the first time, the Queen opened Parliament and the federal cabinet included a woman. The Canada Council began operating and Canadians were making a mark in popular music.

With the opposition parties calling for more spending on social programs, Liberal cabinet ministers differed over whether to introduce a balanced or an expansionary pre-election budget. Public opinion polls reinforced Liberal confidence that they would be re-elected. However, Conservative John Diefenbaker, who had become his party's leader just six months earlier, proved to be an outstanding politician, drawing much larger, more enthusiastic crowds than prime minister Louis St. Laurent. For the first time in a federal election, the Conservatives won more seats while the Liberals won more votes. The CCF and Social Credit parties made marginal gains but enjoyed little support beyond the West. St. Laurent resigned as Liberal leader.

It was a politically tumultuous year as the federal government changed hands after more than two decades of unbroken Liberal rule. It was also an unusual year in that no provincial elections were held. The new Conservative government increased spending on social programs and its novice ministers performed well in the House of Commons. Federal equalization payments replaced Ottawa's tax-rental agreements with the provinces, a shared-cost national hospital insurance program was launched, and Diefenbaker convened his first federal-provincial conference. The fiscal capacity of the provinces increased, but they asked Ottawa for more fiscal transfers and taxing power. With its greater financial resources, the new government accommodated some of their requests.

By-elections in Quebec and Ontario reinforced the dominant positions of their respective Union Nationale and Conservative governments. The Supreme Court struck down Quebec's notorious Padlock Law, the Quebec Federation of Labour was formed, and the Quebec government used the provincial police to quell a major strike. Ontario's Conservatives, boasting that they would have the best hospital insurance program on the continent, played a prominent role in the election of the federal Conservatives. Industrial underdevelopment and weak school systems hampered economic and social development in the Atlantic provinces. Newfoundland's financial condition was particularly acute. Manitoba's Liberal-Progressive government continued its stingy ways and Saskatchewanians witnessed the "debate of the century" between a sitting CCF premier and a future Liberal premier. Albertans and Vancouverites voted in plebiscites on various issues, most notably water fluoridation.

Canada's remaining troops in Korea returned home, and shipping resumed between Canada and China, but Ottawa continued to withhold recognition of China's Communist government. Canada provided West Germany with military jets and turned over to India a major Colombo Plan power project. The United Nations remained a cornerstone of foreign policy under both Liberal and Conservative governments. Lester Pearson received the Nobel Peace Prize for initiating a UN emergency police force in the Middle East commanded by a Canadian general. Canada's ambassador to Egypt committed suicide amidst unsubstantiated American allegations that he was a Communist. Ottawa cooperated with Washington in major continental defence projects, the DEW Line and NORAD. The Conservative government proposed a Commonwealth trade conference but was not favourably disposed to negotiating a free trade agreement with Britain. At a NATO summit, Diefenbaker championed the cause of "captive" Eastern European nations.

1958

Diefenbaker seems to appreciate intuitively what the Canadian people want.[1]

Paul W. Fox

The sag in the booming economy which began when the Conservatives replaced the Liberals in government continued in the first half of the year. Prime minister John Diefenbaker blamed the recession in the United States for Canada's economic woes. University of Toronto economist B.S. Keirstead, although a critic of the Conservative government's policies, concurred: "it is largely an 'imported' depression caused by the slump in world demand for some of our principal exports."[2] High interest rates beset the Maritime and Western provinces in getting their products to market.

Of the nearly six million Canadians in the labour force, 590,000 were unemployed. The drop in business expenditures for non-residential construction, machinery, and equipment put downward pressure on economic growth. On the other hand, consumer spending, an expansion in housing, and government spending counteracted the downward pressures. The gross national product increased by 1 per cent in real terms mainly because of higher production in the farm economy.[3]

Federal, provincial, and municipal governments recorded combined deficits of over a billion dollars after having had combined fiscal surpluses of $70 million ($653 million in 2021) a year earlier.[4] "There is a formidable array of forces in Canada at the present time working in the direction of increased government expenditure," read the first sentence of the first article in the first issue of *Canadian Public Administration*; the author attributed it "to more general awareness of what can be done by government and a greater articulateness in pressing for governments to assume further responsibilities."[5]

By the end of the year, the number of post-war immigrants totalled almost two million. Between 1956 and 1958, 449,000 immigrants arrived, while an estimated 144,000 Canadians emigrated. Anxious about the high unemployment rate, the government limited the intake of immigrants: "There has been no active recruiting. It has been more a matter of limited selection," immigration minister Ellen Fairclough told the House of Commons. After officials denied entry to a Filipino on his way to accept a job with a Canadian mining company, the Philippines government retaliated, barring entry to Canadians, except for visitors, and seeking clarification: Was Canada pursuing a "white Australia" policy?[6]

Reflecting government policy, twenty-four of the twenty-seven offices issuing immigrant visas were in Europe: priority for British subjects and citizens of Ireland, the United States, and France. Nationals of India, Pakistan, and Ceylon qualified as British subjects but were admitted only in specified numbers.[7] Many more Asians than French settled in British Columbia; while historian Arthur Lower's newly published social history, *Canadians in the Making*, offered a sympathetic account of French settlement in Canada, it completely ignored Asians.[8]

Canada's cities were growing horizontally and vertically. Suburban sprawl bedevilled some municipal planning departments; a pamphlet by British Columbia's Lower Mainland Regional Planning Board, *Urban Sprawl*, likened suburbanization to the destructive effect of "termites."[9] Modernist architecture became more common; Finnish architect Viljo Revell won the $25,000 prize for designing Toronto's new city hall and Princess Margaret opened Ottawa's new city hall, whose flush-glazed fenestration "signified contemporary ideas of civic democracy" according to architectural historians because it "opened governance to citizen gaze." Over the course of three days in Montreal, a parade of celebrities under a battery of television lights attended the opening of the twenty-one-storey Queen Elizabeth Hotel, which embodied the high luxury of neoclassical midcentury hotels.[10]

The overwhelming majority of the more than thirty-eight thousand adults charged with almost seventy thousand indictable criminal offences were found guilty. One exception was Kikkik, an Inuit woman from a community about a hundred miles south of the Arctic Circle, acquitted of murdering an Inuit conjuror. Murders doubled from eight a year earlier to sixteen, but manslaughter convictions were down significantly. The conviction rate for all crimes, 311 per 100,000 of population, varied significantly by province: Prince Edward Island had 213, Alberta 489. Under the Opium and Narcotic Drug Act, 488 alleged offenders were charged, in most cases for possessing or trafficking heroin; the overwhelming majority of those charged were Canadian-born men.

British Columbia and Ontario accounted for 62 and 30 per cent respectively of all narcotics convictions.[11]

The summary dismissal of Professor Harry Crowe by the principal of Winnipeg's United College became a cause célèbre in academic circles. The Canadian Association of University Teachers, which designated future Supreme Court chief justice Bora Laskin as one of the investigators of the affair, concluded that Crowe's dismissal lacked proper procedure and a statement of cause, therefore constituting a breach of academic freedom. The imbroglio led fourteen of the College's fifty-two professors, some members of the Board of Regents, and the principal – a former Toronto United Church pastor – to resign. One professor's resignation letter charged that Crowe's dismissal amounted to thought control, and that the college had so disintegrated that it was neither Christian nor a college.[12]

The completion of a coast-to-coast microwave relay system extended telecasting within Atlantic Canada and northern Ontario, resulting in more sales of television sets in those regions. However, sales of television sets nationally declined from the previous year as did sales of radios and record players. CBC's chief engineer said the corporation would consider introducing colour television broadcasts, depending on how popular they became in the United States. The Ontario Association of Curriculum Development considered equipping all new school buildings with televisions; some thought television could help overcome the shortage of teachers as well as lead "to higher standards of education."[13]

With nearly six million telephones, Canadians had more telephone conversations per person than residents of any other country. Direct long-distance telephone dialling began between Toronto and Montreal and soon extended to several cities between New York and Chicago. Coloured telephones became available. Another telephone innovation was a specified phone number (EM 1-1111 in Toronto) for emergencies, but an official reported that in its first day of operation, 99 per cent of the avalanche of calls did not concern emergencies at all: one caller asked for a plumber, another to have his beer bottles carted away.[14]

Set in the northern Quebec tundra of the Inuit, the wilderness novel *Agaguk* by Yves Thériault riveted French Quebec's intellectual class.[15] Destined to become one of the most widely read and taught Quebec novels in the 1960s, the book was translated into six languages, sold three hundred thousand copies, and was twice adapted for film.[16] Describing the cruelties of Inuit life and affirming the plurality of sexual identity, *Agaguk* told of cultural conflict between Inuit and white men of authority, touching on issues of assimilation, alcoholism, and economic and judicial injustice. *Execution*, the only novel of war veteran

Colin McDougall, won the Governor General's Award for English-language fiction.[17] Based on his experience in Italy, the novel told of a Canadian infantry unit whose commander orders the execution of two Italian deserters. The executioners are torn between their obligation to follow orders and their sense that the order is ethically unjustifiable. The book's thesis was that war may make men act inhumanely but cannot expunge their essential goodness.

Three weeks of celebrations marked the 350th anniversary of the founding of Quebec City by Samuel de Champlain in 1608.

Federal Politics

Federal legislation extended financial assistance for the generation of electric power in Atlantic Canada, provided $750 million for housing programs, introduced mandatory price support for various agricultural commodities, and created a revolving fund of $250 million to stabilize farmers' incomes. Employees of federally regulated industries who had worked for at least a year were guaranteed an annual paid vacation of at least two weeks. The National Parole Board was established, and the Board of Broadcast Governors was formed to regulate broadcasting. An amended Indian Act permitted the descendants of Indigenous people who had been allotted half-breed lands or scrip to continue to be registered as Indians.[18]

The Liberal party, confused and disorganized after their stunning defeat in the 1957 election, held a leadership convention to replace Louis St. Laurent. Lester Pearson easily defeated Paul Martin, 1074 votes to 305. Unlike Martin, Pearson expressed eagerness to defeat Diefenbaker's minority government. Defining Liberalism as "the middle way," Pearson contrasted it to the "privilege, discrimination, and class distinction" of the right and the "imposed equality" and "conformity" of the left. He wrote that "the foundation of [the Liberal party's] faith is belief in the dignity and worth of the individual. The state is the creation of man, to protect and serve him; and not the reverse."[19]

Conservative MPs greeted Pearson with derisive laughter during his maiden speech as opposition leader which called on the government to resign and cede power to a government "pledged to implement Liberal policies." Diefenbaker's riposte to Pearson cited a "hidden report" prepared by government economists for the former government, which he suggested the Liberals had deliberately concealed from the public because it contained forecasts of the recession inherited by the new Conservative government. Within days, Diefenbaker succeeded in having Parliament dissolved for a winter election. Liberal MPs jeered; some shouted "Black Saturday," recalling the term "Black Friday" used by the Conservatives in the 1956 pipeline debate.[20] CCFer Stanley Knowles accused the Conservatives of showing even greater contempt for Parliament than the former Liberal government because the new government had not sought spending approval from Parliament, governing instead with governor general's warrants. Social Credit leader Solon Low deemed the government's behaviour "a matter of censure."[21]

The election campaign pointed to trouble for Pearson's Liberals. None of the eight cabinet ministers defeated in the 1957 election stood as a candidate. Nor did nineteen incumbent Liberal MPs, fifteen of whom represented Quebec constituencies. At a party rally of nine hundred in Hamilton, Pearson was heckled half a dozen times; while Martin received two standing ovations, Pearson's one ovation was subdued. His largest crowd in the first three weeks of the campaign, one thousand at Vancouver's airport, "was almost mute. There were few cheers. Just stares." In Halifax, he faced "a politically sedate audience" of eleven hundred. Toronto's Massey Hall was filled for his rally, but the seven hundred overflow seats in a building across the street remained empty. CCF leader M.J. Coldwell, anticipating a Conservative victory, spoke of overtaking the Liberals as official opposition.[22]

If the Liberals were the old guard in Canadian politics, the Conservatives were the new vanguard. Diefenbaker attracted five thousand people to the Winnipeg Auditorium, the largest political rally in the prairie provinces in thirty years; several hundred unable to get in were left standing outside in near-zero cold. More than ten thousand people greeted him over the course of a day in Edmonton. In Cape Breton, he spoke at the largest political rally in the Island's history.[23] At his rally in Trois-Rivières, Conservative candidates and organizers "were ecstatic. For the first time in sixty years they could get all the money they needed, all the candidates and workers they wanted, and the Liberals couldn't."[24]

Diefenbaker promised that a Conservative government would stabilize farmers' incomes, build roads for resource developments in the territories and in the north of provinces, and prevent the textile and agricultural sectors of other countries from exporting goods to Canada at prices lower than in their own countries. He pledged to abolish the closure rule in Commons' debates, reduce the length of federal election campaigns, and increase financial transfers to the provinces. Responding to opposition charges that he was acting without Parliament's budgetary authority, he vowed to convene Parliament soon after the election "for ratification, consideration, amendment or defeat" of the monies spent.[25]

The Liberals highlighted their experience in government, noting "world-wide acclaim of Canada's contribution to peace," and citing Pearson's Nobel Peace Prize. They promised lower taxes, an expanded welfare state, and a "dowry plan," to "take the pressure off many young wives who now feel they must work in order to help establish a home."[26] The CCF called for "economic democracy," public ownership of interprovincial pipelines, a national labour code, abolition of the Senate, and a bill of rights; they proposed that Ottawa pay for 80 per cent of a national health insurance program that would include "full medical, hospital, nursing, dental, optical and other health care."[27] Social Credit underscored the positive fruits of automation while ruing consumers' lack of purchasing power, unemployment, and debt, both personal and public: "Citizens are destined to economic slavery ... [because] Governments use the artificial remedy of spreading public charity through the welfare state in an attempt to buy another term in office resulting in a further load of debt, interest, and tax."[28]

The Gallup poll reported Conservative support at 56 per cent, the Liberals at 32, the CCF 7, and Social Credit 4. The poll led CCF MP Arnold Peters to announce that he would introduce a bill prohibiting the publication of polls during an election campaign: "We feel things like the Gallup poll have some effect on the outcome of an election, which is not right or proper."[29] Surprises in the unsurprising Conservative victory were its size and the level of public engagement. The party won 54 per cent of the popular vote and over 78 per cent of the seats. Voter turnout of nearly 80 per cent was the highest ever, 12 per cent higher than in the last Liberal victory in 1953. The Conservatives won most of the seats in every province except Newfoundland, and they captured all but one in the prairie provinces, where Diefenbaker was seen more as a prairie radical than a conventional Conservative.

The shattered Liberals, losing more than half their seats, failed to win any seats west of Ontario. Pearson attributed his party's defeat to smugness and self-satisfaction. He claimed that voters responded positively to Diefenbaker's optimistic vision of Canada's future only because of the good management Liberal governments had provided for over two decades. Political scientist Paul Fox's view was that "Diefenbaker seems to appreciate intuitively what the Canadian people want."[30]

Despite having lost only 1 per cent in the popular vote, the CCF was reduced from twenty-five MPs to eight. With leader M.J. Coldwell defeated, there was speculation that the party would turn to Saskatchewan premier T.C. Douglas or Stanley Knowles. Douglas decided to remain in Saskatchewan and Knowles, who had also lost his seat, accepted an offer from officials of the Canadian Labour Congress to serve as a vice president, a position he would use to help create the CCF's successor, the New Democratic Party.[31] Hazen Argue, the party's only MP on the prairies, having defeated CCFer-cum-Liberal Ross Thatcher in Assiniboia, became the new party leader. Social Credit lost all nineteen of its seats to the Conservatives, but a half dozen of its defeated MPs insisted their party was as vigorous as ever. When a *Wall Street Journal* reporter exclaimed "balderdash" to party leader Solon Low's assessment of the government's financial policy as "embezzlement and highway robbery," Low retorted, "Ask questions in a gentlemanly manner. Or out you go."[32]

After the election, Diefenbaker refused to table the most recent edition of the annual report written for cabinet by government economists, the annual report he had accused the Liberals of concealing.[33] He introduced a bill of rights, which the opposition parties supported with reservations. Pearson, questioning the bill's necessity, urged that the provinces be invited to comment and join in "a truly national declaration." CCFer Argue wanted to know why the bill lacked a right to employment. Lawyers at the annual meeting of the Canadian Bar Association had their own misgivings; one called the bill "window dressing," another termed it "downright dangerous." Others said that as a federal bill it would apply only in the Northwest Territories and Yukon, and some said that British Columbia's Doukhobors would use the bill's freedom of religion clause to avoid sending their children to school as required by law.[34]

Some opponents of the government expressed anxiety that the CBC would become a tool of the government. For the first time in Canadian history, a prime minister appeared on television to make a direct address to the nation as part of a $375,000 blanket advertising campaign: all but five of the country's TV stations carried the Diefenbaker broadcast urging Canadians to exchange their unmatured Victory Bonds for longer-term savings bonds, with a view to consolidating over 40 per cent of the national debt. Pearson and Martin accused Diefenbaker of censorship for telling a CBC reporter not to ask visiting British prime minister Harold Macmillan whether the United Kingdom would be proposing a free trade agreement with Canada.[35] Social Credit MP Ernest Hansell was concerned that the CBC might be advising the government on which new private television and radio stations ought to be licensed, while CCFer Herbert Herridge lauded the CBC for spending its funds "to the very best effect possible."[36]

Intergovernmental Relations

Ottawa's transfer of personal income taxes to the provinces increased from 10 to 13 per cent. In addition, the Atlantic provinces received increased equalization payments as well as a special annual adjustment grant of $25 million. New Brunswick's Conservative premier Hugh

John Flemming was gratified: "Nothing on this scale and magnitude both with respect to recognition and action has ever happened before." Prince Edward Island's Alex Matheson and Newfoundland's Joey Smallwood, both Liberals, were less impressed: Matheson dismissed the $25 million grant as "the poorest type of arrangement you could imagine" because, he said, Diefenbaker had told the provinces to "fight it out among themselves in dividing it." Smallwood was unhappy because the Royal Commission reviewing Newfoundland's terms of union with Canada recommended that his province receive an additional $8 million annually, less than half of what he had requested.[37]

To alleviate winter unemployment, Ottawa offered to pay half the payroll costs incurred by municipalities for local projects, subject to approval by their provincial governments. Several premiers were "delighted" with the offer. Surprisingly, Quebec's government authorized its municipalities to conclude agreements with Ottawa just days after premier Maurice Duplessis had denounced federal encroachment in areas of provincial jurisdiction, rejecting subsidies for building roads to natural resources and once again refusing federal aid to Quebec's universities.[38]

Lobbying by the Federation of Mayors and Municipalities representing three thousand local governments led Diefenbaker to consider a tri-level federal-provincial-municipal conference to overhaul government tax sharing. Ontario premier Leslie Frost said Queen's Park expected to receive $78 million from Ottawa in addition to the $22 million received a year earlier. However, Diefenbaker refused to commit to such a transfer and the federal-provincial conference that had been scheduled to continue the work of the adjourned 1957 conference was not held. Finance minister Donald Fleming told Parliament the conference would take place "when the time is ripe."[39]

The Canadian Welfare Council identified the lack of an integrated universal social security scheme to replace the separate federal and provincial programs as a notable failure in Canada's welfare system; support programs available in some provinces, such as help for families to meet medical bills, were not available in other provinces. In a second meeting with the executive of the Federation of Mayors and Municipalities, Diefenbaker said that Ottawa's burden of social security costs prevented innovations such as an exemption from paying the 10 per cent federal sales tax on most municipal purchases.[40]

With only 37 per cent of Canadian hospitals accredited (compared with 60 per cent in the United States), five provinces – Newfoundland, British Columbia, Alberta, Saskatchewan, and Manitoba – began operating hospital insurance programs cost-shared with Ottawa. Manitoba urged Ottawa to enlarge the program to cover outpatients requiring minor surgery and British Columbia operated its program under protest because Ottawa would not pay for some diagnostic services. All the provinces except for Prince Edward Island and Quebec were expected to institute programs by 1959, with Ottawa contributing an estimated $160 million to the fifty-fifty shared-cost plan.[41]

While Quebec and Ontario remained aloof, the other eight provinces banded together to appeal to the federal cabinet to reverse a decision by the Board of Transport Commissioners to increase freight rates by 17 per cent. To prevent a strike by railway employees, the three spokespersons for the eight provinces – Saskatchewan's T.C. Douglas, Nova Scotia's Robert Stanfield, and Manitoba's Duff Roblin – proposed that Ottawa provide subsidies to the Canadian Pacific and Canadian National Railways in place of a rate increase.[42]

The Provinces

Formation of the Nova Scotia Civil Service Association signalled a milestone on the road to eventual unionization. The government appointed prominent business executive Frank Sobey to head a new crown corporation to attract industries, but the Springhill mining disaster, in which seventy-five men died, overshadowed all provincial political and economic issues.[43] Premier Smallwood refused to release an American study he had commissioned of Newfoundland's industries, leading the opposition Conservatives to charge that he had refused because the findings fell short of his extravagant predictions.[44]

Excitement rippled through Prince Edward Island about the possibility of an oil discovery. Some Islanders were concerned that the federal Conservative government would not follow through on a feasibility study initiated by the former federal Liberal government regarding construction of a causeway to New Brunswick. New Brunswick's government suggested that new sources of electric power, advanced pulp and paper-making techniques, and a more efficient use of forests could make the province the centre of Maritime economic activity.[45]

Quebec's Union Nationale actively supported the re-election of the federal Conservatives; future Union Nationale premier Daniel Johnson, the legislature's deputy speaker, shared a stage with Diefenbaker and sang his praises. The Liberal-leaning francophone media did not: *Le Devoir* criticized Diefenbaker for refusing to commit to issuing bilingual cheques and funding specific projects in Quebec; Ottawa's *Le Droit* attacked him for implying that Quebec's representation in his cabinet would depend on the election of qualified candidates.[46]

After four thousand Liberal convention delegates elected MP Jean Lesage as party leader, he quickly capitalized on the biggest controversy to shake the Union Nationale government since its first election in 1936: the questionable financial gains made by stockholding UN MLAs in the sale of Montreal's natural gas system. Lesage described the affair as "a shame for all North America," saying Quebecers "hold sufficiently clear the honor of the French-Canadian race to have light thrown on the matter" in a Royal Commission inquiry. Unsurprisingly, Duplessis refused the demand for an inquiry. Lesage also argued that Duplessis had used provincial autonomy "as a mask" for political gain, that "only with a Liberal government in Quebec would provincial prerogatives be truly safeguarded" against the federal Conservatives, "the most centralizing" of all federal governments.[47]

Other opponents of the Union Nationale included La Ligue des Électeurs and Pierre Trudeau. The Ligue had become a bitter enemy of the government after the Union Nationale had organized to defeat the Ligue in Montreal's municipal elections; it announced plans to expand "to the whole of Quebec a campaign for political reform, restoration of democracy and administrative honesty." Trudeau wrote a series of weekly newspaper articles attacking Duplessis for his "trickery," challenging what he said was Duplessis's claim that "we must not criticize the authority he exercises ... because this authority comes from God."[48]

Despite growing opposition, the Union Nationale won all three by-elections. Challenging Duplessis to hold a general election, the Liberals did not contest the by-elections, leading the pro-UN *Montreal Gazette* to criticize them for abdicating the role of opposition. Lesage considered the by-elections a trap set by Duplessis; he expected that since all three were in safe UN ridings, Duplessis would claim vindication in the natural gas corruption controversy after winning them. Duplessis's heir apparent Paul Sauvé made clear the cost of not voting for the government: "You know how to vote if you want to get something out of the government, don't you?"[49]

Seven Ontario by-elections in Conservative-held constituencies resulted in Conservative victories in all of them, two by acclamation. Three of the by-elections had been caused by deaths, two by resignations, and two by appointments, most notably that of provincial treasurer Dana Porter as provincial chief justice by the federal cabinet. In Porter's former Toronto riding, future provincial and federal Conservative minister Allan Lawrence defeated three female candidates, including a Social Crediter opposed to fluoridation.[50]

As in Quebec, controversy surrounding a natural gas company roiled Ontario politics. CCF leader Donald MacDonald aggressively questioned the financial gains made by the president of the company which had received $35 million in government funds. MacDonald also pointed to a "whopping number" of shares in the company held by two cabinet ministers. As in Quebec, the government denied MacDonald's call for a Royal Commission investigation. John Wintermeyer, who replaced Farquhar Oliver after defeating former federal finance minister Walter Harris for the Liberal leadership, also owned some of the company's shares. Delegates at the Liberal convention that elected Wintermeyer urged the teaching of French in all elementary and secondary schools, called for a Royal Commission to study Ontario's liquor laws, and elected future federal cabinet minister Judy LaMarsh to the party's executive.[51]

Manitoba held the year's only provincial election. The results mirrored the 1957 federal election results: Duff Roblin's Conservatives overtook a long-governing Liberal-Progressive regime to form a minority government with the CCF holding the balance of power. The Liberal-Progressives and CCF briefly considered forming a coalition government to keep the Conservatives from taking power, but their negotiations came to naught.[52] Cartoons in the Liberal *Winnipeg Free Press* depicted the young, energetic Roblin in a boy scout's outfit. The Conservative victory was the first since 1914, when Roblin's grandfather, Sir Rodmond Roblin, served as the premier. In addition to infrastructure projects, the new government announced revisions of the minimum wage, vacation with pay, and workmen's compensation legislation.[53]

The federal Conservative triumphs of 1957–8 boosted the morale of provincial Conservatives across the West. However, both the provincial Saskatchewan and Alberta Conservative parties were weak and leaderless. The Alberta and Manitoba Liberals also had no leader. At a convention of over eight hundred delegates and alternates, three hundred guests, and five candidates, W.J.C. Kirby was elected the first Alberta Conservative party leader since 1937.[54] Saskatchewan's Conservatives opted for a thirty-six-year-old farmer and insurance executive, Martin Pederson. He won the leadership with no organization and "not a button or poster" at the largest convention in the party's history, 880 voting delegates with Diefenbaker as the featured speaker.[55]

Many members of the weak British Columbia Conservative party, which had not held power on its own since 1933, wanted to depose leader Deane Finlayson, a thirty-nine-year-old former realtor, and entice federal justice minister Davie Fulton to lead them. Some party members saw Social Credit as a kind of provincial wing of the federal Conservative party and proposed a truce with W.A.C. Bennett's government. Others, including Finlayson, considered Social Credit an adversary and were determined to maintain a separate identity and ride the Diefenbaker wave to provincial victory. The party schism played out at a leadership convention called by Finlayson to settle the dispute; he retained his position narrowly, defeating geologist Desmond Kidd by a vote of 350 to 339.[56]

Canada in the World

Canada continued to distance itself from some British concerns. External affairs minister Sidney Smith repeated that Ottawa had no commitment to defend British oil interests in the Middle East, Diefenbaker retreated from his vow to divert 15 per cent of Canada's trade with the United States to Britain, and Ottawa maintained its chilly attitude to Britain's proposal to negotiate a free trade agreement. However, Smith was onside with the British call for freer world trade at a ministerial meeting of twenty of the participating nations in the General Agreement on Tariffs and Trade, at which criticisms were levelled at the restrictive policies of the United States, West Germany, and the European Economic Community.[57]

Prime minister Harold Macmillan was extended the honour of addressing both houses of Parliament as were West German president Theodor Heuss, the first German head of state to visit Canada, and US president Dwight Eisenhower. Diefenbaker assured Heuss that Canada would maintain its forces in Europe; Eisenhower and Diefenbaker discussed the establishment of a joint cabinet-level defence committee like the existing joint cabinet committee on economic policy, but no decision was reached.[58]

The Conservatives had spoken of fostering Commonwealth and specifically British trade, but their amended Customs Act deleted the exclusion of British goods from some new import duties, troubling the British government. Conversely, Ottawa was unhappy with British restrictions on imports priced in dollars.[59] After some bargaining at the Commonwealth Trade and Economic Conference held in Montreal, Ottawa agreed to maintain its tariff concessions for British goods and the British agreed to eliminate exchange controls on a broad range of Canadian exports. The most significant decision at the conference, which devoted much attention but arrived at no solution for stabilizing low commodity prices, was agreement to a proposal for the construction, largely funded by Britain, of an around-the-world coaxial telephone cable linking member countries.[60]

Domestic political considerations were more influential in the Diefenbaker government's foreign policy than they had been for the Liberals.[61] His thirty-five-thousand-mile, six-week world tour to Europe,

Asia, and the Antipodes, with stops in a dozen Commonwealth capitals, began in New York and London. The *Times* of London opined that Diefenbaker had "no specific business of State to discuss"; rather his motives were to convey Canada's high standing in world affairs and to make himself "be known by the leaders and peoples of all countries."[62] Much of his time in Rome was spent sightseeing. In Lahore, he received an honorary Doctor of Laws degree from the University of the Punjab and, with his brother Elmer, stood on the balcony where the builder of the Taj Mahal had held court. He went fishing in New Zealand. Government officials in Wellington did not expect results from his week-long courtesy visit; there was little to discuss since prime minister Walter Nash had recently talked with Diefenbaker at the Commonwealth trade conference in Montreal. In Australia, Diefenbaker spoke of the Commonwealth as involving a "feeling of oneness, of responsibility of members to each other, and common heritage." Reporting on his world tour in a televised broadcast, he said that international communism had made Malaya one of the vital battlegrounds for the hearts and minds of Asians.[63]

Serving a two-year term on the United Nations Security Council, Canada reaffirmed its shared position with the United States, Britain, and France in disarmament negotiations with the Soviet Union. Ottawa indicated willingness to permit aerial inspection of Canada's Arctic by the Soviets in a reciprocal arrangement: "Since we are neighbors across the Arctic," said Diefenbaker, it would be "in order to provide assurance against the fear of surprise attack."[64] Participation in both the UN Emergency Force in the Sinai Desert and UNOGIL, the observation group on the Lebanese-Syrian border, made Canada a significant player in the Security Council. However, after the overthrow of Iraq's Hashemite dynasty, Sidney Smith admitted that Ottawa suffered for lack of knowledge of the Middle East because of the absence of diplomatic relations with all the countries in the region. Nevertheless, in the strongest charge made by any western leader, he accused Egyptian president Nasser's newly formed United Arab Republic of having plotted to overthrow the governments of Sudan, Libya, Jordan, and Iraq and, in a break with American and French policy, Smith proposed a neutral Lebanon along the lines of the Austrian State Treaty.[65]

The supersonic Avro Arrow interceptor, considered the ultimate manned fighter plane, made its maiden flight. Kurt Stehling, NASA's future senior scientist, opined that the more than $300 million Ottawa had spent on the Arrow's development could have been spent more effectively on high-altitude missiles. After Washington refused to commit to buying the Arrow and the Americans persuaded defence minister

George Pearkes that missiles were a greater threat than manned bombers, Pearkes wrote a memo to that effect to the cabinet's defence committee. He was convinced that the best option would be to purchase
American-built ground-to-air Bomarc missiles. Ontario's Leslie Frost was
aware that the Arrow would almost certainly be terminated, but Diefenbaker postponed publicly announcing the Arrow's fate until 1959.[66]

Irritants in the relationship with the US included the Ford Motor
Company's refusal to let its Canadian subsidiary sell automobiles to
the Communist Chinese regime, Washington's restrictions on foreign
oil imports, and Canada's sale of wheat to China. Trade minister Gordon Churchill and Canadian business leaders urged more trade with
mainland China, and some encouraged political recognition of its government, but finance minister Donald Fleming announced in Tokyo
that Canada had no intention of establishing diplomatic relations with
Peking.[67] Growing criticism in Canada of the US, and incipient protectionist sentiments in both countries, led two congressmen to author a
study bemoaning "an erosion in the traditionally excellent" relationship between the two countries.[68]

Canada established diplomatic representation in Burma, Malaya,
and Iran as well as in the newly formed West Indies Federation, to
which Ottawa offered the gift of a ship to carry passengers and cargo
among the islands. Later, Ottawa also proposed $10 million for tech-
nical assistance and a second ship to facilitate inter-island trade. West
Indies Federation prime minister Sir Grantley Adams warmly acknowledged the announcement of Canada's support during the Commonwealth trade conference. A trade agreement with the Federation
was necessary to consolidate Canada's separate agreements with the
individual island colonies.[69]

Unemployment rose, the federal and provincial governments ran
deficits, and immigration was curtailed. Canada's cities were literally
growing up and out. Per capita criminal convictions varied dramatically by province, while the summary dismissal of a Winnipeg professor without due process dismayed the national academic community.
The National Parole Board and Board of Broadcast Governors were created to operate at arm's length from the government.

Lester Pearson, defeating Paul Martin for the Liberal party leadership, had an inauspicious beginning as the new leader of the opposition. Prime minister John Diefenbaker dissolved Parliament for an
election campaign in which he attracted record crowds. His Conservative party's victory was overwhelming: they won all but one seat west
of Ontario while more than half the Liberal seats were in Quebec.

Ottawa transferred more fiscal capacity to the provinces, supplemented by special grants to the Atlantic provinces whose challenges of economic development and fiscal sustainability were chronic. Municipalities lobbied for a tri-level conference to discuss tax sharing, but neither it nor a planned federal-provincial conference were held. More provinces signed on to join Ottawa's hospital insurance program, while the Canadian Welfare Council drew attention to the country's fragmented social security system. The Diefenbaker government introduced a bill of rights that would apply in areas of federal jurisdiction, but it did not advance beyond first reading in Parliament.

Jean Lesage, Quebec's new Liberal leader, aggressively attacked the aging Duplessis government, which was mired in scandal. By-elections in Ontario confirmed the strong hold of the provincial Conservatives on government. On the prairies, the Diefenbaker sweep energized the provincial Conservative parties: Manitoba elected its first Conservative government since the First World War, Saskatchewan's Conservatives held their largest-ever convention, and the Alberta Conservatives elected their first leader since 1937. British Columbia's Conservatives were torn between making peace or fighting with the Social Credit government.

Ottawa continued to distance itself from British interests, and new irritants arose in Canada's relations with the United States. At a Commonwealth trade and economic conference held in Montreal, agreement was reached to construct a telephone cable linking Commonwealth countries. At the UN, where Canada took a seat at the Security Council for a two-year term, the major issues were the West's disarmament negotiations with the Soviet Union and turbulence in the Middle East. Canada reached out to aid the newly formed West Indies Federation. The prime minister embarked on a six-week world tour that included much sightseeing and little policy substance.

1959

Only when the majority of people have been assured a comparatively high standard of living, with security against unemployment, old age and sickness, is a surplus available for any other purpose.[1]

Globe and Mail

The Dominion Bureau of Statistics estimated Canada's population at 17,408,000, an increase of almost 4 million in the decade. Both fertility and immigration propelled growth. In a post-war peak, 20 per cent of women in their twenties gave birth during the year. Immigrants settled largely in the major cities, but their numbers were fewer: 104,000 compared to 282,000 two years earlier. Italian immigrants outnumbered all Commonwealth immigrants. Fewer than 180,000 Indigenous people, barely 1 per cent of the population, were organized in 562 bands occupying nearly six million acres on 2,200 reserves. For the first time, Ottawa granted some bands the authority to open bank accounts and spend their own revenue.[2]

The 11,500 Inuit scattered over nine hundred thousand square miles in the far north had gained the right to vote in 1950 but had no way of exercising it because their isolated communities were given no ballot boxes. RCMP commissioner Colonel L.H. Nicholson, a member of the federally appointed Northwest Territories Council that held most of its meetings in Ottawa, expressed the "semi-official policy" of the government vis-à-vis Inuit: "He must never be looked upon as a curiosity but as a man and a Canadian." This meant that Inuit should be drawn into national life and simultaneously encouraged to retain their cultural heritage.[3]

Some native-born Canadians claimed that non-British immigrants were taking their jobs, causing a worsening of labour conditions and

weakening trade unions. The president of the British Columbia Federation of Labor charged that "massive immigration" meant that "management's very quick to toss a labor surplus in our teeth." The Immigration
Act allowed for the deportation of immigrants seeking social welfare,
but this rarely occurred. Responding to claims that immigrants were
forming ethnic ghettos, the editor of the Italian semi-weekly *Corriere
Canadese* quipped: "A sort of pizza curtain exists between us. We're
thought of as people who just like to sing and eat queer foods."[4]

Student numbers increased in all types of schools, but the number of
schools remained constant; as newer, larger urban schools were built,
many one-room rural schools closed. Provincial governments controlled only 23 of the 339 institutions offering degree-credit courses.
Most post-secondary institutions were religious establishments, more
than three-quarters of them Catholic. York University was incorporated
in a setting of a record high number of full-time students and increasing
demand for non-denominational higher education. Ontario alone anticipated tripling its thirty thousand post-secondary students within nine
years and the University of Toronto planned to double its enrolments.[5]

More women were running for office and winning. They occupied
hundreds of municipal posts, particularly on school boards. Three
women sat in the House of Commons and five in the Senate. A group
of female newspaper editors, describing Ellen Fairclough as a "cabinet minister, housewife and accountant," selected her as "woman of
the year in public affairs." A Winnipeg school trustee, upset by Fairclough's prediction that the number of female politicians would double
in the following decade remarked, "It looks to me as if women are trying to take over. It would be a major mistake." Pointe Claire mayor Ol-
ive Urquhart lamented that husbands "don't encourage their wives" to
engage in politics.[6] Quebec and the Atlantic provinces, with their more
traditional political cultures, lagged in the representation of women.

Largely due to an economic upsurge in the United States, the gross
national product at mid-year was up by 7 per cent over 1958. Industrial production increased by 10 per cent over its recessionary low two
years earlier, unemployment declined substantially, and sales of new
and used cars jumped by 14 per cent. With Canadian bond interest
rates significantly higher than in the United States, many businesses
and provincial governments turned to foreign borrowing. Sales of uranium, iron ore, asbestos, and forest products increased while sales of
farm products, nickel, copper, petroleum, and aircraft fell. Farmers,
rubber firms, and other industries clamoured for an increase in tariff
rates, but the government resisted pressure to broaden the range of protected goods; rates increased for thirty-two items, decreased for forty,

and sixty-one were unchanged. Overall tariff rates rose slightly. Tariff Board chairman Hector McKinnon declared that free trade or a customs union with the United States "wouldn't be such a bad thing ... I think a customs union would have over-all benefits for us."[7]

The voice of Bay Street, the *Globe and Mail*, editorialized that the business community had come to accept the welfare state as "a first charge on the nation's wealth ... Only when the majority of people have been assured a comparatively high standard of living, with security against unemployment, old age and sickness, is a surplus available for any other purpose."[8] Often funded by a combination of state and private sources, non-profit institutions such as hospitals, churches, and trade unions provided a range of social welfare services to supplement universal government programs such as unemployment insurance and family allowance payments.

Ottawa's cancellation of the Avro Arrow, though expected, still shocked the public: over 14,000 workers were laid off. Drawing on the infamous 1956 pipeline debate, Avro workers termed the cancellation announcement "Black Friday." The *Toronto Daily Star*'s Duncan Macpherson, winner of the year's National Newspaper Award for editorial cartooning, caricatured Diefenbaker as Marie Antoinette intoning, "Let them eat cake." A *Globe and Mail* cartoon had bystanders cheering as prime minister John Diefenbaker, involuntarily strapped to a rocket, was shot into space. More than a thousand of the Avro workers applied for a US visa, and NASA immediately hired the company's lead engineer and thirty-one others. Described as "alien scientists having special qualifications," they were put to work on the Mercury man-in-space program. However, over eight thousand of the former Avro employees were still jobless two months after the Arrow's demise.[9]

A strike by 74 Montreal CBC producers led to 1,500 unionists marching on Parliament Hill. Singing French Canadian folk songs, their noisy demonstration lent a tone of French Canadian nationalism to the strike. Seven CBC unions honoured the producers' picket line, French language CBC stars including René Lévesque supported the strikers, and most of *The Plouffe Family* cast, whose popular program was broadcast in English and French, spent a night on the picket line.[10]

The Queen and Prince Philip embarked on a forty-five-day, fifteen-thousand-mile cross-Canada tour. Highlights included the Calgary Stampede and a review of Toronto's 48th Highlanders at the Canadian National Exhibition where a crowd of twenty thousand gave the royal couple a rousing cheer. To mark the visit, Ottawa reduced the sentences for most federal prisoners.[11] Along with US president Dwight Eisenhower, the Queen officially opened the already crowded St. Lawrence Seaway, the most important official function on her itinerary.

After two extensions of Vincent Massey's term and two days after the two hundredth anniversary of the battle of the Plains of Abraham, Georges Vanier became the first French Canadian and first Catholic governor general. A distinguished war veteran, diplomat, and Chevalier of the French Legion of Honour, Vanier spoke of looking to France to aid "our mission of safeguarding and spreading French culture in Canada."[12]

Canadians continued to talk on their telephones more than any other people. Guests at Toronto's Royal York hotel were now able to dial city numbers directly without the hotel operator. Even bigger innovations were on the horizon according to Bell Telephone Company engineers. They were testing phones to be worn on the wrist, phones that could take photographs, hands-free phones, push-button dialling, phones that could emit a musical tone when called, and a single phone key that could dial preset numbers. The automobile industry was also innovating, introducing compact cars like the Ford Frontenac, an exclusive Canadian model. An out-of-the-world advance was Eisenhower's use of an ultra-high-frequency klystron tube to transmit a radio message to Diefenbaker via the moon on the occasion of the opening of the Prince Albert Radar Laboratory, a joint defence project. Since the Prince Albert transmitter was not yet in operation, Diefenbaker responded via a land line.[13]

Industrialist K.C. Irving outlined a program to revitalize the Maritime economy. He called on Ottawa to reduce the value of the dollar, lower interest rates, and construct the Chignecto Canal as a shortcut for ocean-going ships travelling between US ports and the Great Lakes, avoiding the need to travel around Nova Scotia. Manitoba's government weighed a proposal to move the fourteen hundred residents of Churchill, located on muskeg, rock, and permafrost near the mouth of the Churchill River, to a gravel ridge five miles away.[14]

Poet, critic, historian, philosopher, and essayist George Woodcock founded *Canadian Literature*, the first literary journal exploring the works of Canadian authors. The first issue included articles on Gabrielle Roy and Ralph Connor. Literary theorist Northrop Frye asked whether Canadian poets should be evaluated "in Canadian proportions or in world proportions" and concluded that they had to be judged "as though no other contemporary poetry were available for Canadian readers."[15] *The Double Hook* by British Columbian novelist Sheila Watson was hailed as a landmark work of Canadian modernism.[16] *La belle bête* established twenty-year-old Marie-Claire Blais as a new talent in Quebec literary circles.[17] Fellow Quebecer Mordecai Richler's *The Apprenticeship of*

Duddy Kravitz, a rags-to-riches story gone askew, explored the Jewish immigrant experience, anti-Semitism, and the corruption of relentless pursuit of higher social status and monetary success.

Emphasizing continuity, loyalty, and organic growth, historian W.L. Morton equated conservatism with recognition of human fallibility: "the individual man is weak, imperfect and limited."[18] Discomforted by American notions of popular sovereignty, the general will, and majoritarian democracy, Morton, like Diefenbaker, considered monarchy a constructive feature of Canadian parliamentary government. The president of the Toronto Assembly of the Native Sons of Canada viewed Canada's British connection and British symbols as reflections of a "miserable inferiority complex." He called for *O Canada* as the national anthem, the abandonment of the Red Ensign, and the adoption of a distinctive Canadian flag.[19]

Federal Politics

The CBC strike divided the Conservative government: revenue minister George Nowlan termed the strike "illegal," solicitor-general Leon Balcer insisted it was not, and labour minister Michael Starr, refusing to intervene, said, "I have never expressed an opinion as to the legality of this strike." The party's Quebec MPs used the strike to argue for an autonomous French language CBC network while opposition house leader Lionel Chevrier asserted that a Liberal government would have averted a strike. Picket lines and alleged threats of violence prevented some employees from going to work. Citing news reports that CBC management had hired a hundred private police, CCF parliamentary leader Hazen Argue asked Starr to invite the parties to Starr's office to see whether the strike could be settled.[20]

To embarrass Quebec's forty-two French Canadian Conservative MPs, many of whom supported Quebec premier Maurice Duplessis, the Liberals called for recorded votes on measures that they and the Conservatives had agreed to but that Duplessis opposed.[21] Liberal ranks were also divided: Newfoundland MP Jack Pickersgill, who had been Louis St. Laurent's counsellor and aide, threatened to take the province's MPs out of the caucus because other Liberal MPs were criticizing premier Joey Smallwood's negative reaction to a strike by loggers of the International Woodworkers of America. A member of the Newfoundland constabulary was injured fatally in a confrontation with the strikers, and Smallwood's government used legislation to strip the union of its bargaining rights. The RCMP commissioner resigned because of Diefenbaker's refusal to send RCMP reinforcements requested by St.

John's; to do so, said Diefenbaker, would be "provocative and likely to cause further outbreaks of violence."[22]

The Arrow was terminated in part because of the government's fiscal situation: Ottawa was borrowing more than $100 million a month to meet its cash deficit.[23] Liberal leader Lester Pearson attacked the government for its "confusion, uncertainty and fumbling," while his party and the CCF characterized the Arrow's replacement with the American Bomarc missile as an injury to national sovereignty.[24] The Arrow's demise also discomforted Conservative backbenchers; they sat silent as defence production minister Raymond O'Hurley tried to distract from the cancellation by citing two small previously announced defence contracts that the US had placed with Canadian companies. The backbench rallied however when Diefenbaker cited a speech made by Pearson months earlier, implying that the Bomarc would be adopted.[25]

Soon after the Arrow imbroglio, over a thousand westerners, mainly Saskatchewan farmers, arrived in Ottawa to press for subsidies compensating them for reduced crop receipts. Greeting them, Diefenbaker and sixteen of his ministers were warmly received and applauded; the farmers laughed at his jokes, but he made no commitment, noting that subsidies would lead the United States to impose countervailing duties or ban the import of Canadian grains altogether. Even before the farmers arrived, agriculture minister Douglas Harkness had denounced the idea of subsidies on the CBC program, "The Nation's Business": "they would provide the greatest assistance to those who need it the least."[26]

"He never administered anything more complicated than a walk-up law office," wrote Peter Newman, a leading journalist, of Diefenbaker. However, Blair Fraser of *Maclean's* reported that while Diefenbaker was much more assertive on policy issues than St. Laurent had been, he did not act without his cabinet. Some pundits said he was running "a one-man government," but the cabinet was meeting more often and longer than any in memory. Asked how many meetings had been held, a deputy minister replied, "Just one. It started on June 22, 1957, and it's still going on – with occasional brief adjournments."[27]

Hazen Argue insisted that the proposed partnership of the CCF and CLC entailed no "watering down of CCF policy," dismissing as "nonsense" talk that the CLC might "gobble up" the party. The public however, including two-thirds of labour union households, were opposed to union activity in politics, according to the Gallup organization.[28] Though shut out of Parliament, some Social Crediters believed their party could fill a vacuum if the Conservative government faltered and the Liberals were unable to revive themselves. Pressed to take the helm of the leaderless national party, Alberta premier Ernest Manning declined.[29]

The bill creating the National Energy Board (NEB) to advise and carry out research made the government the final arbiter of the rules regarding the engineering, construction, and financing of pipelines and international power lines. The *Globe and Mail* thought the NEB unnecessary but saluted the appointment of its first chairman, the head of the Alberta Oil and Gas Conservation Board. A failed Liberal amendment would have prohibited lower prices for gas exports to the US than those charged domestically. The CCF's Argue proposed that all interprovincial pipelines be brought under public ownership and the "buccaneers" in the energy sector – a term Diefenbaker had used when in opposition – not be permitted "to reap fabulous profits."[30]

Amendments to the Criminal Code included for the first time a legal definition of obscenity. Until then, courts had applied a test for obscenity laid down by an English court in 1868. Subject to consent by the provincial attorneys general, the bill empowered courts to impound obscene material without a charge being laid. Another element in the bill changed the standard of proof required to charge a man with seducing a fourteen-to-sixteen-year-old girl or a female employee under twenty-one.[31] Courts also gained jurisdiction over indictable offences committed on an aircraft even if the offence occurred outside of Canada so long as the flight began or ended in Canada. Other bills passed by Parliament allowed more spending for the Trans-Canada Highway and housing programs.

A representative of the Canadian Construction Association on Ottawa's unemployment insurance advisory committee criticized proposed amendments to the Unemployment Insurance Act that would increase payments and extend seasonal payment periods. These would make it too easy for some to avoid work, he claimed, citing Quebec carpenters who used to work also as loggers in the winter but now did not, and fishermen who earned large sums of money in a short period and collected insurance payments during periods when they were not fishing.[32]

Diefenbaker told the Canadian Bar Association that his long-cherished bill of rights would be reintroduced in 1960. Justice Joseph Thorson of the Exchequer Court argued for a constitutional amendment to entrench any bill of rights, saying this was essential because freedom of association was in danger in British Columbia, Quebec, and possibly Newfoundland. Diefenbaker responded, "when the provinces are prepared to abdicate their constitutional rights ... I expect there will have been several more prime ministers."[33] The Bar Association decided not to formulate a position on the issue.

CCF MP Douglas Fisher criticized as inadequate the $8,000 indemnity ($73,725 in 2021) and tax-free allowance ($2,000) received by MPs.

Two Conservative backbenchers rose in the Commons to endorse Fisher's views; John MacLean noted that he had graduated from law school in debt and that serving as an MP put him further in debt: "I say this for the benefit of the cabinet." According to Blair Fraser of *Maclean's*, the complaint was symptomatic of a deeper malaise, that backbenchers did not amount to much, that ministers were uninterested in their views: "All that the ruling party really wants of the private member is his vote, from time to time. The rest of the time he can go to sleep."[34]

Two by-elections yielded predictable results in which the Liberals and Conservatives easily retained their seats: Russell, a riding in eastern Ontario, had been in the Liberal column continuously for seventy-two years; Hastings-Frontenac, where the CCF did not field a candidate, had been the constituency of external affairs minister Sidney Smith. In the polls, the Conservatives maintained a healthy lead over the Liberals all year although their margin had narrowed slightly since their 1958 landslide and following what Denis Smith termed the "political poison" of the Arrow's termination. Support for the CCF rose in Ontario, but the party was truly competitive only in the West, where Social Credit had some lingering support.[35]

Intergovernmental Relations

Insisting that Ottawa's fiscal situation forbade it, finance minister Donald Fleming rejected demands by provincial treasurers for an immediate increase in tax-sharing payments at a federal-provincial conference. Some treasurers complained that high interest rates and federal borrowing were crowding them and their municipalities out of the bond market, and that Ottawa's increase in the amount individuals could purchase in Canada Savings Bonds, from $5,000 to $20,000, had a similar effect.[36]

At the annual meeting of Atlantic premiers, New Brunswick's Hugh John Flemming suggested that lower federal corporate taxes would aid economic development, Prince Edward Island's premier-elect Walter Shaw repeated his predecessor's request that Ottawa consider building a causeway to the island, and Nova Scotia's Robert Stanfield proposed the appointment of an agent-general for the new West Indies Federation, augmenting the Atlantic region's representation in London. Federal legislation provided additional grants to Newfoundland in accordance with its Terms of Union, but Smallwood and Jack Pickersgill criticized Diefenbaker's insistence that the grants were "final and irrevocable."[37] The federal-provincial hospital insurance plan went into effect in Nova Scotia, PEI, and Ontario.

Quebec premier Maurice Duplessis contended that the Conservatives were perpetuating the federal Liberal practice of taxing Quebecers to pay for hospital insurance and grants to universities, fields properly under provincial jurisdiction. This was thievery, Duplessis said, because his province had not joined either program. Duplessis's successor Paul Sauvé, however, was keen to receive the $25 million in grants accumulated since 1952 by Ottawa and earmarked for Quebec's universities; he and Diefenbaker negotiated a mutually satisfactory agreement.[38]

To little avail, Ontario premier Leslie Frost contended that Ottawa was obliged to provide substitute employment for the laid-off Avro workers. He also complained to Diefenbaker about the Bank of Canada's tight money policy. Disillusioned with Diefenbaker, Frost decided not to attend the federal Conservative party's annual meeting, relenting only after being persuaded that his absence would stir speculation about divisions in Conservative ranks and do him no good.[39]

Conservative intra-party harmony was also at risk in Manitoba because Ottawa's anticipated announcements about funding the Red River Floodway and the appointment of former Conservative leader Errick Willis as lieutenant governor – Willis had resigned as an MLA expecting to immediately occupy the position – were delayed or did not occur. Premier Duff Roblin, acting as his own provincial treasurer, let it be known that he had found the federal-provincial fiscal conference "pretty disappointing." Saskatchewan CCF treasurer Clarence Fines accused Diefenbaker of "a breach of faith" for having broken his promises to hold a tax-sharing conference in 1958 and to consider favourably the positions of the provinces. "All the provinces are unhappy," he said, because Ottawa refused to consider any adjustments to the tax-sharing arrangements before 1962.[40]

Alberta and British Columbia squabbled with Ottawa. Diefenbaker blamed Edmonton for delays in approving oil and natural gas export permits, while Manning blamed Ottawa's delayed establishment of the National Energy Board. Diefenbaker said a challenge was finding capable Board appointees who would "accept salaries far below what they could secure in private life." After the *Vancouver Sun* quoted British Columbia premier W.A.C. Bennett saying that federal public works minister Howard Green had refused to sign an agreement for hydroelectric development on the Columbia River, Green called Bennett "a very impetuous and, might I say, impatient man." To the glee of Bennett's opponents, Ottawa appointed the former manager of the provincial power commission whom Bennett had fired for criticizing his policies to the National Energy Board.[41]

The Provinces

Five elections were held, and speculation abounded that they would also be held in New Brunswick and Nova Scotia. New Brunswick's hospital insurance program was working smoothly and unemployment had decreased, but rural road repairs led a long-time resident to conclude, "That is something that only happens in an election year." In Nova Scotia, premier Robert Stanfield ended months of election rumours when he called a by-election.[42]

The popular vote for Newfoundland's easily re-elected Liberals dropped from 66 per cent in 1956 to 58 per cent. After the loggers' strike ended and Smallwood decertified their union, the Newfoundland Federation of Labour ran candidates under the Newfoundland Democratic Party banner. Endorsed by the CCF, they all lost. Two Conservatives supporting Smallwood's fight with Ottawa over the Terms of Union won seats as the United Newfoundland Party while Conservative leader Malcolm Hollett, supporting Diefenbaker's position, was defeated after Smallwood challenged him in his own riding.[43] Also re-elected was Smallwood's son, William.

PEI's governing Liberals entered the election campaign with twenty-six seats to the Conservatives' four. They pledged to pay for textbooks from grades one through eight while the Conservatives, led by former deputy agriculture minister Walter Shaw, promised to help school boards pay for teachers. Shaw accused premier Alex Matheson of negotiating "with hostility" toward Ottawa. Benefitting from the Diefenbaker tide, the Conservatives won twenty-two seats, ending twenty-five years of continuous Liberal government.[44] The result reinforced Islanders' tradition of choosing a government of the same stripe as the federal governing party.[45]

Ontario's Conservatives were re-elected but lost twelve seats, including those of the two cabinet ministers implicated in the Northern Ontario Natural Gas scandal. The party's lacklustre campaign led the *Ottawa Citizen* to describe Frost, who offered no new proposals, as a "great tranquilizer." Running on his party's record of achievement, he boasted that Ontario's rate of growth in the decade was double that of the United States. The most colourful campaign event was a Toronto Liberal rally featuring a fifteen-piece band, majorettes, balloons, confetti, an Italian tenor singing "Sunny Italy," and placards reading "Votate Liberale."[46]

Holding the balance of power, the Manitoba CCF was not inclined to bring down Duff Roblin's minority Conservative government. A prominent CCFer explained: "Look at our position. The Roblin government is putting into effect good legislation. The people want it: they need it, and they should have it. Are we going to defeat them and face the charge that we obstructed the very things we have been calling for over the years?"[47] But Roblin engineered his government's defeat on a procedural motion and the subsequent election produced a strong Conservative majority. The result confirmed the realignment of the party system that had occurred a year earlier.[48] A fading force, the opposition Liberal-Progressives lost votes and seats while the CCF increased its popular vote but lost a seat.

Social Credit routed its opposition in Alberta's election, winning sixty-one of the sixty-five seats; no other party won more than a single seat. Manning's peculiar assessment of the results was that "public acceptance of the [federal] Conservative party is steadily going downhill in this part of the country. It shows growing western disillusionment." British Columbia's Bennett concurred: "no party collapsed as quickly and so completely as the Conservative party in Western Canada." These were odd appraisals because although Alberta's Conservatives lost two of their three seats, their popular vote climbed sharply to 24 per cent from 9 per cent in the 1955 election. Moreover, the federal Conservatives stood at 50 per cent in the polls, not far from their performance in the 1958 election.[49]

Maurice Duplessis died and, unopposed, Paul Sauvé was chosen Union Nationale leader and Quebec premier by the UN cabinet and caucus.[50] Sauvé expressed admiration for Duplessis as his mentor and committed himself to Duplessisism. Emphatically defending the partnership of church and state in the school system, he even extended financial assistance to some religious classical colleges that Duplessis had refused to support. Sauvé also restated Duplessis's positions that the Union Nationale would remain independent of all federal parties and pursue Quebec's constitutional rights.[51] The weak Quebec civil service that Sauvé inherited had fewer than twelve economists and hardly any statisticians.[52]

The proposal to create a new party that would institutionalize a prominent role for trade unions divided party members of the governing Saskatchewan CCF: rural members were opposed; urban members were in favour. Party members were also divided over Canada's membership in NATO. Several senior cabinet ministers announced they would not stand in the next election. Conservatives and Liberals talked about whether their constituency associations would cooperate to defeat CCF candidates. The Liberal leader said it "was none of my business" if his party's local associations pursued cooperation, but the Conservative leader insisted his party would field a full slate of candidates.[53]

Premier Bennett, boasting that British Columbia was now debt free, marked the occasion with a bond-burning event in Kelowna. In exchange for maintenance of the Alaska Highway traversing the province, he suggested Ottawa cede one-fifth of the Northwest Territories to the province. The opposition CCF rejected provincial ownership of the forest industry and fought off efforts by Communists and Communist-led unions to infiltrate its ranks.[54] Howard Green, the new secretary of state for external affairs, became the first British Columbian appointed to a senior federal cabinet portfolio.

Indigenous people gained the right to purchase alcohol in the Northwest Territories, and an Alberta royal commission proposed studying the integration of Aboriginal children into the public school system. Yukon MP Conservative Erik Nielsen urged the creation of a party system in the territory, called on the Diefenbaker government to invest more power in the Yukon Territorial Council, and oil was discovered in the territory.[55]

Canada in the World

Parliament increased Canada's subscriptions to the IMF and the International Bank for Reconstruction and Development. Stepping down as commander of the UN Emergency Force in the Sinai Desert, General E.L.M. Burns was appointed to represent Canada in forthcoming ten-power disarmament talks. Backed by a majority of Asian and African countries, John MacAulay was elected as the first Canadian to head the International Red Cross.[56]

Diefenbaker predicted that by 1979, "We will then no longer be a middle power but one of the leading powers of the West." However, Canada's relative standing was actually declining. Sidney Smith and his successor Howard Green did not get the attention and respect in the US, at the UN, or at NATO that Lester Pearson had received. According to senior external affairs official Peter Dobell, Green did not realize that Croatia was part of Yugoslavia and thought Albania was. *The Times* of London thought Smith had not made "any great mark," questioned Green's qualifications, ventured that Davie Fulton or Commons speaker Roland Michener would have been a better choice for the external affairs portfolio, and opined that Canada's contributions at NATO meetings were no longer as significant as they had been. In Paris and London, Green lobbied for a Canadian presence at a summit of the US, Britain, and France but was unsuccessful after arguing that Canada's role was to counsel NATO's larger members while assisting the smaller members. Future assistant undersecretary of state for external affairs Max Yalden thought "Diefenbaker was preoccupied with being

flamboyant, with showmanship. He enjoyed making spectacular out-
bursts. He had this thing in his head that he was a great international
figure, that he was a much bigger figure than in fact he was. He thought
he was a great protagonist in the Cold War. He wasn't."[57]

Decisions had already been made which assumed that Canada's
armed forces would have nuclear weapons capability, but Green, more
influential in cabinet than Smith had been, was concerned about radioactive fallout from nuclear weapons tests; he promoted limited nuclear
disarmament as the centrepiece of Ottawa's foreign policy and spoke
against France's plan to detonate an atomic bomb. Under UN aegis,
Canada became a member of the Ten Nation Committee on Disarmament, but it was short-lived. Exemplifying growing public antipathy
to nuclear weapons, the Combined Universities Committee for Nuclear Disarmament was formed, its slogan "Let Canada Lead the Peace
Race!"[58] Ottawa signed an agreement with Tokyo for cooperation in
harnessing atomic energy for peaceful purposes.

The Arrow's demise contributed to the increasing integration of the
defence industry as part of a continental industry. A new Defence Production Sharing Agreement allowed Canadian firms to bid on American military contracts, exempt from tariff barriers and the Buy America
Act. Canada's purchase of some American military hardware drew criticism: former associate defence minister Paul Hellyer decried the government's choice of Lockheed's F-104 interceptor because of its high
accident rate and lack of manoeuvrability. There were more American
than Canadian soldiers in the far North as the DEW Line was completed. Because the American nuclear umbrella covered Canada and because of speculation that Canada would withdraw its forces in Europe,
some observers characterized defence spending as "simply our annual
NATO club dues." Canada and West Germany agreed on aircraft standardization for the RCAF and the Luftwaffe, and the defence department
trained with French missiles and considered purchasing them.[59]

Resolving a long-standing dispute, Canada and the US agreed to
share the benefits of harnessing the Columbia River system. The terms
were favourable to Canada, which retained the right to divert waters
for her own needs, and the US agreed to pay for some flood control
works in British Columbia. Ottawa carried Britain's brief at a US-
Canada joint cabinet committee on trade and economic development,
asking the Americans to use their influence with the Organization for
European Economic Co-operation to persuade the Europeans to adopt
a more conciliatory orientation in trade relations with the British.[60]

Attitudes toward the Communist bloc softened somewhat: Toronto's
Empire Club invited a talk by the Soviet ambassador; the president of

National Research Council signed an agreement on the exchange of researchers with the Soviet Academy of Science; and the government allowed the first Chinese Communist trade union official to come to Canada. At the UN, Canada voted for Poland, not for NATO ally and US candidate Turkey, as its replacement on the Security Council. Regretting that the matter had become a Cold War issue, Green proposed that Turkey and Poland split the two-year term.[61]

Expressing anxiety about a "Communist trade offensive" in Asia and Africa, Diefenbaker called on free nations to issue a collective declaration of freedom's creed "so that uncommitted peoples can understand the worth and superiority of freedom when compared to communism." He cautioned that despite reduced tensions with the Soviet Union, its grip on Eastern Europe had not relaxed and that nothing Nikita Khrushchev says, "justifies the view that any of the basic Soviet positions have been abandoned or modified."[62] Diefenbaker endorsed suggestions by Britain's Harold Macmillan that the western powers negotiate with the Soviets to lower tensions over Berlin and freeze armaments in parts of Central Europe.[63]

Unlike most years in the 1950s, no Commonwealth prime ministers' meeting was held. However, at a Commonwealth education conference in London, former Conservative leader and high commissioner to the United Kingdom George Drew proposed a thousand exchange scholarships, an idea Sidney Smith had originally promoted as a "University of the Commonwealth."[64] Trinidad asked Canada to consider a customs union with the new West Indies Federation, where Canada's chief investment was in bauxite.

Births were at a post-war peak, more women were engaging in politics, the economy was bouncing back from its recessionary low, and the entrenchment of the welfare state continued with more provinces joining the federally initiated hospitalization program. The first French Canadian governor general was appointed, the Queen undertook a forty-five-day tour, and a more self-consciously mature literary scene was developing.

Both the Conservative government and the Liberal party were divided, the Conservatives over a CBC strike, the Liberals over a loggers' strike. CCF members were divided over a proposed political partnership with the trade union movement. John Diefenbaker was very assertive in the cabinet, but it met frequently, and he did not act on policy without their knowledge and backing. Parliament created a National Energy Board and amended the Criminal Code, defining obscenity and changing the standard of proof for convicting a man for seducing a minor. Diefenbaker told the Canadian Bar Association he would proceed with a bill of rights as a statute, and some MPs complained of inadequate compensation.

Ottawa rejected provincial demands for an increased share of tax revenues. The most contentious issue in Atlantic Canada was Ottawa's financial obligations under Newfoundland's Terms of Union. Quebec's Paul Sauvé, the only premier to attend the federal-provincial fiscal conference of finance ministers, was more agreeable than his predecessor Maurice Duplessis had been in dealing with Ottawa. Manitoba's Conservative government was unhappy about delayed announcements by Ottawa's Conservative government, and Saskatchewan's CCF finance minister accused Diefenbaker of breaking his promises. Ottawa and Edmonton blamed each other for delays in issuing energy export permits, while British Columbia's premier and the province's senior federal cabinet minister attacked each other personally.

Four of the five provincial elections returned incumbent parties. The upset in Prince Edward Island did not upset the convention that Islanders vote for a provincial government with the same name as the governing federal party. Provincial Conservative parties generally benefitted from the continuing popularity of the federal Conservatives. The death of the longest-serving premier, Maurice Duplessis, was a prelude to Quebec's Quiet Revolution.

Canada signed several bilateral agreements, but Canadian influence on the world stage shrank; Diefenbaker had an inflated view of his himself as a world statesman. The Commonwealth became to some extent less important; for the first time in the decade, no prime minsters' meeting was held for two successive years. As attitudes to the Communist bloc softened, the demise of the Avro Arrow, the pride of the aerospace industry, and a new Defence Production Sharing Agreement further integrated Canada's defence industry with that of the US. The Canada-US joint cabinet committee on trade and economic development met and the two countries cooperated on developing hydropower on the Columbia River.

Conclusion: Politics and
Public Affairs in the 1950s

The 1950s, but a chapter in Canadian history and part of a larger historical plot, are best understood in their own terms and not judged by contemporary standards. They were years of social conformity but also of political, economic, and technological change. They rapidly altered the fabric of Canadian life. Against a background of growing prosperity, federal and provincial politics became more competitive, intergovernmental relations grew more contentious, and Canada's presence in the world expanded. There was more leisure time, more food to eat, better housing, and there were better health and hygienic standards. The life expectancy of Canadians increased as the social pathologies of poverty, crime, racial, ethnic, and gender discrimination were in retreat. Economic abundance contributed to building and sustaining a more democratic and socially progressive polity.

The 1950s were also a time of apprehension about communism. There was fear of the existential threat of thermonuclear war; the government commissioned the "Diefenbunker," the massive four-story reinforced underground sanctuary near Ottawa where top officials were expected to take shelter during a nuclear attack. As the atomic bomb gave way to the hydrogen bomb and aircraft interceptors gave way to missiles, Canada contributed to an armaments race. Cold War tensions between East and West intensified.

Rock and roll became the dominant style of popular music. Jet passenger travel, television, the transistor radio, direct long-distance telephone dialling, tranquilizers, a nuclear power station, and a vaccine for polio made their first appearance. Air travel began to complement train travel while television undermined movie going. The Stratford Festival arose, modernist structures like Toronto's City Hall were designed, and massive buildings like Montreal's Queen Elizabeth Hotel were built. Small towns continued to give way to ever-larger cities. Suburban growth led to the creation of Metropolitan Toronto, the first new upper tier level of municipal government in North America.

Media and public policy promoted residential stability, the nuclear family, sexual discretion, the work ethic, temperance, and church attendance. Stirrings of discontent among women, youth, and Indigenous Peoples were barely discernible. Advertisements portrayed loyal wives and stay at home mothers. Young women were expected to find husbands rather than careers; the law barred married women from employment in the federal civil service until mid-decade. Conservative party leader George Drew gave credence to allegations that corrupt Canadian government officials extorted thousands of dollars to smuggle Italians into Canada, and a Liberal citizenship minister justified denying Indigenous Peoples the right to vote on the grounds that they, unlike Inuit, were exempt from taxation.[1]

The old attachment to British Canada began to fray but was not dislodged. After a leading CBC personality told an American television audience that she thought most Canadians were indifferent to a forthcoming visit by the Queen, she received a barrage of criticism: eggs and rocks were thrown at her house, the mayor of Toronto demanded that she apologize, and the sponsors of her television program dropped her. In the end, however, after announcing that she was quitting the program 'to save the CBC from grief,' she and her daughters joined with thousands of other Canadians to greet the Queen.[2]

Canadians continued to be British subjects, but Britain's empire completely collapsed during the decade. The global backdrop was the beginning of the decolonization of Africa and Asia. The appointment of the first native-born governor general and the creation of the Canada Council, whose purpose was to highlight and nurture Canada's cultural and intellectual life, reflected a drive to cultivate a distinctive sense of Canadian community.

As the population grew from fourteen to eighteen million, the number of Canadians professing no religion grew modestly from 60,000 to 95,000. (The number exploded tenfold, to 930,000, in the more secular 1960s.) Religion continued to play a large role in the society of the 1950s: some, including academics, demanded regular radio broadcasts of Bible readings, and some organizations and many listeners scorned the CBC for what they deemed to be anti-religious broadcasts. Government MPs sang "Onward Christian Soldiers" during a parliamentary debate in which closure was imposed to speed construction of a pipeline. The Imperial Order Daughters of the Empire called on Ottawa to outlaw sex and love comics and, for the first time, the Criminal Code legally defined obscenity.[3]

Wartime controls were still in force when prime minister Louis St. Laurent ushered in the decade with buoyant confidence about Canada's prospects. The rate of population growth exceeded that of the United States, and though many social scientists fretted about global overpopulation and food shortages, these were not Canadian concerns. In the same year that George Drew opined that Canada could easily feed, clothe, and house 100 million people, a man-made shortage of food and milk occurred when a strike by railway workers led to "mercy" trains and planes making deliveries to some communities.[4]

A commodity-driven economy benefitted Canada. Ottawa ran more budgetary surpluses than in any other decade before or since, and commercial and industrial opportunities abounded amidst a labour shortage. Service industries, where women had become more prominent, were the fastest growing sector of the economy; office positions and "white collar" jobs proliferated, family farms continued to disappear, and the number of workers in the manufacturing sector stagnated.[5] Service sector labour unions gained members while industrial unions declined.

Productivity soared and the labour force expanded rapidly but, as usual, development was regionally uneven. Ontario grew at a faster pace economically and demographically than the rest of the country while Atlantic Canada was in relative and apparently chronic decline. There were, of course, economic fluctuations; inflation, above 10 per cent in 1951, gave way to deflation the following year.[6] There were also brief recessionary bursts. Sharply decelerating economic growth late in the decade contributed to a sense of economic precariousness and coincided with the election of a Conservative government, which killed the Canadian designed and built Avro Arrow, one of the world's most advanced high-altitude aircraft interceptors.

The natural resources boom, augmented by a baby boom and immigration boom, fed an investment boom. A young, fast-growing, immigrant population served as an inexpensive labour pool employed mostly in manufacturing and construction. Infrastructure projects such as the Trans-Canada Highway, a trans-Canada pipeline, the St. Lawrence Seaway, the Don Valley Parkway, and the Macdonald–Cartier Freeway boosted the economy, as did the steady growth of foreign trade and foreign investment. Concern by the Royal Commission on Canada's Economic Prospects about growing foreign ownership in the economy and regional economic disparities led to increased attention by the federal government to regional development. The Royal Commission on National Development in the Arts, Letters, and Sciences served as an important turning point in Canada's cultural history, leading Ottawa, after hesitating for most of the decade, to underwrite a range of activities to preserve, nurture, and promote Canadian culture.

Defence expenditures increased dramatically during the Korean War and accounted for about 40 per cent of the federal budget at mid-decade, but government policy became increasingly more distributive as health and welfare programs such as family allowances and old-age pensions assumed a steadily larger share of Ottawa's spending.[7] In response to a growing public belief that government should provide citizens with a guaranteed level of social and economic security, federal and provincial governments of all partisan stripes contributed to the development of a growing network of social services. The operating and capital expenditures of governments grew even during economic recessions.

The warfare state at the beginning of the decade increasingly gave way to the welfare state. All the federal political parties and provincial governments endorsed a universal federal pension program with no means test for seventy-year-olds at a time when the life expectancy for men was sixty-six. Ottawa then augmented the benefits of its universal unemployment insurance program and old-age pension plan, introduced assistance for the blind and disabled, and launched a national hospital insurance program modelled on a program pioneered by Saskatchewan.

One-room schools largely disappeared, and teachers became better trained and more specialized. Nevertheless, at the beginning of the decade fewer than half of fifteen-to-nineteen-year-olds were in school and less than 10 per cent of the college and university aged cohort attended post-secondary institutions. Educational purists among the country's elites, thinking low participation rates in higher education an agreeable situation, equated the democratic extension of education with the dilution of standards. By the end of the decade undergraduate enrolments in post-secondary institutions had ballooned from 64,000 to 107,000. To address what St. Laurent termed a crisis in higher education, Ottawa increased federal grants to universities and their operating and capital expenditures quintupled.[8]

The decade began with no women in Parliament; by decade's end a woman had been chosen to move acceptance of the Speech from the Throne, three sat in the House of Commons, one served as a minister, and hundreds held municipal posts, mainly on school boards. However, Atlantic Canada elected no female legislator at any time during the decade, a reflection of the more traditional political culture of this oldest region of English Canada.

At the beginning of the decade, University of Toronto professor and administrator Harold Innis continued working to develop a cadre of

Canadian academics to make universities less dependent on British teachers. His ground-breaking books, *Empire and Communications* and *The Bias of Communication*, brought a distinctly Canadian perspective to the study of media. Shifting his focus from the world's trade routes to the trade routes of culture, he discerned how communications technologies such as newspapers and radio shaped societies. At a time when television was being introduced to Canadian homes, Innis's acolyte Marshall McLuhan picked up this theme in *The Mechanical Bride*, casting light on technology's effects on sensory organization.[9]

At the end of the decade, literary critic Northrop Frye's *Anatomy of Criticism* became highly influential internationally. Demonstrating a rare breadth of knowledge, he formulated a radically bold view of the scope, principles, and techniques of literary criticism. In an era when Canada's universities were still largely elite institutions, Frye was saddened by the "personable, docile, polite young people" he was teaching, criticizing their view of education as simply a means of gaining greater comfort, security, and "stupefied satisfaction with what we call our own way of life."[10]

Historical and political science works published during the decade focussed on the "two founding races" of the English and French. However, the appeal of Canada's British cultural heritage subsided somewhat as the decade wore on in the context of Canada's increasingly Americanized and multicultural society. A Senator and former minister responsible for Indian affairs denounced a proposal to extend the franchise to Indigenous Peoples, "especially the primitive tribes," when the decade began. But by 1957, an Indigenous person sat in the Senate, a year later the government advocated enfranchising Indigenous people without endangering their treaty rights or other privileges, and a year after that the government introduced a statute giving them the right to vote in federal elections.[11] In 1950, only British Columbia's Indigenous people could vote in provincial elections (granted in 1949); by 1960, Indigenous people acquired that right in Manitoba, Ontario, and Saskatchewan.

Federal Politics

The decade began with four parties and eight Independents in the House of Commons. It ended with three parties and no Independents. Television became a major source of news, revolutionizing political coverage and political marketing. CBC's "The Nation's Business," established in consultation with the major political parties, offered each of them fifteen minutes of free broadcast time. Political journalism also improved, offering more analytical coverage by the end of the decade. The focus of television on party leaders contributed to presidential-style election-eering; voters were identifying more with parties and leaders and less with local candidates. MPs were thus pulled along in the slipstream of their leaders, contributing to increasing party discipline.

Nevertheless, differences of opinion within parties were sometimes aired publicly by MPs, and they were not expelled from their caucus for breaking ranks. MPs could be less compliant because party discipline, while sturdier than in the past, was not as robust as it was to become in later decades: the nomination of MPs for office did not depend on their party leader's approval as it has since the 1970s. Cabinet minis-ters were more prominent and the prime minister's office was smaller and less powerful than it was to become. A consequence of the end of the Liberal regime in 1957 was the attenuation of the system of cabinet governance through more or less autonomous regional ministers.[12] As the administrative state grew, both St. Laurent and his successor John Diefenbaker spoke of the challenge they faced in finding capable ap-pointees for newly created government boards like the National Parole Board and crown corporations like the Canada Council.

Politics became more combative as the decade wore on, but par-liamentary debate was more constructive and political jousting more genteel than they are today. Debate, however heated, remained civil. Ideological rivalry between the Liberals and Conservatives was muted, with the more philosophically abstruse Liberals stressing their expe-rience in governing and celebrating French-English amity, while the Conservatives called for a more decentralized federal system, thrifty government, and lower taxes. The Conservatives expressed greater affinity for Britain, the Commonwealth, and parliamentary traditions. The Cooperative Commonwealth Federation (CCF), championing the interests of the less wealthy and the trade union movement, was the party most supportive of public ownership and of a more expansive, more distributive, state. Social Credit, in which evangelical Christians were particularly prominent, blamed organized labour for price infla-tion and proposed boosting the purchasing power of consumers and inflating the money supply as tonics for economic ills.

The Liberal cabinet was divided at first about introducing a universal hospital insurance plan. There were also differences about engaging in the Korean War. Cautious and fearful of alienating Catholic Quebec, the Liberals rebuffed attempts by the other parties to liberalize the archaic divorce law that applied in the province. Liberal MPs also opposed St. Laurent's proposal to appoint some members of other parties, as well as distinguished Canadians, to the Senate, where only seven Con-servatives sat on the opposition benches. Rejected too by the Liberals was a proposed independent commission to determine the redistribution of parliamentary seats; they opted instead for the redistribution recommended by a Liberal-dominated parliamentary committee.

By mid-decade, all opposition parties favoured enhancing unemployment insurance benefits and family allowances. Burgeoning fiscal resources, a by-product of economic growth, allowed the government to take on greater responsibilities. Both Liberal and Conservative administrations steadily deployed public funds to stimulate home ownership. The Conservatives, in both opposition and government, were more sympathetic than the Liberals to the interests of farmers and more concerned about American ownership of Canada's natural resources. Although the Conservatives vowed to divert some of Canada's trade with the United States to Britain, they were unable to do so.

Public fervour regarding pipelines was intense. Indeed, an infamous parliamentary debate regarding the financing of a pipeline by a company that continues to be a major player in the political economy of Canada (TC Energy, formerly TransCanada Pipelines), proved pivotal in the downfall of the Liberal government after they repeatedly imposed closure on debate. The opposition parties succeeded in turning the debate into a fight over the rights of Parliament. Perceived as behaving as if they had a divine right to govern, the Liberals misread the public's mood. Trust in their leadership collapsed.

The 1957 election campaign resulted in the end of over two decades of uninterrupted Liberal government, with the first minority government since 1925. The campaign highlighted the contrast between the avuncular, languorous seventy-five-year-old St. Laurent and the sixty-one-year-old Diefenbaker, an eloquent parliamentarian. His charismatic populist style was very different than the patrician demeanour of his predecessor, George Drew, whose tenure as party leader had ended just months earlier. The Liberals were less able to adapt, personified by St. Laurent's refusal to wear make-up or use a teleprompter during his free-time television broadcasts; he preferred to stare downward at his written text rather than look at the camera.[13]

Diefenbaker proved to be an electrifying speaker with a thunderous tone on the hustings. His allure added a dimension of fascination to federal politics. Although his party cast a critical eye at the CBC as the "monopoly" television broadcaster, Diefenbaker was an excellent fit for the new medium; St. Laurent and CCF and Social Credit leaders M.J. Coldwell and Solon Low were not. Diefenbaker redefined his party: his name and heritage were unlike those of his predecessors – Robert Borden, Arthur Meighen, R.J. Manion, John Bracken, and Drew. George Pearkes, an MP who served under both Drew and Diefenbaker, understood that Drew "was considered too closely associated with the Toronto financiers and too far removed from the common man," while Diefenbaker had concern for the "man on the street."[14] Diefenbaker spurned talk of hyphenated Canadians. His formulation of "unhyphenated Canadians" attracted Ukrainian, Polish, German, and other "ethnic" Canadians who were concentrated in western Canada. He also played to them as foes of Soviet Communism, vowing that "those behind the Iron Curtain would not be forgotten" and met with a delegation of the Assembly of Captive European Nations.[15]

Although the Conservatives won fewer votes than the Liberals in 1957, they won seven more seats. Their minority government was secure because, as Diefenbaker's popularity soared, the opposition parties feared returning to the polls. He easily upstaged St. Laurent's easy-going successor Lester Pearson, mocking him for calling on the Conservatives to effectively turn power back to the Liberals without an election. To capitalize on his political saleability, Diefenbaker had Parliament dissolved for a snap election. He captivated record audiences in the campaign; an observer noted that his "appeal to the emotions of the voters seems to have had an almost hypnotic effect."[16] Riding on his coattails, the Conservatives scored the largest-ever victory in seats. Their 54 per cent of the vote and 78 per cent of the seats in the 1958 election still stand as record highs since the emergence of a multi-party system a century ago.

The CCF and Social Credit leaders lost their seats, and their parties were soundly defeated. The decimated CCF soon responded positively to a proposal from the Canadian Labour Congress to forge a partnership with a view to forming a new party. The complete collapse of Social Credit, which lost all its seats, was the result of its supporters switching their allegiance to the Conservatives, a party they had rejected in the past.

The enthusiasm for Diefenbaker in the 1958 election was akin to the Trudeaumania election a decade later; indeed, Diefenbaker's popularity exceeded that of Trudeau. Contemporary Conservatives celebrate Diefenbaker in a way that Liberals do not celebrate Mackenzie King, although King was a much more successful, astute, and transformative prime minister. Part of Diefenbaker's legacy, his long-championed Bill of Rights introduced late in the decade, and which became law in 1960, was constitutionalized with some modifications in 1982 as the Charter of Rights and Freedoms. The Conservatives maintained their healthy lead in the polls as the 1950s ended despite the setback they suffered after terminating the popular supersonic Avro Arrow.

At the beginning of the decade, Conservative MPs had accused the CBC of broadcasting "leftist propaganda" and employing Communist fellow travellers. At the end of the decade, a strike by 74 Montreal CBC producers led to 1,500 unionists marching on Parliament Hill singing French Canadian folk songs while three Conservative ministers publicly staked out three conflicting positions on the strike's legality.[17] Soon after, when dozens of English language producers also resigned or threatened to resign, Liberal MPs charged the Conservative government with political interference with the CBC.[18]

Intergovernmental Relations

At the beginning of the decade, the prime minister and the premiers held three federal-provincial conferences, two of which were dedicated to finding a formula for amending the Constitution. Without a formula, constitutional patriation from Britain could not proceed. Failure to agree resulted in the issue not being revisited until the 1960s. However, the first ministers did agree to ask Britain for an amendment transferring responsibility for old-age pensions from the provincial legislatures to Parliament.[19]

As the decade unfolded, the federal and provincial governments played increasingly large roles in economic and social development. Most intergovernmental discussions focussed on fiscal issues with the provinces charging that the federal government was overbearing; throughout the decade, they clamoured for Ottawa to share more of its revenues. Wielding its spending power under Section 106 of the British North America Act, Ottawa induced provinces to adopt provincially administered shared-cost programs such as a universal hospital insurance scheme and physical infrastructure projects including highways and housing. Ottawa also made direct grants to universities under provincial jurisdiction. In effect, constitutional tinkering proceeded through administrative means.

The wealthier provinces of Ontario, British Columbia, and Alberta, as well as Quebec, were the most critical of the federal government's deployment of its superior resources to influence provincial priorities. The poorer Atlantic and prairie provinces were more like beseeching supplicants in dealing with Ottawa, although Saskatchewan took the initiative in prodding Ottawa on social policy, urging a national labour code and a bill of rights.[20]

Public finance changed significantly during the decade. Conditional federal grants accounted for a significant increase in provincial government revenues. As the provinces steadily acquired more fiscal capacity, including a greater share of the personal income tax collected by Ottawa, the federal system became more decentralized. Originating during the Second World War, the tax-rental agreements, in which provinces gave up their power to collect personal and corporate taxes and succession duties in exchange for certain fixed sums of money, ended in 1957 when Ottawa replaced the agreements with equalization payments. These non-negotiable, unconditional grants raised the per capita yield of the three taxes in each province to match their average yield in wealthy Ontario and British Columbia. One result was that Quebec, which had rebuffed the tax-rental agreements, was no longer disadvantaged by forfeiting federal transfers. By the end of the decade, Quebec agreed to accept federal grants for its universities.

As the fiscal resources of both levels of government grew dramatically, provincial governments spent unprecedented amounts on social services and physical infrastructure. The provinces were pressed to assemble the human resources required to develop a welfare state. Federal personal income tax revenues more than tripled, and Ottawa's unconditional and cash transfers to the provinces nearly quadrupled in the decade. The net revenues as well as the deficits of the provinces more than doubled. In some years, all ten provincial governments tabled budgets with record high revenues and expenditures. Nevertheless, regional disparities persisted; the debt of Newfoundland, for example, increased by more than ten-fold while that of resource-rich Alberta less than doubled.[21]

Quebec's Maurice Duplessis was the leading provincial protagonist in federal-provincial relations during the St. Laurent years. Newfoundland's Joey Smallwood filled that role during the Diefenbaker period. Duplessis criticized what he deemed Ottawa's unwarranted intrusion in areas of provincial jurisdiction. To buttress his position, he created a Royal Commission of Inquiry on Constitutional Problems to study tax sharing between different levels of government and to make explicit Quebec's vision of Canada. Smallwood fought with Diefenbaker over financial aspects of his province's Terms of Union with Canada. Saskatchewan premier T.C. Douglas was the most supportive of Ottawa's initiation of national social programs, Duplessis the most resistant. Ontario's Leslie Frost argued that his province should not be judged a "have" province in calculating federal fiscal transfers simply because of its concentration of large industries. After Duplessis's death, the Quebec City-Ottawa agreement regarding federal funds for Quebec's universities became the model for Ottawa's subsequent asymmetrical arrangements with the province for other programs.

During the decade, premiers gained power as provincial spokesmen at the expense of regional ministers in the federal cabinet. The annual meeting of the Atlantic premiers, which began in 1956 as the Atlantic

Provinces Economic Council, was an innovation in interprovincial relations. The council, whose purpose was to coordinate regional policies and postures vis-à-vis Ottawa, was a precursor to the annual assembly of prairie premiers in the Prairie Economic Conference, expanded later to the annual Western Premiers Conference in the 1970s. The Atlantic premiers also held joint conferences with New England's governors with a view to expanding trade between their regions. Canada's municipalities asked, and Diefenbaker agreed, to hold a tri-level federal-provincial-municipal conference to discuss government tax sharing, but none was convened.

The Diefenbaker government proved more supportive than St. Laurent's of programs benefitting the Atlantic and western provinces. Most intergovernmental relations were bilateral, dealing with issues specific to a province, such as Prince Edward Island's perennial request that Ottawa consider building a causeway to the province. British Columbia premier W.A.C. Bennett made the bizarre proposal that Ottawa cede some of the Northwest Territories as compensation for B.C.'s maintenance of the Alaska Highway that traversed his province.

The Provinces

A weak education system impeded Atlantic Canada's development, while feeble public administration did so in Quebec. Ontario was preoccupied with building infrastructure to accommodate its dynamic economic growth, while the midwestern provinces of Manitoba and Saskatchewan, like the Atlantic region, suffered economic and demographic stagnation. The far western provinces of Alberta and British Columbia experienced burgeoning development of their natural resources.

Dire economic and financial conditions persisted in Atlantic Canada despite repeated forays at economic diversification. A shortage of human capital was perhaps the region's greatest challenge. All four provinces experienced net interprovincial out-migration. Uncritical acceptance of political patronage was deeply engrained, and dubious electioneering practices were common. The sons of well-known, long-established families governed: a Stanfield in Nova Scotia, a Flemming in New Brunswick. Choosing his party's candidates, Newfoundland's Joey Smallwood arranged his son's election as an MHA. Religion played a particularly large role in voting behaviour.

Nova Scotia ended 150 years of segregated black schools but only after fears arose that the turbulence surrounding segregated schooling in the United States south would be reprised locally. Unlike the rest of

Canada, where parties of various stripes either governed or functioned as the official opposition, Atlantic Canada's original parties, the Liberals and Conservatives, operated as an ensconced political oligopoly, practicing a politics devoid of programmatic content; elections represented little beyond ins versus outs. Newfoundland maintained a constitutionalized denominational system of representation, with remarkably uncompetitive elections; the Liberals repeatedly won landslides even though Smallwood scarcely bothered to campaign.

Quebec, like the Atlantic provinces, experienced election irregularities and questionable behaviour during campaigns. In both Atlantic Canada and Quebec, voters were led to believe that if they failed to elect government MLAs, their constituencies would receive no benefits. Goon squads, strong-arm tactics, and stuffed ballot boxes marred the 1956 provincial and 1957 federal elections in Quebec. Illegal premarked ballots were common in New Brunswick, a roadblock prevented a returning officer from moving ballot boxes in Nova Scotia, and a wandering ballot box was found at the headquarters of Newfoundland's Liberal party.[22]

Quebec's political culture was no less traditional than that of Atlantic Canada, but was exceptionally distinctive in language, religion, ethnicity, and temperament. The Québécois strove to protect and preserve their identity as a French and Catholic nation in North America. A darling of the Catholic clergy, premier Duplessis was determined to persecute and prosecute Communists and Jehovah's Witnesses. His party's traditionalist appeal was, however, increasingly challenged by counternarratives. Quebec's culturally segmented society with English and French living in separate universes, and an economic structure in which the minority Anglos were dominant – an Anglophone held the provincial finance portfolio continuously from Confederation through the 1950s – became harder to sustain as the Québécois moved from their farms and parishes to the factories, tenements, and office towers of Montreal.

CBC's French language service, Radio-Canada, began to broadcast viewpoints that questioned clerical control of the welfare and education systems. Publications such as *Refus global, Maintenant, Cité Libre*, and *Liberté*, founded by CBC and National Film Board producers, challenged the established order. An increasingly assertive labour movement became disillusioned with Duplessis, who deployed police as agents of big corporations in labour disputes. His aging Union Nationale government exhibited typical characteristics of an ancien regime: incompetence, inertia, and resistance to modernization.

Ontario and Quebec were like "two solitudes."[23] While Quebec's government resisted modernization, Ontario was in the forefront of the transformation of Canada's economy. A torrent of economic energy and expansion bestowed political capital on premier Leslie Frost. He cultivated the image of an unpretentious, down-to-earth small-town lawyer while admiring and winning the confidence of corporate titans, particularly bankers. His ideal in running government was the prosperous firm "that was managed cautiously, invested wisely in future expansion, and paid close personal attention to details."[24] Ontario was the only province that began and ended the decade with a Conservative government: it governed continuously from 1943 to 1985. Ontario outpaced Quebec: at the beginning of the 1950s, Ontario had a half million more residents; at the end, it had almost a million more. It attracted more than three times as many immigrants, and migrants from other parts of Canada, as Quebec. Both provincial governments endured scandals related to natural gas distribution companies.

While both Manitoba and Saskatchewan suffered net interprovincial migration losses, Winnipeg, Regina, and Saskatoon grew significantly. In Manitoba, a redistribution of legislative seats, less discriminatory against urban voters than in the past, enabled a progressive, revitalized Conservative party to defeat the incumbent Liberal-Progressives in 1958, a party originally elected as a farmers' party in 1922 and which remained opposed to social reform. Despite increasing urbanization, agriculture remained prominent in the political economies of both Manitoba and Saskatchewan. The base of support for the social democratic Saskatchewan CCF became unmistakably urban: in the 1952 and 1956 elections, the party's urban votes exceeded its rural votes even though the four largest cities – Regina, Saskatoon, Moose Jaw, and Prince Albert – constituted less than a fifth of the population.

In contrast to the out-migration from the midwestern provinces, the far western provinces of Alberta and British Columbia lured Canadians from elsewhere. British Columbia, which had a quarter of Quebec's population at the beginning of the decade, gained many more interprovincial migrants during the decade than Quebec.[25] The far western provinces exhibited a penchant for plebiscites absent in the other regions: voters went to the polls to weigh in on issues such as water fluoridation, liquor control, and whether to permit commercial sporting events on Sundays.

Passivity characterized Manitoba premier Douglas Campbell and many of Atlantic Canada's premiers. Nova Scotia's Robert Stanfield, Saskatchewan's T.C. Douglas, and Manitoba's Duff Roblin were more active in shaping their provinces. Stanfield did not eliminate patronage but was prepared to denounce and diminish it; he did not resort to the wholesale replacement of the previous government's appointees with supporters of his party, as had been the custom. Douglas, who had realized his dream of public hospital insurance in the 1940s, laid out a plan for a public medicare insurance scheme before the 1950s ended. Roblin, with the support of the CCF, enacted a series of progressive reforms and was eventually voted "the greatest Manitoban" by fellow Manitobans.[26] British Columbia's Bennett and Newfoundland's Smallwood were politically astute blusterers; Bennett benefitted politically from his province's resource wealth while Smallwood touted economic schemes that did not materialize. Nevertheless, Newfoundlanders credited him for the social benefits, like unemployment insurance and family allowances, brought by union with Canada.

When the decade began, Ontario had the only provincial Conservative party in power. When the decade ended, Conservative governments held sway in five provinces. The popularity of the governing federal Conservatives after 1957 greatly aided the New Brunswick and Manitoba Conservative parties. At the beginning of the 1950s, there were coalition governments in British Columbia and Manitoba. By the end of the decade, there were none. Unlike the Liberals and Conservatives, the only parties that had governed federally, five different parties won office in six provinces in 1956: Liberal, Conservative, Union Nationale, CCF, and Social Credit.

Canada in the World

The appointments of the first native-born governors general and membership in the United Nations Security Council raised national self-esteem. Canada was allied with the United States and its NATO partners and active at the UN. Indeed, at the UN, "the 1950s was remarkable for creative innovations by second-rank countries such as Canada."[27] However, Canada was usually a spectator in the tug of war between the US and the USSR. Separated from the rest of the world by two oceans and shielded under an American nuclear umbrella, Canada benefitted from proximity to the US but was also limited in its foreign policy options by that proximity.

The CCF was the only party critical of Washington's foreign policy, and the most supportive of trade in non-strategic goods with the Soviet Union and China. These positions so discomfited CCF MP (and future Saskatchewan Liberal premier) Ross Thatcher that he quit the party. The Conservative and Social Credit parties were the most anxious about the Communist threat domestically and internationally; some of their MPs alleged at the beginning of the decade that the International Monetary Fund was a subversive communist innovation.

As one of the "Big Four" western powers in the first half of the decade, Canada sometimes acted as the spokesperson for the other three – the US, Britain, and France – in disarmament negotiations with the Soviet Union. By the end of the decade, however, Ottawa's lobbying without success to participate at a summit of the three suggested Canada's diminished status. Western Europe's recovery by the end of the decade reduced Canada's relative importance; its GDP, roughly equivalent to Italy's, was far exceeded by that of West Germany. At the beginning of the decade, Canada and Germany were still formally at war and Bonn was hoping to import steel and agricultural products, while Canada was hoping to collect on a pre-war German debt of hundreds of millions of dollars. By the end of the decade, Germany was a NATO ally and the RCAF and the Luftwaffe were standardizing their equipment.

Canada's network of international relations widened as overseas trade grew, and Ottawa steadily expanded its diplomatic representation abroad. It recognized new governments and began paying attention to regions that had been ignored. Nevertheless, Canada was still largely uninvolved with the global periphery, only marginally engaged diplomatically with Africa, South America, and the Middle East. Canadians and their leaders believed the nations of the world fell into two camps – those that treasured freedom and those that did not – and that Canada could play a constructive role in winning over the peoples of newly independent states to the freedom-loving camp. The US encouraged Canada in that role. Ottawa's contribution to the Colombo Plan was made with a view to retarding the spread of communism in Southeast Asia. Ottawa extended material and technical assistance to India and Pakistan but refused to take sides regarding their dispute about Kashmir.

Another facet of Canadian activity in Asia was the Korean War, which Canada entered under the auspices of the UN. From the beginning of the conflict, Ottawa was more cautious and more supportive of a negotiated settlement than Washington. However, in dealing with the new Communist Chinese regime, St. Laurent was determined to not differ with the US; he told the Indian government, which had recognized Peking, that even though recognition seemed to be "the common-sense realistic approach," Canada was not prepared to follow suit.[28]

The public and officialdom saw the US as a benign, well-meaning imperial power. St. Laurent described the US as "the most unselfish country ... with no other ambition than to live and let others live in mutually helpful intercourse."[29] The two countries took common positions on most international issues and Ottawa accommodated many American requests, although the relationship was at times difficult. Some of

Ottawa's policymakers thought the Americans were arrogant, unlike themselves. Their policies differed vis-à-vis China and the UN, with Canada more committed to multilateral initiatives. Knowing that the Americans would not be receptive, Ottawa was reluctant to make the case to Washington that NATO could be more than a military alliance.

Military and economic ties with the US deepened, but the Americans criticized what they felt was a deficiency in Canadian military capacity. Part of the Canadian response was to reopen military enrolment for women in some limited fields. The two countries had a joint cabinet committee on trade and economic development, they jointly constructed and managed the St. Lawrence Seaway, and two-thirds of Canada's trade was with the US throughout the decade.[30] One irritant in the relationship was the subjection of Canadian subsidiaries of American corporations to American legislation forbidding trading with some countries with which Canada had a normal trade relationship.

Steady integration of defence production culminated with the integration of military personnel in the North American Aerospace Defense Command (NORAD), with a Canadian serving as the deputy commander. During the decade Canada and the US jointly built and manned three radar warning systems in Canada's north to alert against Soviet bombers carrying nuclear weapons. By the end of the decade, however, the major threat was redefined as intercontinental ballistic missiles. Consequently, the manned Canadian Arrow interceptor was jettisoned in favour of the American-built surface-to-air Bomarc missile.

Canada played a critical part in NATO's deterrence and containment project: an infantry brigade and a dozen jet fighter squadrons were stationed in West Germany, the navy assigned dozens of ships to defence duties and the protection of Atlantic convoys, and hundreds of pilots and navigators from various NATO countries trained in Canada.[31] Nevertheless, Canada's NATO contribution was dramatically smaller than the large number of brigades that had been considered necessary and promised at the beginning of the decade. As the Soviet Union developed its nuclear arsenal, a sense of "mutually assured destruction" helped calm fears of a hot war.

The Cold War persisted, but the Soviet Union seemed less menacing as an imminent threat. The vociferous attacks on the USSR and its allies in the early part of the decade subsided somewhat in the second half; Canada made grain sales to the USSR and the National Research Council signed an agreement with the Soviet Academy of Science. At the beginning of the decade, a highly esteemed Canadian professor, a colleague and collaborator of Albert Einstein, was castigated in Parliament and investigated for having accepted an invitation to lecture in

Soviet-allied Poland; by the end of the decade, Canada was supporting the bid of Warsaw Pact member Poland rather than that of NATO ally Turkey for a seat on the Security Council.

As ties to the US strengthened, ties to Britain loosened. In addition to deeply disappointing Britain by not rallying to her side during the Suez Crisis, Ottawa rebuffed a British proposal to create a joint Commonwealth military presence in Asia. Nothing like the Commonwealth Division in the Korean War, in which Canadian troops fought alongside troops from the United Kingdom, Australia, New Zealand, and India, was repeated.

Lester Pearson was Canada's face on the international stage until the Conservatives took office in 1957. Repeatedly approached to serve as secretary general of NATO, which he repeatedly turned down, Pearson served as president of the UN General Assembly in 1953. The first NATO foreign minister to be invited to Moscow, Pearson was the pivotal figure in resolving the 1956 Suez Crisis, for which he received the Nobel Peace Prize. Health minister Paul Martin, representing Canada at the UN while Pearson travelled abroad, proved to be a helpful fixer when he resolved a 1955 deadlock between the US and the Soviet Union regarding the admission of twenty-one new applicants for membership. This earned Martin a standing ovation at the General Assembly.

At the beginning of the decade the Liberal government pressed for more trade with Britain and the Conservatives made it a centrepiece of their platform, promising to shift a significant percentage of trade from the US to Britain. In office, the Conservatives backed down and were every bit as cool to British overtures to negotiate a free trade agreement as the Liberals had been. Nevertheless, the Conservatives championed the British and Commonwealth connections and criticized the Liberals for not standing with the British in the Suez Crisis. Canadian foreign and trade policies did not change under the Conservatives, but they were more vocal in hostility to the Soviet Union's occupation of Eastern Europe. Unlike the Liberals, they also expressed "regret and concern" with South Africa's apartheid policies.[32] Conservative external affairs ministers Sidney Smith and Howard Green were not given the attention or respect that Pearson received on the international stage.

Politics and public affairs during the 1950s were conditioned by what came before and by the new post-war international environment. The complexity and rapidity of material progress produced an accelerated rise in standards of living, war time controls disappeared, the consumer society surged, and an economic miracle unfolded. Canadians became able to travel across the country on paved roads and by air, and they gained greater control over the Arctic.

During the decade, cultural survival simmered as a concern in the societies of English and French Canada. In Quebec, where the 1950s came to be identified with *la grande noiceur* (the great darkness), the traditional Québécois family, historically tied to a particular rural setting, began to disintegrate. Some Quebec nationalists, like André Laurendeau, wanting to defend their culture and Quebec's autonomy, argued that an alliance with English Canada could offer more security against the cultural influence of the United States.[33] In English Canada, unease also grew about the cultural and economic penetration of the United States; American ownership of Canada's physical assets grew steadily, and American publications dominated the market for magazines. If the two societies of English and French shared a common creed, it was built around deference to authority and respectful acceptance of established institutions.

The decade was a time of social progress and political change. Women, ethnic minorities, and Aboriginals made gains although impediments remained to their advancement. The first Italian Canadian cabinet minister was appointed in British Columbia in 1952, the 1953 federal election returned an unprecedented four female MPs, and the first Italian Canadian MP was elected in 1958. The Senate welcomed its first Jewish and Ukrainian members in 1955. Indigenous Peoples gained the right to sue the government in 1951, some provinces enfranchised them, and some bands were allowed to open bank accounts and spend their own revenue. Federally and in many provinces, governments changed hands as new political personalities emerged in a context of changing social and economic conditions.

The changes of the 1950s informed many developments in subsequent decades. The constitutionalized Charter of Rights of the 1980s was in part the result of the debate that swirled around the limitations of the proposed Bill of Rights introduced in the 1950s. Medicare in the 1960s was heir to the national hospital insurance program of the 1950s. And a direct line may be drawn from the Royal Commission on Canada's Economic Prospects in the 1950s, to the Task Force on Foreign Ownership in the 1960s, and to the Foreign Investment Review Agency in the 1970s. The capture of the prairies by John Diefenbaker's Conservatives and the shattering of Liberal hegemony in the 1950s reconfigured the political map in a way that persists to this day, while the defeat of the long-governing Liberal party led to its adoption of a more nationalist, urban orientation.

Appendix 1: Population

	1950	1959
Newfoundland	351,000	449,000
PEI	96,000	102,000
Nova Scotia	638,000	716,000
New Brunswick	512,000	590,000
Quebec	3,969,000	4,999,000
Ontario	4,471,000	5,952,000
Manitoba	768,000	885,000
Saskatchewan	833,000	902,000
Alberta	913,000	1,243,000
British Columbia	1,137,000	1,510,000
Yukon	8,000	13,000
Northwest Terr.	16,000	21,000
Canada	13,712,000	17,442,000

Source: *Canada Year Book, 1960*

Appendix 2: Prime Ministers and Premiers

Canada	Louis St. Laurent (1948–57) Liberal
	John Diefenbaker (1957–63) Prog. Conservative
Newfoundland	Joey Smallwood (1949–72) Liberal
PEI	J. Walter Jones (1943–53) Liberal
	Alex Matheson (1943–59) Liberal
	Walter Shaw (1959–66) Prog. Conservative
Nova Scotia	Angus Macdonald (1945–54) Liberal
	Harold Connolly (1954) Liberal
	Henry Hicks (1954–56) Liberal
	Robert Stanfield (1956–67) Prog. Conservative
New Brunswick	John McNair (1940–52) Liberal
	Hugh J. Flemming (1952–60) Prog. Conservative
Quebec	Maurice Duplessis (1944–59) Union Nationale
	Paul Sauvé (1959–60) Union Nationale
Ontario	Leslie Frost (1949–61) Prog. Conservative
Manitoba	Douglas Campbell (1948–58) Liberal-Progressive
	Duff Roblin (1958–67) Prog. Conservative
Saskatchewan	Tommy Douglas (1944–61) CCF
Alberta	Ernest Manning (1943–68) Social Credit
British Columbia	Boss Johnson (1947–52) Liberal (Coalition)
	W.A.C. Bennett (1952–72) Social Credit

Appendix 3: Elections

Canada	Party, Seats (& Pop. Vote)
1953	Liberal, 169 (48%) P. Cons., 51 (31%) CCF, 23 (11%) Social Credit, 15 (5%)
1957	P. Cons., 112 (39%) Liberal, 105 (41%) CCF, 25 (11%) Social Credit, 19 (7%)
1958	P. Cons., 208 (54%) Liberal, 48 (34%) CCF, 8 (10%)

Newfoundland

1951	Liberal, 24 (64%) P. Cons., 4 (36%)
1956	Liberal, 32 (66%) P. Cons., 4 (32%)
1959	Liberal, 31 (58%) P. Cons., 3 (25%) United Nfld. & Others, 2 (10%)

PEI

1951	Liberal, 24 (52%) P. Cons., 6 (47%)
1955	Liberal, 27 (55%) P. Cons., 3 (45%)
1959	P. Cons., 22 (51%) Liberal, 8 (49%)

Nova Scotia

1953	Liberal, 22 (49%) P. Cons., 13 (44%) CCF, 2 (7%)
1956	P. Cons., 24 (49%) Liberal, 18 (48%) CCF, 1 (3%)

New Brunswick

1952	P. Cons., 36 (49%) Liberal, 16 (49%)
1956	P. Cons., 37 (52%) Liberal, 15 (46%)

Quebec

1952	Union Nationale, 68 (51%) Liberal, 23 (46%)
1956	Union Nationale, 72 (53%) Liberal, 20 (45%)

Ontario

1951	P. Cons., 79 (49%) Liberal, 8 (32%) CCF, 2 (19%) LPP, 1 (1%)
1955	P. Cons., 83 (50%) Liberal, 11 (33%) CCF, 3 (17%) Indep. P.C., 1 (< 1%)
1959	P. Cons., 71 (46%) Liberal, 22 (37%) CCF, 5 (17%)

Manitoba

1953	Lib. Prog, 35 (44%) P. Cons., 12 (21%) CCF, 5 (17%) Social Credit, 2 (13%) LPP, 1 (1%)
1958	P. Cons., 26 (41%) Lib. Prog., 19 (35%) CCF, 11 (20%)
1959	P. Cons., 36 (47%) Lib. Prog., 11 (30%) CCF, 10 (22%)

Saskatchewan

1952	CCF, 42 (54%) Liberal, 11 (39%)
1956	CCF, 36 (45%) Liberal, 14 (30%) Social Credit, 3 (22%)

Alberta

1952	Social Credit, 54 (58%)* Liberal, 3 (22%) CCF, 2 (14%) Cons., 2 (4%)[†]
1955	Social Credit, 38 (47%)[‡] Liberal, 16 (33%) Cons. 3 (9%) CCF, 3 (9%) Ind., 1 (1%)
1959	Social Credit, 62 (56%)** P. Cons., 1 (24%) Liberal, 1 (14%); Coalition, 1 (1%)

British Columbia

1952	Social Credit, 19 (30%) CCF, 18 (34%) Liberal, 6 (25%) P.C., 4 (10%) Labour, 1 (<1%)
1953	Social Credit, 28 (46%) CCF, 14 (29%) Liberal, 4 (23%) P.C., 1 (1%) Labour, 1 (<1%)
1956	Social Credit, 39 (46%) CCF, 10 (28%) Liberal, 2 (22%) Labour, 1 (<1%)

---

* Includes 1 Independent Social Credit
† Includes 1 Prog. Conservative
‡ Includes 1 Ind. Social Credit, 1 Lib. Cons., and 1 Coalition
** Includes 1 Ind. Social Credit

Appendix 4: Immigrant Arrivals

1950	73,912
1951	194,391
1952	164,498
1953	168,868
1954	154,227
1955	109,946
1956	164,857
1957	282,164
1958	124,851
1959	106,928

Appendix 5: Foreign Representation Established and New Consulates

Foreign Representation Established, 1950–9

1950   Germany, Pakistan
1952   Austria, Portugal, Uruguay, Venezuela
1953   Ceylon, Colombia, Indonesia, Israel, Spain
1954   Dominican Republic, Haiti, Lebanon, United Arab Republic
1957   Ghana
1958   Burma, Iran, Malaya, West Indies

New Consulates

1952   New Orleans
1953   Los Angeles, Seattle
1956   Hamburg

Appendix 6: Average Family Expenditure per Person in Nine Cities, 1957

(St. John's, Halifax, Trois-Rivières, Montreal, Toronto, Kitchener-Waterloo, Winnipeg, Edmonton, Vancouver)

	Dollars per Person	2021 Dollars
Food	346	3,319
Housing, fuel, light, water	244	2,340
Household operation	52	499
Furnishings & equipment	81	777
Clothing	127	1,161
Other commodities & services	380	3,645
Gifts, contributions, personal taxes, security	101	969
Total	1,421	13,630

Source: *Canada Year Book, 1961*

Appendix 7: Gross National Product in Millions of Constant (1949) Dollars

1950	17,471
1951	18,547
1952	20,027
1953	20,794
1954	20,186
1955	21,920
1956	23.821
1957	24,117
1958	24,397
1959	25,157

Source: *Canada Year Book, 1962*

Appendix 8: Leading Industries in 1950
(by Gross Value of Products in $)

Newfoundland
 1. Pulp & Paper 2. Sawmills 3. Planing Mills, Sash, Doors, etc.
Prince Edward Island
 1. Butter & Cheese 2. Fish Processing 3. Feeds, Stock and Poultry
Nova Scotia
 1. Fish Processing 2. Primary Iron & Steel 3. Sawmills
New Brunswick
 1. Pulp & Paper 2. Sawmills 3. Fish Processing
Quebec
 1. Pulp & Paper 2. Non-Ferrous Metal Smelting/Refining
 3. Petroleum Products
Ontario
 1. Motor Vehicles 2. Pulp & Paper 3. Slaughtering & Meat Packing
Manitoba
 1. Slaughtering & Meat Packing 2. Railway Rolling Stock 3. Butter
 & Cheese
Saskatchewan
 1.   Petroleum Products 2. Flour Mills 3. Slaughtering & Meat
 Packing
Alberta
 1. Slaughtering & Meat Packing 2. Petroleum Products 3. Flour
 Mills
British Columbia
 1. Sawmills 2. Pulp & Paper 3. Fish Processing

Source: *Canada Year Book, 1954*

Appendix 9: Manufactures by Industrial Group, 1959 (Selling Value of Factory Shipments $)

Newfoundland
1. Paper & Allied Industries 2. Foods & Beverages 3. Wood
Prince Edward Island
1. Foods & Beverages 2. Leather 3. Printing, Publishing & Allied Industries
Nova Scotia
1. Foods & Beverages 2. Transportation Equipment 3. Wood
New Brunswick
1. Foods & Beverages 2. Paper & Allied Industries 3. Wood
Quebec
1. Foods & Beverages 2. Paper & Allied Industries 3. Primary Metal
Ontario
1. Foods & Beverages 2. Primary Metal 3. Machinery (except electrical)
Manitoba
1. Foods & Beverages 2. Transportation Equipment 3. Metal Fabricating (except machinery & transportation equipment)
Saskatchewan
2. Foods & Beverages 2. Petroleum & Coal Products 3. Primary Metal
Alberta
2. Foods & Beverages 2. Petroleum & Coal Products 3. Chemicals and Chemical Products
British Columbia
1. Wood 2. Foods & Beverages 3. Paper & Allied Industries

Source: *Canada Year Book, 1962*

Notes

Introduction

1 Jack Shafer, "Who Said It First? Journalism Is the 'First Rough Draft of History,'" *Slate*, 30 Aug. 2010, https://slate.com/news-and-politics /2010/08/on-the-trail-of-the-question-who-first-said-or-wrote-that -journalism-is-the-first-rough-draft-of-history.html.

2 Voltaire, *Oeuvres complètes de Voltaire* (Paris: Firmin-Didot Frères, 1875), 6:65.

3 Patrick Scott, "Jazz Scene: Now Here Is Waste of Talent," *Globe and Mail* (hereafter *G&M*), 2 Nov. 1957, 16; and Patrick Scott, "Jazz Scene: Handsome Does as Handsome Is in Grab-Bag," *G&M*, 7 Dec. 1957, 15.

4 John Porter, *The Vertical Mosaic: An Analysis of Social Class and Power in Canada* (Toronto: University of Toronto Press. 1965).

5 W.L. Morton, "Canadian Conservatism Now," *Conservative Concepts* 1 (Spring 1959), 7–8; and George Grant, *Lament for a Nation: The Defeat of Canadian Nationalism* (Toronto: McClelland & Stewart, 1965).

6 Michael Hayday, "CBC Television and Dominion Day Celebrations, 1958–1980," in *Communicating in Canada's Past: Essays in Media History*, ed. Gene Allen and Daniel J. Robinson (Toronto: University of Toronto Press, 2009), 173; and Myron Momryk, "Michael Starr, 89, Ukrainian Canadian Political Pioneer, Dies," *Ukrainian Weekly* 68, no. 14 (April 2000), https://web .archive.org/web/20040907201740/http://www.ukrweekly.com /Archive/2000/140004.shtml.

7 Greg Donaghy and Michael D. Stevenson, "The Limits of Alliance: Cold War Solidarity and Canadian Wheat Exports to China, 1950–1963," *Agricultural History* 83, no. 1 (2009), 29–50.

8 John Meisel, *The Canadian General Election of 1957* (Toronto: University of Toronto Press, 1962); Peter Regenstreif, *The Diefenbaker Interlude: Parties and Voting in Canada, an Interpretation* (Toronto: Longmans, 1965); and Lester

B. Pearson, *Mike: The Memoirs of the Rt. Hon. Lester B. Pearson, vol. 2: 1948–1957* (Toronto: University of Toronto Press, 2015).

9 House of Commons, *Debates*, 28 Apr. 1959.

10 "Tommy Douglas Crowned 'Greatest Canadian,'" CBC, 30 Nov. 2004, https://www.cbc.ca/news/entertainment/tommy-douglas-crowned -greatest-canadian-1.510403; Angus McLaren, *Our Own Master Race: Eugenics in Canada, 1885–1945* (Toronto: University of Toronto Press, 2014), 8; and F. Laurie Barron, "The CCF and the Development of Métis Colonies in Southern Saskatchewan During the Premiership of T.C. Douglas, 1944–1961," *Canadian Journal of Native Studies* 10, no. 2 (1990), 244.

11 F. Laurie Barron, *Walking in Indian Moccasins: The Native Policies of Tommy Douglas and the CCF* (Vancouver: UBC Press, 1997), xiii.

12 Walter Sullivan, "Study Shows Sun Grows Brighter," *New York Times* (hereafter *NYT*), 5 May 1959, 18; and "Palms for the Arctic," *G&M*, 30 July 1955, 6.

13 Robert Bothwell, "Minister of Everything," *International Journal* 31, no. 4 (1976), 692–702.

14 Geoffrey Barraclough, *An Introduction to Contemporary History* (London: C.A. Watts, 1964), 27–8, 148.

15 Ramsay Cook, *Canada and the French-Canadian Question* (Toronto: Macmillan, 1966), 119–21.

16 Pierre Berton, *Vimy* (Toronto: McClelland & Stewart, 1986); and John Ralston Saul, *A Fair Country: Telling Truths about Canada* (Toronto: Viking, 2008).

17 Margaret Atwood, *Survival: A Thematic Guide to Canadian Literature* (Toronto: Anansi, 1972); and Margaret Atwood, "After *Survival* … Excerpts from a Speech Delivered at Princeton University, April 29, 1985," *The CEA Critic* 50, no. 1 (1987), 36.

18 Pierre Vallières, *White N[******] of America* (New York: Monthly Review Press, 1971).

19 Lionel Groulx, *La naissance d'une race* (Montréal: Bibliothèque de l'Action française, 1919).

20 Gérard Pelletier, *Years of Impatience, 1950–1960*, trans. by Alan Brown (Toronto: Methuen, 1984); and Pierre Elliott Trudeau, *Federalism and the French Canadians* (Toronto: Macmillan, 1968), 211–12.

21 "School History," Ryerson School of Journalism, accessed 27 Feb. 2022, https://www.ryerson.ca/journalism/about/school-history/.

22 Publisher's Preface, J. Castell Hopkins, ed., *Morang's Annual Register of Canadian Affairs* (Toronto: Morang, 1902), v.

23 Jeffrey A. Keshen, "Hopkins, John Castell," in *Dictionary of Canadian Biography*, vol. 15 (University of Toronto/Université Laval), accessed 8 Mar. 2022, http://www.biographi.ca/en/bio/hopkins_john_castell_15E .html.

24 Stephen Leacock, *The Social Criticism of Stephen Leacock*, intro. by Alan
    Bowker (Toronto: University of Toronto Press, 1973), xxxix; and quoted
    in Robert C. Sibley, *Northern Spirits: John Watson, George Grant, and Charles
    Taylor: Appropriations of Hegelian Political Thought* (Montreal: McGill-
    Queen's University Press, 2008), 44.
25 Trudeau, *Federalism and the French Canadians*.
26 Norman Ward, "Canadian Annual Review for 1961: A Reference Guide
    and Record," *Canadian Historical Review* 44, no. 1 (1963), 53.
27 Nelson Wiseman, "The Pattern of Prairie Politics," *Queen's Quarterly* 88,
    no. 2 (1981), 298–315.
28 James B. Hartman, "The Growth of Music in Early Winnipeg to 1920,"
    Manitoba History, no. 40 (Autumn/Winter 2000–1), accessed 27 Feb. 2022,
    http://www.mhs.mb.ca/docs/mb_history/40/earlywinnipegmusic.shtml.
29 Frank H. Underhill, *The Image of Confederation* (Toronto: CBC Massey
    Lectures, 1964), 63.

1950

1 "New Cause for Concern Noted by St. Laurent," *G&M*, 3 Jan. 1950, 3.
2 "Like the Life of a Rose Is the Policy of Mr. Borden," *The Globe*, 15 Oct.
   1904, 1, 17.
3 *Canada Year Book, 1951*, 978–9.
4 "Motor Vehicle Registrations, by Province, 1903 to 1975," T147–194,
   Statistics Canada, accessed 27 Feb. 2022, https://www150.statcan.gc.ca
   /n1/pub/11-516-x/sectiont/4147444-eng.htm; and Warren Baldwin,
   "Personal Income Tax Unchanged: Cars, Drinks, Candy Hit; Business Levy
   Up, No Sales Tax Boost," *G&M*, 8 Sept. 1950, 1.
5 C.B. Macpherson, *Democracy in Alberta: The Theory and Practice of a Quasi-
   party System* (Toronto: University of Toronto Press, 1953), 249.
6 "Cross-Section Represented at Alexander's Annual Levee," *G&M*, 3 Jan.
   1950, 3.
7 Quoted in "New Cause for Concern Noted by St. Laurent," *G&M*, 3 Jan.
   1950, 3; "St. Laurent Predicts: 'No New War in My Lifetime,'" and "Armed
   Forces May Again Enlist Women," *G&M*, 30 Dec. 1950, 1.
8 Advertisements, *Toronto Daily Star* (hereafter *TDS*), 20 Sept. 1950, 18; *G&M*,
   12 Dec. 1950, 38, and 14 Dec. 1950, 11.
9 "Decontrol Is Ottawa's Job," *G&M*, 2 Mar. 1950, 6; and Warren Baldwin,
   "Howe Plans to Follow U.S. Example," *G&M*, 27 Oct. 1950, 3.
10 "Drew Confident Canada Can Feed 100,000,000 People," *G&M*, 9 Nov.
   1950, 3.
11 Joseph Ryan, "Mariner Mounties: RCMP Boat in New York on Way to Being
   First Craft to Circumnavigate North America," *G&M*, 26 May 1950, 15.

12 British North America (No. 2) Act, ch. 81, 12, 13 & 14 Geo. 6 (1949); and
    Canadian Intergovernmental Conference Secretariat, "First Ministers'
    Conferences, 1906–2004," accessed 27 Feb. 2022, www.scics.gc.ca/CMFiles
    /fmp_e.pdf.
13 *Canada Year Book, 1951,* 141; and "Jobs without Men," *G&M,* 23 Dec. 1950, 6.
14 *Canada Year Book, 1951,* 121; and *Canada Year Book 1952–53,* 130.
15 "Defense Needs Point to Labor Shortages," *G&M,* 30 Dec. 1950, 1; "5
    Jobless Fined for Police Clash," *G&M,* 13 Jan. 1950, 5; "Unemployed Ask
    DP's Be Kept Out; Shameful: Croll," *G&M,* 14 Jan. 1950, 21; "261,000
    Hunting Work; Labor Force Is Larger," *G&M,* 9 Jan. 1950, 3; and
    Advertisement, *TDS,* 11 Oct. 1950, 14.
16 Quoted in "Women Deserve Larger Role in Politics, PM Emphasizes,"
    G&M, 2 June 1950, 11.
17 "IODE Urges St. Laurent Ban Sex and Love Comics," *G&M,* 30 May 1950, 13.
18 "Discrimination Evils," *TDS,* 19 June 1950, 6; and quoted in "The
    Neglected Minority," *G&M,* 4 May 1950, 6.
19 "Canada Wants Its 'Own TV Culture': Fears 'Carbon Copy' of U.S.
    Programs," *Variety,* 18 Jan. 1950, 24.
20 Communic@tions Management Inc., "Requiem for the Print Edition," 30
    Nov. 2017, Figure 2, 4.
21 Robert Taylor, "Blame Liberals for UK's Anti-Canada Policy – Tory," *TDS,*
    18 Jan. 1950, 44.
22 "A City Submerged: Winnipeg and the Flood of 1950," CBC Archives,
    accessed 8 Mar. 2022, https://www.cbc.ca/archives/entry/a-city
    -submerged-winnipeg-and-the-flood-of-1950; "Flood-Besieged Residents
    of Winnipeg Battle to Curb River," *G&M,* 10 May 1950, 13; "Key Bridges
    and Subways Cut Off in Winnipeg as Flood Keeps Rising," *G&M,* 11 May
    1950, 17; "U.S. Senators Urge Congress Aid Manitoba Flood Victims:
    River Level Rises Again at Winnipeg," *G&M,* 17 May 1950, 1; and "2,000
    Homeless in Rimouski: City Burns 30 Hours, $20,000,000 Damage, over
    300 Homes Lost," *G&M,* 8 May 1950, 1.
23 Julie Guard, *Radical Housewives: Price Wars and Food Politics in Mid-
    Twentieth-Century Canada* (Toronto: University of Toronto Press, 2019),
    197.
24 Douglas How, "Canada May State Position on Korea Today," *G&M,* 28
    June 1950, 1; and "Two Ousted from Forces for Red Tinge," *G&M,* 9 June
    1950, 1.
25 Frank Flaherty, "Vote on Drew's Motion to Outlaw Communism Expected
    in House Today," *G&M,* 3 May 1950, 1; and quoted in Warren Baldwin,
    "Infeld Denials Not Quite Clear, Drew Asserts," *G&M,* 20 May 1950, 3.
26 Wilfred List, "'Economic Philosophy' Policy of CCL Angers Left Wingers,
    Scores Right," *G&M,* 27 Sept. 1950, 15.

27 Canadian Institute of Public Opinion, "Citizens Give Their Views on Three Political Parties," *TDS*, 13 Sept. 1950, 11.

28 Canadian Institute of Public Opinion, "Majority of Canadians Favors Army Training 6 Years Polls Show," *TDS*, 11 Nov. 1950, 2; and Warren Baldwin, "Three By-elections Expected in May," *G&M*, 20 May 1950, 3.

29 Quoted in "Canada's Racial Harmony World Example – St. Laurent," *TDS*, 27 Mar. 1950, 1–2.

30 House of Commons, *Debates*, 26 Apr. 1950; and "Keep Pension Promise, Liberals Challenged," *G&M*, 25 Mar. 1950, 2.

31 "Coldwell Scores Policy on Trade with Britain," *G&M*, 10 Jan. 1950, 4; Frank Flaherty, "House Rejects CCF Motion For Price Control," 4 Sept. 1950, 4; "Agenda Now Shaping For Commons Session," *G&M*, 14 Dec. 1950, 10; Frank Flaherty, "Low Re-elected As Socred Head; Hansell President," *G&M*, 21 Oct. 1950, 15; and Warren Baldwin, "CCF Wants Higher Tax on All Pay over $3,000; PC's Also Rap Budget," *G&M*, 13 Sept. 1950, 1–2.

32 G.H. Ross, quoted in "Senators Turn Tables, Ask Commons Reform," *G&M*, 26 May 1950, 1.

33 John Brehl, "'Drew Insults Houde' So Pouliot Says 'How Times Have Changed,'" *TDS*, 14 Sept. 1950, 1; "Has Power to Mobilize All Transport Aircraft," *TDS*, 24 Aug. 1950, 1; John Brehl, "Send All Workers Back Satisfied, Ottawa Desire," *TDS*, 31 Aug. 1950, 1–2; and Dennis Braithwaite, "Railway Bill Dead after Arbitrator Named," *TDS*, 11 Oct. 1950, 14.

34 Warren Baldwin, "Spy Strangers: House Spurns Drew Move for Secrecy," *G&M*, 8 Sept. 1950, 15.

35 Frank Flaherty, "Toronto-Led Demonstrators Ejected by Commons Police: Claim They Represent Unemployed," *G&M*, 28 April 1950, 1.

36 Warren Baldwin, "PC Motion for Hoist of Indian Act Changes Rejected by Commons," *G&M*, 22 June 1950, 1.

37 Warren Baldwin, "Filibuster over Pipelines Shows Sign of Ending," *G&M*, 9 May 1950, 3, and Frank Flaherty, "Division Bells Ring as Pipeline Filibuster Ended," *G&M*, 16 May 1950, 3.

38 "May Ask Court If Governments Can Swap Powers," *G&M*, 13 Jan. 1950, 3; and "Mr. Duplessis' 'Compact,'" *TDS*, 11 Jan. 1950, 6; and Frank Flaherty, "Supreme Court Judgment Blocks Provinces, Ottawa from Delegating Powers," *G&M*, 4 Oct. 1950, 1.

39 Robert Taylor, "Quebec Won't Give Up Any of its Powers Declares Duplessis," *TDS*, 10 Jan. 1950, 1; "Duplessis Is in Accord with Conference Aims, Will Argue Some Points," *G&M*, 10 Jan. 1950, 1–2; "Agenda Not Yet Ready for Provincial Talks," *G&M*, 25 May 1950, 8; and Warren Baldwin, "Ontario to Get Power at Manitoba Border," *G&M*, 12 Jan. 1950, 3.

40 Robert Taylor, "Provinces Won't Agree to Giving Veto Power," *TDS*, 25 Sept. 1950, 4.

41 Warren Baldwin, "Defense Program Seen Softening Tax Pact Pleas," *G&M*, 4 Dec. 1950, 9.

42 William Baldwin, "Uniform Age Pension Plan Said Many Months Away," *G&M*, 7 Dec. 1950, 1–2; "No Means Test at 70," *G&M*, 7 Dec. 1950, 6; and British North America Act, 1951 – Enactment no. 23, accessed 28 Feb. 2022, http://www.justice.gc.ca/eng/rp-pr/csj-sjc/constitution/lawreg-loireg /p1t231.html.

43 Quoted in William Baldwin, "Hopes of Nfld. Said Postponed," *G&M*, 6 Dec. 1950, 6.

44 Quoted in "'Fathers Forgot First Loyalty': Confederation a Curse: N.S. Premier," *G&M*, 25 Mar. 1950, 1; "Senate Beckons Premier Jones," *Windsor Daily Star*, 6 Feb. 1950, 22; "Agenda Not Yet Ready for Provincial Talks," *G&M*, 25 May 1950, 8; "Howe to Seek Pitprop Orders Claim Maritimers Starving," *G&M*, 10 Jan. 1950, 13; quoted in William Baldwin, "Hopes of Nfld. Said Postponed," *G&M*, 6 Dec. 1950, 6; and quoted in "Asks Place in Sun For Maritimes," *G&M*, 6 Nov. 1950, 14.

45 Quoted in Charles Foran, *Extraordinary Canadians: Maurice Richard* (Toronto: Penguin, 2011), 70.

46 Pelletier, *Years of Impatience, 1950–1960*, 68.

47 William Stewart, "Lapalme Is New Leader of Liberals in Quebec," *G&M*, 22 May 1950, 3.

48 "Social Crediters Quit in Quebec," *G&M*, 12 Dec. 1950, 38.

49 Sid Noel, "The Ontario Political Culture: An Interpretation," in *The Government and Politics of Ontario*, ed. Graham White, 5th ed. (Toronto: University of Toronto Press, 1997), 60; and Ross Harkness, "St. Laurent, Frost Sit Down in Amity to Sign Niagara River 'Treaty,'" *TDS*, 27 Mar. 1950, 1.

50 Dan Azoulay, *Keeping the Dream Alive: The Survival of the Ontario CCF/NDP, 1950–1953* (Montreal: McGill-Queen's University Press, 1997), 19; and Dan Azoulay, "Winning Women for Socialism: The Ontario CCF and Women, 1947–1961," *Labour/Le Travail* 36 (1995), 64.

51 Warren Baldwin, "Liberals Fear Early Election in Ontario," *G&M*, 24 May 1950, 19; Warren Baldwin, "Ontario Liberals Want June Vote, Thomson States," *G&M*, 15 Dec. 1950, 5; and "Thomson Backs Oliver as Party House Leader," *G&M*, 13 Dec. 1950, 5.

52 "Two PC Members Stick to Coalition in Manitoba," *G&M*, 12 Aug. 1950, 3; "Crisis Is Over for Coalition, Events Indicate," *G&M*, 9 Feb. 1950, 3; and Nelson Wiseman, *Social Democracy in Manitoba* (Winnipeg: University of Manitoba Press, 1983), chap. 3.

53 Nelson Wiseman, "The Socialist Imprint on Saskatchewan Politics," *Saskatchewan History* 65, no. 2 (2013), 26–33, 43–4; and quoted in George Bain, "Social Security, Labor Approach PC Parley Topics," *G&M*, 5 Aug. 1950, 4.

54 "No Job for the State," *G&M*, 17 Mar. 1950, 6; quoted in A.W. Johnson, *Dream No Little Dreams: A Biography of the Douglas Government of Saskatchewan, 1944–1961* (Toronto: University of Toronto Press, 2004), 154; and "Urges Canadian Study of Rail Nationalization; Would Grant Subsidies," *G&M*, 5 May 1950, 8.

55 James G. MacGregor, *A History of Alberta* (Edmonton: Hurtig, 1972), 292; and Alvin Finkel, *The Social Credit Phenomenon in Alberta* (Toronto: University of Toronto Press, 1996), 125–6.

56 "Manning Called Judas of Socred Movement," *G&M*, 11 Mar. 1950, 2; and quoted in "Old-Fashioned Religion Need: Alberta Premier," *G&M*, 16 Jan. 1950, 1.

57 Donald E. Blake, "The Politics of Polarization: Parties and Elections in British Columbia," in *Politics, Policy, and Government in British Columbia*, ed. R.K. Carty (Vancouver: UBC Press, 1996), 71; Dennis Pilon, "Democracy, BC-Style," in *British Columbia Politics and Government*, ed. Michael Howlett, Dennis Pilon, and Tracy Summerville (Toronto: Emond Montgomery, 2010), 93; and "Quits, Then Wins Vote; Heads West Coast PC's," *G&M*, 9 Oct. 1950, 11.

58 Pearson, *Mike: The Memoirs, vol. 2: 1948–1957* (Scarborough, ON: New American Library, 1975), 165.

59 "Canada Elected to Chairmanship of Monetary Fund," *G&M*, 15 Sept. 1950, 3.

60 Quoted in "Forces at UN Balk Unity, Pearson Says," *G&M*, 14 Jan. 1950, 21.

61 Quoted in "UN World Force Canadian Idea, Pearson Stresses," *G&M*, 25 Oct. 1950, 1.

62 *Canada Year Book 1952–53*, 1092; and quoted in "Two-Year Layoff on Bellicose Talk Urged by Pearson," *G&M*, 31 Oct. 1950, 3.

63 House of Commons, *Debates*, 6 Sept. 1950.

64 Quoted in "Canada Had to Help in Korea: McNaughton," *G&M*, 15 July 1950, 3; Warren Baldwin, "Canada's Korea Policy Urges Military Caution," *G&M*, 4 Dec. 1950, 1; and "Canada's Troops Head to Korea," CBC Archives, accessed 28 Feb. 2022, https://www.cbc.ca/archives/entry/1950-canadas-troops-head-to-korea.

65 "Pearson Advises: Unwise Now to Have Pact Cover World," *G&M*, 8 Sept. 1950, 1; and "Home from N.Z., Diefenbaker Asks for Pacific Pact," *G&M*, 22 Dec. 1950, 24.

66 House of Commons, *Debates*, 4 Sept. 1950; Frank Flaherty, "House Rejects CCF Motion for Price Control," 4 Sept. 1950, 4; Frank Flaherty, "Commons Endorses Korean Plans, Defeats Drew Amendment, 147–59," *G&M*, 6 Sept. 1950, 3; "Quebec Members Differ in Views on Korean War," *G&M*, 5 Sept. 1950, 10; "The CCF Takes Stock," *G&M*, 2 Aug. 1950, 6; and "Quebec Socreds Oppose Sending Men to Korea," *G&M*, 21 July 1950, 4.

67 "Brigade Troops Leave Canada for Fort Lewis," *G&M*, 13 Nov. 1950, 1; National Film Board, "Minister of Everything," https://www.nfb.ca /film/minister_of_everything/; Warren Baldwin, "Howe Member of Joint Group on Mobilization," *G&M*, 6 Sept. 1950, 3; and "Two Nations Lift Barriers to Pool Arms," *G&M*, 27 Oct. 1950, 1.

68 "Prime Minister Discloses: Canada as Atlantic Partner Will Send Troops to Europe," *G&M*, 7 Oct. 1950, 1; Peter C. Newman, *The Establishment Man: A Portrait of Power* (Toronto: McClelland & Stewart, 1982), 146; and "Duncan Urges Canada, U.S. Send Troops to Europe," *G&M*, 13 Sept. 1950, 5.

69 "Canada Allows West Germany Send Consul to Ottawa," *G&M*, 9 Nov. 1950, 3; and "Canada to End State of War with Germany in Near Future," *G&M*, 27 Oct. 1950, 1.

70 "Canada Foresees Restored Trade with Former Foes," *G&M*, 18 May 1950, 8.

71 House of Commons, *Debates,* 12 June 1950.

72 "Canada Bans Exports to China, Hong Kong," *G&M*, 11 Dec. 1950, 11; and "Call Council Meet to Take Up Formosa, Korea," *G&M*, 25 Nov. 1950, 30.

73 Rev. G.M. Lamont, quoted in "Reds Block Work, So Presbyterians Home from China," *G&M*, 25 Oct. 1950, 9; and "Missionaries Urge Canada Recognize Mao," *G&M*, 20 May 1950, 2.

74 Norman Altstedter, "India Turns Down McNaughton Plan on Kashmir Issue," *G&M*, 8 Feb. 1950, 9; and "Canada Pledges $850,000 to Aid Backward Areas," *G&M*, 13 June 1950, 1.

75 Statistics Canada, Table H52–74, "All Governments, Net General Revenue by Major Source, Selected Years, 1933 to 1969," https://www150.statcan. gc.ca/n1/pub/11-516-x/sectionh/4057752-eng.htm#2.

76 Reginald Whitaker, *The Government Party: Organizing and Financing the Liberal Party of Canada, 1930–58* (Toronto: University of Toronto Press, 1977).

77 Lester B. Pearson, "In Reply to a USSR Peace Resolution" (1950), *Words and Occasions* (Toronto: University of Toronto Press, 1970), 95.

1951

1 "Inflation by Invitation Result of Inaction: Drew," *G&M*, 5 May 1951, 17.

2 *Census of Canada, 1951* (Ottawa: Dominion Bureau of Statistics, 1956) 10:7, 9, 10; and Harvey Hickey, "Census Finds 1,108,532 in Greater Toronto," *G&M*, 9 Nov. 1951, 1.

3 *Census of Canada, 1951,* vol. 1, table 31, and vol. 10, table 137; and Porter, *The Vertical Mosaic,* 166, 286.

4 See, for example, Frank Tumpane, "Women Drive Differently," *G&M*, 12 Jan. 1951, 3.

5 Eva-Lis Wuorio, "Last of the Battling Suffragettes," *Maclean's*, 1 March 1951, 10, 11, 60; "Charlotte Whitton Becomes Canada's First Big-City Woman Mayor," CBC Archives, accessed 1 Mar. 2022, https://www.cbc.ca/archives/entry/1951-charlotte-whitton-becomes-canadas-first-big-city-woman-mayor; "Woman Party Leader Greets Women Candidates," *G&M*, 13 Nov. 1951, 12; and "Charlotte Whitton Named by Canadian Press Poll," *G&M*, 28 Dec. 1951, 1.

6 Arthur R.M. Lower, *Canadians in the Making: A Social History of Canada* (Toronto: Longmans, Green, 1958), 393–4; House of Commons, *Debates*, 18 June 1951; and Louis Rosenberg, "Canada," *American Jewish Yearbook* 53 (1952), 261–2.

7 *Census of Canada, 1951*, 10:5, 11.

8 Warren Baldwin, "Defense Budget of $1,500,000,000 Likely This Year," *G&M*, 15 Jan. 1951, 17; and Historic Inflation Canada – CPI Inflation, https://www.inflation.eu/inflation-rates/canada/historic-inflation/cpi-inflation-canada.aspx.

9 "Restoration of Controls on Prices, Rents Asked by Heads of Four Unions," *G&M*, 3 Jan. 1951, 1.

10 "Gasoline War Price Lines Hold," *G&M*, 5 Oct. 1951, 11.

11 Frank W. Peers, *The Politics of Canadian Broadcasting, 1920–1951* (Toronto: University of Toronto Press, 1969), 421; and Advertisement, *TDS*, 27 Aug. 1951, 4.

12 Peers, *The Politics of Canadian Broadcasting, 1920–1951*, 423.

13 House of Commons, *Debates*, 14 May, 29 June, and 20 Nov. 1951; and "$6,250,000 CBC Grant Opposed," *G&M*, 5 Dec. 1951, 9.

14 Canada, *Report of the Royal Commission on National Development in the Arts, Letters and Sciences, 1949–1951* (Ottawa: King's Printer, 1951); and Frank H. Underhill, "Notes on the Massey Report," *In Search of Canadian Liberalism* (Toronto: Macmillan, 1960), 209–13.

15 Pierre Berton, "There'll Always Be a Massey," *Maclean's*, 15 Oct. 1951, 8.

16 "May Day Tradition: Prime Minister Moves to New Home," *G&M*, 1 May 1951, 15.

17 *Canada Year Book, 1952–53*, 60, 65, 66, 67, 71.

18 Eva-Lis Wuorio, "The Edinburgs," *Maclean's*, 1 Oct. 1951, 7; "Well Guarded: Seven Ships on Duty Along Royal Route," *G&M*, 5 Oct. 1951, 11; Jean Shaw, "Likes Her Games Exciting: Princess Sorry to Miss Montreal Hockey Fight," *G&M*, 10 Nov. 1951, 17; "Caribou Slippers for Prince Charles," CBC Archives, accessed 8 Mar. 2022, https://www.cbc.ca/archives/entry/1951-caribou-slippers-for-prince-charles; and House of Commons, *Debates*, 12 Nov. 1951.

19 "Debut of the Cobalt Bomb," CBC Archives, accessed 1 Mar. 2022, https://www.cbc.ca/archives/entry/1951-debut-of-the-cobalt-bomb; Robert K.

Plumb, "New Cobalt Bomb Aids Cancer Fight," *NYT*, 13 Nov. 1951, 35; Wellington Jeffers, "Finance at Large," *G&M*, 29 Jan. 1951, 24; and "N.Y. Group Seeks to Loosen Bars on Cobalt Export," *G&M*, 20 June 1951, 19.

20 "St. Laurent Sees 1951 Bringing Deprivations, but Progress to Peace," *G&M*, 1 Jan. 1951, 3; "Must Continue Buildup, PM's Message for 1952," *G&M*, 31 Dec. 1951, 7; and "PM Foresees Period of Price Wars to Clear Loaded Shelves of Stocks," *G&M*, 16 Oct. 1951, 1.

21 "Civil Servants Again Press for Higher Pay," *G&M*, 4 Oct. 1951, 3.

22 Bruce Hutchison, "Are We Heading for a 20 Cent Dollar?," *Maclean's*, 1 Jan. 1951, 5.

23 Quoted in "Frost Sees Great Ontario Future," *TDS*, 27 Aug. 1951, 4; and "Inflation by Invitation Result of Inaction: Drew," *G&M*, 5 May 1951, 17.

24 Quoted in "Be Cost-Conscious or Lose Freedom, Solon Low Warns," *G&M*, 24 Jan. 1951, 3.

25 William Jenoves, quoted in Wilfred List, "Labor Rejects Abbott on Longer-Hours Plea," *G&M*, 8 May 1951, 1.

26 John Brehl, "'Go Where Money Is – to Big Firms' for Funds to Finance Defence M.J. Coldwell Tells Government," *TDS*, 18 May 1951, 19; and quoted in "New Law Will Strike at Abuses, St. Laurent Says," *TDS*, 21 Feb. 1951, 4.

27 Quoted in "Be Cost-Conscious or Lose Freedom, Solon Low Warns," *G&M*, 24 Jan. 1951, 3.

28 Frank Flaherty, "Ottawa Wheat Marketing Policy 'Colossal Failure,' Rowe Declares," *G&M*, 10 Mar. 1951, 3; and Frank Flaherty, "Motion Condemning Wheat Policy Rejected in Commons, 112 to 42," *G&M*, 17 Mar. 1951, 1.

29 Warren Baldwin, "17 Liberals Fail to Swing Checkoff Bill," *G&M*, 1 March 1951, 1.

30 Quoted in "New Law Will Strike at Abuses, St. Laurent Says," *TDS*, 21 Feb. 1951, 4.

31 John Brehl, "Filibuster Shapes Up on Price-Fixing Ban Tories Only Opposition," *TDS*, 19 Dec. 1951, 13; "All 3 Opposition Parties Demand Halt to Price Rise," *TDS*, 5 July 1951, 1; and Harvey Hickey, "Three Parties Demand Price Control; Drew Urges Repeal of Sales Tax Boost," *G&M*, 16 Oct. 1951, 1.

32 "Pensions Bill Is Given Third Reading," *G&M*, 9 Nov. 1951, 1; "Much Greater Security," and "Locked Up in Mental Hospitals," *TDS*, 21 Nov. 1951, 6.

33 British North America Act, 1951, 14–15 George VI, c. 32 (UK); and Speech from the Throne, *Senate Debates*, 9 Oct. 1951, 3.

34 Blair Fraser, "Backstage at Ottawa," *Maclean's*, 15 Aug. 1951, 5, 30.

35 "St. Laurent Announces: New Bill Gives Power to Retain Rent Control; Also Covers National Registration," *G&M*, 21 Feb. 1951, 1.

36 "Indigenous Foundations," First Nations and Indigenous Studies, University of British Columbia, accessed 1 Mar. 2022, https://indigenous foundations.arts.ubc.ca/the_indian_act/#amendments; Frank Flaherty, "Six-Year Proceeding: New Indian Law Passes Commons," *G&M*, 18 May 1951, 3; and "CBC-TV Visits a Residential School in 1955," CBC Archives, accessed 1 Mar. 2022, https://www.cbc.ca/archives/cbc-tv-visits-a -residential-school-in-1955-1.4667021.

37 Canadian Institute of Public Opinion, "Popularity of Liberals Slipping, Mostly in West," *TDS*, 11 Aug. 1951, 9.

38 "Honor Prime Minister for 10 Years at Ottawa," *G&M*, 6 Dec. 1951, 3; Warren Baldwin, "Most Fantastic Day: Closure Threat Stymies Progress in Commons," *G&M*, 21 Dec. 1951, 1; John Brehl, "Filibuster Shapes Up on Price-Fixing Ban Tories Only Opposition," *TDS*, 19 Dec. 1951; and House of Commons, *Debates*, 18 Dec. 1951.

39 "Young Liberals Approve Design of National Flag," *G&M*, 12 Nov. 1951, 12; and Harvey Hickey, "Drop Word Dominion as Canada Substituted; 7 PC's Object in Vain," *G&M*, 15 Dec. 1951, 1.

40 "Bill on Pensions for 'This Year,' Martin Indicates," *G&M*, 24 May 1951, 3; Robert Taylor, "Three Avenues Seen to Finance Old Age Pension," *TDS*, 5 June 1951, 1; and Harold Greer, "Drop Means Test Below 70 Is Demand by C.C.F. Party," *TDS*, 23 May 1951, 9.

41 R.M. Burns, *The Acceptable Mean: The Tax Rental Agreements, 1941–1962* (Toronto: Canadian Tax Foundation, 1980); Warren Baldwin, "Divide $387,627,000 If All Provinces Signed Tax Pacts," *G&M*, 17 Nov. 1951, 19; British North America Act, 1867, 30–1 Vict., c. 3 (UK), Section 92 (2); and J. Harvey Perry, *Taxation in Canada* (Toronto: University of Toronto Press, 1951), 5.

42 "Concealing the Sales Tax," *G&M*, 25 Jan. 1951, 6; "Turnover Tax Criticized Across Canada," *G&M*, 24 March 1951, 6; George Drew, House of Commons, *Debates*, 25 April 1951; and "Duplessis Aping Vishinsky, Premier Douglas Complains," *G&M*, 5 May 1951, 2.

43 Robert Taylor, "Frost Proposes Big Home-Building Plan to Ottawa," *TDS*, 26 May 1951, 41.

44 "Surprise Nfld. Election Called by Smallwood," *G&M*, 2 Nov. 1951, 8; "Liberals Retain Power in Newfoundland Vote," *G&M*, 28 Nov. 1951, 1; Eric Seymour, "Out of Date Election List Hot Issue in Newfoundland," *G&M*, 28 Nov. 1951, 2; and quoted in "Nfld. Minister Quits after Tiff with Smallwood," *G&M*, 14 Dec. 1951, 9.

45 "Liberals Returned in PEI Election with 1-Seat Gain," *G&M*, 27 April 1951, 1; and "Own Enough of PEI, You Can Cast 30 Votes," *G&M*, 27 April 1951, 10.

46 Elections PEI, https://www.princeedwardisland.ca/en/information /legislative-assembly/elections-pei; and Frank MacKinnon, "Prince

Edward Island: Big Engine, Little Body," in *Canadian Provincial Politics: Party Systems in the Ten Provinces*, ed. Martin Robin (Scarborough: Prentice-Hall, 1978).

47 "Premier vs. Premier: Douglas Aid to Jolliffe Unethical," *G&M*, 2 Nov. 1951, 8; and quoted in J.T. Morley, *Secular Socialists: The CCF/NDP in Ontario, A Biography* (Montreal: McGill-Queen's University Press, 1984), 57. Emphasis in original.

48 Ian Mackay and Robin Bates, *In the Province of History: The Making of the Public Past in Twentieth-Century Nova Scotia* (Montreal: McGill-Queen's University Press, 2010), 308; T. Stephen Henderson, *Angus L. Macdonald: A Provincial Liberal* (Toronto: University of Toronto Press, 2007), 202; and "N.S. Raises Taxes on Gas, Liquor," *G&M*, 3 June 1951, 9.

49 R.A. Young, "'And the People Will Sink into Despair': Reconstruction in New Brunswick, 1942–52," *Canadian Historical Review* 69, no. 2 (1988), 165.

50 "Duplessis Calls Newsprint Talk," *G&M*, 7 July 1951, 9; "Duplessis Orders Sect Cases Tried," *G&M*, 5 May 1951, 26; "Court Rules Duplessis Overstepped Authority," *G&M*, 3 May 1951, 15; and Roncarelli v. Duplessis, [1959] S.C.R. 121, 27 Jan. 1959.

51 André Laurendeau, "The Conditions for the Existence of a National Culture," in *Canadian Political Thought*, ed. H.D. Forbes (Toronto: Oxford University Press, 1985), 276.

52 James H. Gray, "Farmers Endorse Wheat Pool as Agency for Coarse Grains," *Windsor Daily Star*, 1 Dec. 1951, 4.

53 Frank Flaherty, "Freight Rates Up 12 p.c. Despite Protests Raised by Maritimes and West," *G&M*, 5 July 1951, 1.

54 "To Refine First Manitoba Crude," *G&M*, 4 June 1951, 25; and "Saskatchewan Seen Becoming Big Uranium Area," *G&M*, 27 July 1951, 18.

55 Aleck Ostry, "The Foundations of National Public Hospital Insurance," *Canadian Bulletin of Medical History* 26, no. 2 (Winter 2009), 261–81.

56 "Taxes, Auto Fees Pared $3,000,000 for Albertans," *G&M*, 6 March 1951, 25.

57 Quoted in "Opposes Canada's War Role: Alberta MPP Called Communist," *G&M*, 31 March 1951, 7.

58 "Coalition Rapped," *G&M*, 3 March 1951, 3; "Woman Changes Mind, Independent," *G&M*, 30 March 1951, 19; and Donald E. Blake, *Two Political Worlds: Parties and Voting in British Columbia* (Vancouver: University of British Columbia Press, 1985), 183.

59 House of Commons, *Debates*, 2 Feb. 1951; and "Canada Broadcasts behind the Iron Curtain," CBC Archives, accessed 8 Mar. 2022, https://www.cbc.ca/archives/entry/1958-canada-broadcasts-behind-the-iron-curtain.

60 Wallace Goforth and Sidney Katz, "If the Russians Attack Canada," *Maclean's*, 15 June 1951, 7; and Gerald Anglin, "The Russian Subs on Our Coastline," *Maclean's*, 1 Apr. 1951, 14.

61 Quoted in "Soviet Terms Canada U.S. Patrimonial State," *G&M*, 15 Sept. 1951, 15.

62 Peter Gellman, "Lester B. Pearson, Collective Security, and the World Order Tradition of Canadian Foreign Policy," *International Journal* 44, no. 1 (1988–9), 68–101; and Blair Fraser, "Meet Mike Pearson," *Maclean's*, 15 April 1951, 7.

63 Mildred A. Schwartz, *Public Opinion and Canadian Identity* (Scarborough, ON: Fitzhenry & Whiteside, 1967), 70.

64 L.B. Pearson, House of Commons, *Debates*, 2 Feb. 1951; "Trade with China Reds until All Hope for Peace Is Gone – Pearson," *TDS*, 5 June 1951, 4; and "Young Liberals Approve Design of National Flag," *G&M*, 12 Nov. 1951, 12.

65 Jack Brehl, "'Greatest Danger' Just Ahead, Europe Is Prize Russians Eye – Pearson," *TDS*, 3 Feb. 1951, 4; and Frank Flaherty, "No Talks with Peiping on Formosa, Jap Peace While War On: Pearson," *G&M*, 8 May 1951, 1.

66 John Melady, *Korea: Canada's Forgotten War* (Toronto: Dundurn, 2011), 103; and "Lessons from Korea War: Clark Offers U.S. Data to Canadian Soldiers," *G&M*, 24 Jan. 1951, 3.

67 Pierre Berton, "Colonel Dunphy's War," *Maclean's*, 1 June 1951, 57.

68 "Report Britain Paid $470,200,000 on Canadian Loan," *G&M*, 9 Nov. 1951, 1.

69 Melady, *Korea: Canada's Forgotten War*, 44; and *Canada Year Book, 1952–53*, 1065.

70 Dale C. Thomson, *Louis St. Laurent: Canadian* (Toronto: Macmillan, 1967), 304–6.

71 Quoted in Blair Fraser, "Why NATO Needs the Twelve Apostles," *Maclean's*, 1 Nov. 1951, 5, 46.

72 Quoted in "Canada Tags $1 Billion for Aircraft, Millions More for Radar, Arms," *TDS*, 15 May 1951, 16.

73 Daniel Macfarlane, *Negotiating a River: Canada, the US, and the Creation of the St. Lawrence Seaway* (Vancouver: UBC Press, 2014), 211; "Need U.S. Co-operation on Power, Can Build Seaway Alone – Howe," *TDS*, 29 Nov. 1951, 1; and Claire Parham "The St. Lawrence Seaway: A Bi-national Political Marathon, a Local and State Initiative," *New York History* 85, no. 4 (2004), 360.

74 "Canada Makes $10 Million Gift to Famine-Threatened India," *G&M*, 9 Nov. 1951, 1; and Thomson, *Louis St. Laurent: Canadian*, 304.

75 "Canada, Allies Soon to End State of War with Germany," *G&M*, 14 June 1951, 2.

76 Quoted in Richard H. Parke, "Cannot Quarrel with U.S. Strategy, St. Laurent Says," *G&M*, 20 Nov. 1951, 1–2.

1952

1 "Canada, a Sleeping Giant, Awakes and Stretches," *NYT*, 27 July 1952, F1.

2 An Act Respecting Immigration, 1952 1 Elizabeth II, chap. 42; and Ninette Kelley and Michael Trebilcock, *The Making of the Mosaic: A History of*

Canadian Immigration Policy (Toronto: University of Toronto Press, 1998), 314, 324.

3 Statistics Canada, "Canadian Statistics in 1955," https://www65.statcan .gc.ca/acyb07/acyb07_0011-eng.htm.

4 John G. Forrest, "Canada, a Sleeping Giant, Awakes and Stretches," *NYT*, 27 July 1952, F1; "Reserve Bank Calls Canada's Economy Sound: Says Nation Stands on Threshold of New Era," *New York Herald Tribune*, 4 Nov. 1952, 32; and "Lauds Canada's Efforts to Keep Economy Free," *G&M*, 12 Mar. 1952, 7.

5 J.W. Pickersgill, *My Years with Louis St. Laurent* (Toronto: University of Toronto Press, 1975), 191.

6 Wilfred List, "Industries Recalling Employees, Ontario Unemployment Drops 2,568," *G&M*, 12 Mar. 1952, 15.

7 "Inflation.eu Inflation Canada 1952," accessed 2 Mar. 2022, https://www .inflation.eu/inflation-rates/canada/historic-inflation/cpi-inflation-canada -1952.aspx.

8 Robert Taylor, "St. Laurent Rejects Idea Canadian Is Not Good Enough for Post," *TDS*, 25 Jan. 1952, 1, 2; "Drew Criticizes Appointment of Massey," *G&M*, 25 Jan. 1952, 8; "What Makes News: King's Death Rated Top Story of 1952 by Telegraph Editors of Canadian Papers," *G&M*, 24 Dec. 1952, 11; and quoted in Harvey Hickey, "Restore Tax Powers to Provinces," *G&M*, 26 Mar. 1952, 1.

9 House of Commons, *Debates*, 6 Mar. 1952.

10 G.V. Ferguson, "TV Gives Canada a Headache," *Washington Post*, 14 Sept. 1952, B2; "Ross Sees Dictatorship," *G&M*, 8 Dec. 1952, 2; and "'Thanks for Nothing'": No Private TV in Big Cities; Monopoly by CBC Protested Station Heads Complain 'Bone Picked,'" *G&M*, 21 Nov. 1952, 1.

11 "CBC Television Debuts," CBC Archives, accessed 2 Mar. 2022, https://www. cbc.ca/archives/entry/1952-cbc-television-debuts; and Alex Barris, "From Puppets to PM: TV Sample Cluttered but Promising," *G&M*, 9 Sept. 1952, 1.

12 "Gang's Second Jailbreak Becomes CBC's First TV News Story," CBC Archives, accessed 2 Mar. 2022, https://www.cbc.ca/archives/entry /gangs-second-jailbreak-becomes-cbcs-first-tv-news-story; and quoted in James Y. Nicol, "Had Three Guns, 96 Bullets but All Four Caught Cold Then Whimper 'Don't Shoot!,'" *TDS*, 17 Sept. 1952, 1.

13 "Religious Censorship and the CBC," *Maclean's*, 1 Jan. 1952, 2.

14 Ken Barker, "Canadian Fundamentalism and T.T. Shields," *Owen Sound Sun Times*, 10 June 2005, B4; and Doug A. Adams, "The War of the Worlds: The Militant Fundamentalism of Dr. Thomas Todhunter Shields and the Paradox of Modernity," PhD diss., Western University (August 2015), 240.

15 Wilfred List, "Clergy in Quebec Taking Stand in Support of Labor Unionism," *G&M*, 29 Oct. 1952, 13; and Blair Fraser, "Labor and Church in Quebec," *Foreign Affairs* 28 (1950), 247.

16 Blair Fraser, "How Dr. Endicott Fronts for the Reds," *Maclean's*, 15 July 1952, 7; and A. Stewart Allen, "I Was a Prisoner of the Chinese Reds," *Maclean's*, 15 Apr. 1952, 15.

17 "The New Law of Treason," *G&M*, 16 May 1952, 6.

18 David Jay Bercuson, *True Patriot: The Life of Brooke Claxton, 1898–1960* (Toronto: University of Toronto Press, 1993), 234; George Bain, "Five Arrested in Theft Case at Petawawa," *G&M*, 19 Apr. 1952, 1; George Bain, "House Adjourns to Jan. 12: PM Admits Report Altered: Currie Paper Changes Laid to Defense Dept.," *G&M*, 18 Dec. 1952, 1; Bruce MacDonald, "'Frailty' Not System Caused Army Thefts Garson Tells House," *TDS*, 17 Dec. 1952, 12, and House of Commons, *Debates*, 16 Dec. 1952.

19 Thomson, *Louis St. Laurent: Canadian*, 332.

20 Quoted in Harvey Hickey, "Restore Tax Powers to Provinces," *G&M*, 26 Mar. 1952, 1, 2.

21 Evelyn McDonald, "Mr. St. Laurent's Remarkable Feat," *G&M*, 18 Sept. 1952, 6.

22 Quoted in "Use of Word Progressive Unnecessary, Drew Feels," *G&M*, 26 Mar. 1952, 1.

23 House of Commons, *Debates*, 6 Mar. 1952.

24 "Monetary Reform Seen SC Platform," *G&M*, 31 Oct. 1952, 5; and Bob Hesketh, *Major Douglas and Alberta Social Credit* (Toronto: University of Toronto Press, 1997), chap. 5.

25 "Easier Exchange to Boost Trade Urged by MP's," *G&M*, 12 Sept. 1952, 4.

26 House of Commons, *Debates*, 11 Dec. 1952.

27 Quoted in "Young Politicians Back Principles of Human Rights," *G&M*, 13 Dec. 1952, 5.

28 House of Commons, *Debates*, 24 Mar. and 4 July 1952; Harvey Hicks, "Croll Raps South Africa's Stand: 15,000 in Pretoria Rioting against Malan Race Policies," *G&M*, 25 Mar. 1952, 1; and Blair Fraser, "How Racketeers Sold Entry into Canada," *Maclean's*, 15 Mar. 1952, 11, 61.

29 Blair Fraser, "Backstage at Ottawa," *Maclean's*, 1 July 1952, 44; Thomson, *Louis St. Laurent: Canadian*, 328–9; and "Liberals Hoping St. Laurent Stays for Next Vote," *G&M*, 7 July 1952, 8.

30 Quoted in Thomson, *Louis St. Laurent: Canadian*, 328.

31 Quoted in "Redistribution Termed Jimmymander, Butchery," *G&M*, 1 July 1952, 2; House of Commons, *Debates*, 28 June 1952; Harvey Hickey, "Canada Amends Its Constitution for First Time," *G&M*, 16 June 1952, 3; and Norman Ward, "The Redistribution of 1952," *Canadian Journal of Economics and Political Science* 19, no. 2 (1953), 341–60.

32 "St. Laurent Urges Young Canadians to Join Army," *G&M*, 21 Jan. 1952, 8; Harvey Hickey, "Defense Costs Prevent Large Tax Reductions, St. Laurent's Warning," *G&M*, 10 Sept. 1952, 7; Harvey Hickey, "N.B. Vote

Held Tip to Ottawa on Tax Cuts," *G&M*, 24 Sept. 1952, 1; and "Old Soldiers Argue: Is Bayonet Obsolete? Debated by Committee," *G&M*, 4 June 1952, 2.

33 Harvey Hickey, "Parliamentarians Find 300 Divorce Actions Cluttering Up Agenda," *G&M*, 22 Feb. 1952, 13.

34 Ronald M. Burns, "Intergovernmental Relations in Canada," *Canadian Public Administration* 33, no. 1 (1973), 15.

35 Harold Greer, "Ontario Seen Refusing to Rent Taxes Again: 4 Year Loss $23,000,000," *TDS*, 28 Feb. 1952, 2; and Robert Taylor, "$40,000,000 Loss Seen for Ontario as Taxes Not Rented to Ottawa," *TDS*, 29 Feb. 1952, 3.

36 Quoted in Harvey Hickey, "Restore Tax Powers to Provinces," *G&M*, 26 Mar. 1952, 1–2; "Hogging the Tax Dollar," *G&M*, 22 Mar. 1952, 6; Corey Slumkoski, *Inventing Atlantic Canada: Regionalism and the Maritime Reaction to Newfoundland's Entry into Canadian Confederation* (Toronto: University of Toronto Press, 2011), 79–80; and R.A. Young, "'And the People Will Sink into Despair,'" 146.

37 N.L. Nicholson, "The Federal Government and Canadian Universities: A Review," *Canadian Journal of Higher Education* 3, no. 1 (1973), 22; Gerard V. La Forest, *The Allocation of Taxing Power under the Canadian Constitution* (Toronto: Canadian Tax Foundation, 1967), 26; "Abbott Seeking Tax Renewals with Provinces," *G&M*, 16 June 1952, 12; "No Federal Ties, Duplessis Pleads," *G&M*, 16 June 1952, 3.

38 "Aid in Farm Research," *G&M*, 6 Mar. 1952, 8; "Douglas Promises Rural Lighting, Better Roads," *G&M*, 30 Apr. 1952, 7; and "Tenders for Canso Causeway Called Amid Desk Thumping," *G&M*, 4 Apr. 1952, 12.

39 A.O.C. Cole, "Ontario Gas Pipeline Might Be Influenced by Alberta Vote Result," *G&M*, 6 Aug. 1952, 7.

40 Harvey Hickey, "Predict Election in B.C. as Coalition Premier Asks PC Leader to Quit," *G&M*, 19 Jan. 1952, 3.

41 Nelson Wiseman, *In Search of Canadian Political Culture* (Vancouver: UBC Press, 2007), chaps. 6 and 10.

42 Quoted in "Socred Plug in B.C.," *G&M*, 8 Mar. 1952, 3.

43 Gordon McCallum, "B.C. Coalition Collapses as Conservatives Quit," and "Winch Urges Early Election," *Vancouver Daily Province*, 18 Jan. 1952, 1.

44 Quoted in "Alternative Voting Damned, Praised by B.C. Politicians," *G&M*, 14 June 1952, 29.

45 "No Federal Ties, Duplessis Pleads," *G&M*, 16 June 1952, 3.

46 Quoted in Conrad Black, *Duplessis* (Toronto: McClelland & Stewart, 1977), 352.

47 "Union Bargaining Election Issue in New Brunswick," *G&M*, 17 July 1952, 2; G.V. Ferguson, "Canada's 'Ins' Take New Beating," *Washington Post*, 28 Sept. 1952, B2; Harvey Hickey, "N.B. Vote Held Tip to Ottawa on Tax

Cuts," *G&M*, 24 Sept. 1952, 1; and "Canadian Liberals Lose," *NYT*, 24 Sept. 1952, 3.

48 Seymour Martin Lipset, *Agrarian Socialism* (Berkeley, CA: University of California Press, 1950); *Census of Canada, 1951*, vol. 1, tables 9, 13; and Wiseman, "The Socialist Imprint on Saskatchewan Politics," 31.

49 A.O.C. Cole, "Ontario Gas Pipeline Might be Influenced by Alberta Vote Result," *G&M*, 6 Aug. 1952, 7.

50 Finkel, *The Social Credit Phenomenon in Alberta*, 127.

51 "Nfld. By-Election to Settle Dispute," *G&M*, 26 Sept. 1952, 3.

52 "Newfoundland May Receive Aid from Rothschild," *G&M*, 16 Sept. 1952, 22; "Record Real Estate Deal: Rothschild Interests Plan Nfld. Operations, Says Smallwood," *G&M*, 9 Dec. 1952, 9; and "Pledges Votes of PEI to Party Promising Aid," *G&M*, 21 Nov. 1952, 8.

53 "Solidly behind Quebec Strikers CCL Announces," *TDS*, 23 Dec. 1952, 2; "Tear Gas, Guns Used on Quebec Strikers by Police, Read Riot Act," *TDS*, 11 Dec. 1952, 1–2; and quoted in Pat McNenley, "Strike by 100,000 Legal as 'Terror' Protest in Quebec – Official," *TDS*, 16 Dec. 1952, 1–2.

54 Harold Greer, "Ontario Seen Refusing to Rent Taxes Again: 4 Year Loss $23,000,000," *TDS*, 28 Feb. 1952, 2.

55 Quoted in Roger Graham, *Old Man Ontario: Leslie M. Frost* (Toronto: University of Toronto Press, 1990), 193.

56 John Hilliker and Donald Barry, *Canada's Department of External Affairs: Coming of Age, 1946–1968* (Toronto: Institute of Public Administration of Canada, 1990), 25, 51, 54, 56, 69, 74, 114–15; and "Canada Moves to Boost Trade with West Indies," *G&M*, 24 Apr. 1952, 3.

57 John English, *The Worldly Years: The Life of Lester Pearson, 1949–1972* (Toronto: Knopf, 1992), 63; and Henry Harris, "U.N. General Assembly Elects Pearson President," *Daily Boston Globe*, 15 Oct. 1952, 27.

58 Harvey Hickey, "'Irresponsible and Disastrous': NATO Arms Objective Is Condemned by CCF," *G&M*, 13 Mar. 1952, 1–2; and English, *The Worldly Years*, 75.

59 Hilliker and Barry, *Canada's Department of External Affairs*, 122.

60 House of Commons, *Debates*, 12 Mar. 1952.

61 B.K. Sandwell, "North Atlantic – Community or Treaty?," *International Journal* 7, no. 3 (1952), 169–70.

62 Quoted in Pearson, *Mike: The Memoirs, vol. 2: 1948–1957*, 184.

63 Quoted in Michael L. Hoffman, "Canada Maps Fight on U. S. Dairy Quota," *NYT*, 29 Feb. 1952, 28; and Harvey Hickey, "Howe Reports Canada Not Ready to Retaliate on Import Issue Now," *G&M*, 1 Mar. 1952, 1.

64 Hilliker and Barry, *Canada's Department of External Affairs*, 111.

65 James Hornick, "Canada, U.S. Join to Test Defense in Air Attack," *G&M*, 15 July 1952, 1.

66 Harvey Hickey, "Canada Building 27-Foot Waterway: Seaway Power
    Preliminaries Launched by 2 Governments," *G&M*, 1 July 1952, 1.
67 Beland Honderich, "Prosperity Is Example Canadian Advice Seen
    Dominating at London," *TDS*, 29 Nov. 1952, 1, 16; Daniel Clifton, "Closer Ties
    Urged at British Parley," *NYT*, 1 Dec. 1952, 23; and Blair Fraser, "Backstage at
    Ottawa: Are We Really Helping Britain?" *Maclean's*, 1 Oct. 1952, 5.
68 Greg Donaghy, "Blessed Are the Peacemakers: Canada, the United
    Nations, and the Search for a Korean Armistice, 1952–53," *War & Society*
    30, no. 2 (2011), 134–46; House of Commons, *Debates*, 3 Apr. 1952; George
    Bain, "Claxton Claims Canada Meeting Defense Quota; Pearkes Not
    Satisfied," *G&M*, 4 Apr. 1952, 3; and Harvey Hickey, "Peacetime Record
    for Canada: Abbott Asks $4,335,800,000; Estimates for Defense up 23 p.c.,"
    G&M, 20 Mar. 1952, 1.
69 House of Commons, *Debates*, 9 Apr. 1952.
70 "Canada to Attend Conference on German Debts," *G&M*, 15 Jan. 1952,
    3; George Bain, "Canada Ratifies Plan Offering Atlantic Link to Western
    Germany," *G&M*, 18 June 1952, 1; and "PM May Present 2nd Fichier Wing
    to NATO Heads," *G&M*, 9 Sept. 1952, 3.

1953

 1 Quoted in "Quebec Declines Ottawa Grants for Universities," *G&M*, 17
    Feb. 1953, 8.
 2 Statistics Canada, "Table H1–18, Federal Government Budgetary Revenue,
    by Major Source, 1867 to 1975," accessed 3 Mar. 2022, https://www150.
    statcan.gc.ca/n1/pub/11-516-x/sectionh/4057752-eng.htm#1; and Robert
    Bothwell, Ian Drummond, and John English, *Canada since 1945: Power,
    Politics, and Provincialism* (Toronto: University of Toronto Press, 1989), 169.
 3 *Canada Year Book, 1955*, 166, 784, 1026, 1027, 1029; "Labor Income in
    September Over Billion for First Time," *G&M*, 17 Dec. 1953, 8; "Inflation.
    eu Inflation Canada 1953," accessed 3 Mar. 2022, https://www.inflation
    .eu/inflation-rates/canada/historic-inflation/cpi-inflation-canada-1953
    .aspx; and "Backstage at Ottawa," *Maclean's*, 1 Oct. 1953, 6.
 4 Statistics Canada, Table E175–177: "Union Membership in Canada, in
    Total and as a Percentage of Non-agricultural Paid Workers and Union
    Members with International Affiliation, 1911 to 1975," https://www150.
    statcan.gc.ca/n1/pub/11-516-x/sectione/E175_177-eng.csv; and Harvey
    Hickey, "Railway Strike Averted: Union Given 12 Per Cent Pay Increase,"
    G&M, 30 Jan. 1953, 1.
 5 Statistics Canada, "Canadian Statistics in 1955," https://www65.statcan.
    gc.ca/acyb07/acyb07_0011-eng.htm; "Frost Sees Population 6,000,000
    in Five Years," *G&M*, 18 Sept. 1953, 3; Neil. B. Freeman, *The Politics of*

Power: Ontario Hydro and Its Government, 1906–1995 (Toronto: University of Toronto Press, 1996), 102; and "Canadian Jet at Karachi: 11 Die in Comet Crash," *G&M*, 3 Mar. 1953, 1.

6 *Canada Year Book, 1954*, 159; and *Canada Year Book, 1955*, 165–76.

7 "Telephone, TV Hookup Benefit by New Tower," *G&M*, 19 Feb. 1953, 5; "3-City TV Link Due Next Month," *G&M*, 24 Apr. 1953, 36; and *Canada Year Book, 1955*, 916–18.

8 A.F.W. Peart, "Canada's Sickness Survey: Review of Methods," *Canadian Journal of Public Health* 43, no. 10 (1952), 401–14; Harold Greer, "$82 Spent on Health Care by Average Canadian Family during the Year," *TDS*, 12 May 1953, 3; Malcolm Taylor, *Health Insurance and Canadian Public Policy* (Montreal: McGill-Queen's University Press, 1978), 116; and "History of Public Health," Canadian Public Health Association, accessed 3 Mar. 2022, https://www.cpha.ca/story-polio.

9 Quoted in Tina Loo, *Moved by the State: Forced Relocation and Making a Good Life in Postwar Canada* (Vancouver: UBC Press, 2019), 33.

10 Canada, *Report of the Royal Commission on National Development in the Arts, Letters and Sciences, 1949–1951* (Ottawa: King's Printer, 1951), 102–3.

11 Hilda Neatby, "Canadian Culture Needs Forums to Exchange Ideas," *G&M*, 5 Dec. 1953.

12 Herbert Whittaker, "Man of 1,000 Faces Dons New Ones at Festival: Guinness' Creation Towering," *G&M*, 14 July 1953, 15; "The Debut of the Stratford Festival in 1953," CBC Archives, accessed 3 Mar. 2022, https://www.cbc.ca/archives/the-debut-of-the-stratford-festival-in-1953-1.4739154; and Iris Nowell, *P11: Painters Eleven: The Wild Ones of Canadian Art* (Vancouver: Douglas & McIntyre, 2010).

13 "Howe, Drew Sail Friday with Coronation Group," *G&M*, 14 May 1953, 15; Alan Harvey, "400 from Canada Occupy Abbey Seats," *G&M*, 2 June 1953, 9; and House of Commons, *Debates*, 22 April 1953.

14 House of Commons, *Debates*, 3 Feb. 1953.

15 Barry West, "Parents First Thought: Thousands in Montreal Greet Cardinal Leger," *G&M*, 30 Jan. 1953, 15.

16 "Gallup Canada," MacOdrum Library, Carleton University (May, 1953) https://library.carleton.ca/find/data/gallup-canada; and "There's Only One," *G&M*, 10 Jan. 1953, 6.

17 A.O.C. Cole, "Little Faith in White Men: Indians Fear Help, Committee Told," *G&M*, 28 May 1953, 21; "Alter Only Nuisance Laws: Wets Left High as Drys by Liquor Act Changes," *G&M*, 20 Mar. 1953, 15; and "B.C. Liquor Probe Deals Hard Blow to Beer Parlors," *G&M*, 14 Jan. 1953, 8.

18 M. Taylor, *Health Insurance and Canadian Public Policy*, 205; and "On the Hustings: Hees Says PC's Seek Medical Conference to Formulate Health Plan," *G&M*, 1 Aug. 1953, 8.

19 G.V. Ferguson, "St. Laurent Nips Election Urge," *Washington Post*, 29 Mar. 1953, B2.

20 "Political Role of Television Still in Doubt," *G&M*, 9 Aug. 1954, 3.

21 "46 P.C. Say Liberal 31 P.C. Conservative, 13 P.C. Select CCF," *TDS*, 6 May 1953, 3.

22 Hugh MacLennan, "Why I'm Voting Liberal," *Maclean's*, 1 Aug. 1953, 10.

23 "Liberal Platform of 1953," in D. Owen Carrigan, *Canadian Party Platforms, 1867–1968* (Toronto: Copp Clark, 1968), 208–10.

24 "Progressive Conservative Platform of 1953," in Carrigan, *Canadian Party Platforms, 1867–1968*, 210–11; and House of Commons, *Debates*, 20 Feb. 1953.

25 "Humanity First," in Carrigan, *Canadian Party Platforms, 1867–1968*, 198–205; quoted in "Social Credit Plans Ontario Office," *G&M*, 6 Oct. 1953, 8; "Solon Low: Former Head of Socred Party," *G&M*, 24 Dec. 1962, 1; and Social Credit Association of Canada, "Why Canada Needs Social Credit" (Edmonton, 1953).

26 Quoted in "St. Laurent Jibes at GOP 'Hot Air,'" *Washington Post*, 14 July 1953, 11.

27 George Bain, "West Apathetic Over Campaign; Uncertain of Date," *G&M*, 4 July 1953, 3.

28 Pearson, *Mike: The Memoirs, vol. 2: 1948–1957*, 14.

29 "George Hees: PM Questioned on Cabinet Gap in South Ontario," *G&M*, 5 Aug. 1953, 3; House of Commons, *Debates*, 11 May 1953; and Ken W. MacTaggart, "PC Leader Defends Pearkes: Drew Says Libellous Letter Sent to Soldiers in Korea Demands St. Laurent Repudiate It," *G&M*, 31 July 1953, 1.

30 "Party Record Reviewed: St. Laurent Says Economic Strength, Unity Achieved during Liberal Regime," *G&M*, 23 June 1953, 9; "Provincial Rights Election Issue, Drew Stresses," *G&M*, 11 May 1953, 3; Ken MacTaggart, "Prime Minister St. Laurent: Constitution in Peril If Drew's Tax Proposal Ended Aid to Provinces," *G&M*, 1 July 1953, 4; and "Party Record Reviewed: St. Laurent Says Economic Strength, Unity Achieved during Liberal Regime," *G&M*, 23 June 1953, 9.

31 Quoted in Thomson, *Louis St. Laurent: Canadian*, 351; and quoted in Eldon Stonehouse, "PC Speakers Critical: Immigrants Fill Jails, Barb Aimed at Liberals," *G&M*, 6 July 1953, 8.

32 George Bain, "West Apathetic Over Campaign; Uncertain of Date," *G&M*, 4 July 1953, 3.

33 "Once Talked of March on Ottawa," *G&M*, 2 Aug. 1967, 36.

34 Harold Morrison, "Long-Range Plan Urged: Prairie Irrigation Move Rejected," *G&M*, 20 Jan. 1953, 3; "Still Undecided on Prairie Power, St. Laurent Says," *G&M*, 7 July 1953, 7; and "'Tomorrow, Tomorrow,'" *G&M*, 17 July 1953, 6.

35 Pearson, *Mike: The Memoirs, vol. 2: 1948–1957*, 26.

36 Thomson, *Louis St. Laurent: Canadian*, 192.

37 "Mutual Problems: Maritimes, Nfld. Talk Ways to Improve Economy,"
    G&M, 15 Sept. 1953, 1.

38 Margaret Conrad, "The 1950s, The Decade of Development," in *The
    Atlantic Provinces in Confederation*, ed. E.R. Forbes and D.A. Muise
    (Toronto: University of Toronto Press, 1993), 403; and "Former Adviser to
    PM Said Slated for Cabinet," *G&M*, 14 May 1953, 17.

39 "Liberal Platform of 1953," and "Progressive Conservative Platform of
    1953," in Carrigan, *Canadian Party Platforms, 1867–1968*, 208, 210.

40 Quoted in "Ontario Forced to Sign Tax Pact, Says Duplessis," *G&M*, 23
    Jan. 1953, 8.

41 Quoted in "Premier Douglas: Ottawa Charged with Welshing on Tax
    Rentals," *G&M*, 4 Aug. 1953, 7.

42 "Alter Only Nuisance Laws," *G&M*, 20 Mar. 1953, 15; and "No Borrowing in
    B.C.: Social Credit Unveils Pay-as-You-Go Budget," *G&M*, 19 Feb. 1953, 1.

43 "Praise for New Health Grants," *TDS*, 26 Nov. 1953, 26; and "A.G. Kuziak:
    CCF Influenced Ottawa to Make Health Grants," *G&M*, 11 July 1953, 3.

44 Quoted in "Quebec Declines Ottawa Grants for Universities," *G&M*, 17
    Feb. 1953, 8; An Act to Institute a Royal Commission on Constitutional
    Problems (1953), 1 & 2 Eliz. II, c. 4 (P.Q.); and "Duplessis Asks Ottawa-
    Province Relations Probed," *G&M*, 14 Jan. 1953, 8.

45 "Alter Only Nuisance Laws," *G&M*, 20 Mar. 1953, 15.

46 Dalton Camp, *Gentlemen, Players, and Politicians* (Toronto: McClelland &
    Stewart, 1970), 111.

47 Peter Clancy, "The Last Pre-Modern Premier," *Acadiensis* 37, no. 1 (2008), 131.

48 Henderson, *Angus L. Macdonald*, 206–7.

49 "PC's Gain Five Seats: Liberals Win in N.S.," *G&M*, 27 May 1953, 1.

50 "Willis Issues Statement," *Winnipeg Free Press*, 29 Sept. 1952, 10.

51 Quoted in "Major Issue Missing in Manitoba Election," *G&M*, 6 June 1953, 3.

52 "Manitoba Vote June 8: Coalition Dead Issue," *G&M*, 25 Apr. 1953, 1.

53 W.L. Morton, *Manitoba: A History* (Toronto: University of Toronto Press,
    1967), 463.

54 Jean Barman, *The West beyond the West: A History of British Columbia*
    (Toronto: University of Toronto Press, 2007), 12.

55 "Woman Minister Defeated in B.C. by Liberal Leader," *G&M*, 8 July 1953,
    3; "Vote at a Glance," *Victoria Daily Times*, 25 Nov. 1953, 1; and "Minister
    Beaten in B.C. Vote," *Evening Citizen* (Ottawa), 25 Nov. 1953, 20.

56 S.B.C. 1931 c.21, and S.B.C. 1953, c.5, s. 4; and R. Jeremy Wilson, "The
    Impact of Communications Developments on British Columbia Electoral
    Patterns, 1903–1975," *Canadian Journal of Political Science* 13, no. 3 (1980),
    534.

57 James P. Feehan, "Smallwood, Churchill Falls, and the Power Corridor through Quebec," *Acadiensis* 40, no. 2 (2011), 112; Gerhard P. Bassler, *Alfred Valdmanis and the Politics of Survival* (Toronto: University of Toronto Press, 2000), 249; "Ex-newspaperman Gets Economic Post in Newfoundland," *G&M*, 3 Apr. 1953, 3; James Lawrence Kenny, "Politics and Persistence: New Brunswick's Hugh John Flemming and the 'Atlantic Revolution,' 1952–1960," master's thesis, St. Francis Xavier University (1986), 15–16; Wayne E. MacKinnon, *J. Walter Jones: The Farmer Premier* (Summerside: Williams & Crue, 1974); Richard J. Needham, "Canada's Stepchildren: Maritime Economy on Shaky Base," *G&M*, 16 July 1953, 6; and "Health Minister Succeeds Jones as PEI Premier," *G&M*, 21 May 1953, 9.

58 Wilfred List, "CCCL Tie-Up Could Rival 1919 Winnipeg Walkout," *G&M*, 9 Jan. 1953, 9; and quoted in "Threat of Unions Call to Crime, Duplessis Charges," *G&M*, 15 Jan. 1953, 15.

59 "Frost Sees Population 6,000,000 in Five Years," *G&M*, 18 Sept. 1953, 3; and Clive Kidd, quoted in "Union Official Terms Premier Utter Hypocrite," *G&M*, 10 Nov. 1953, 5.

60 "Favor Extending Ontario Vote to 23,000 Indians," *G&M*, 24 Nov. 1953, 30; and A.O.C. Cole, "Little Faith in White Men: Indians Fear Help, Committee Told," *G&M*, 28 May 1953, 21.

61 "Prairies Prosper, Set Up Records for Expenditures," *G&M*, 13 Mar. 1953, 17; "Ottawa Ponders B.C. Expansion Aid for Roads, Rails," *G&M*, 15 Dec. 1953, 3; and Finkel, *The Social Credit Phenomenon in Alberta*, 101.

62 David J. Bercuson, *Blood on the Hills: The Canadian Army in the Korean War* (Toronto: University of Toronto Press, 1999), 221–2.

63 *Canada Year Book, 1955*, 132.

64 J.L. Black, "The Stalinist Image of Canada the Cominform and Soviet Press, 1947–1955," *Labour/Le Travail* 21 (1988), 161–2.

65 Stuart Garson quoted in House of Commons, *Debates*, 18 Feb. 1953; and "Powers Act Extension Justified, Says Garson," *G&M*, 19 Feb. 1953, 17.

66 Pearson, *Words and Occasions*, 124.

67 "Plum Discovery Starts New Rush East of the Peach," *G&M*, 10 Sept. 1953, 20.

68 Quoted in John W. Holmes, "The Unquiet Diplomat – Lester B. Pearson," *International Journal* 62, no. 2 (2007), 304; and Thomas J. Hamilton, "Pearson Rules Out Korea Unification by the Use of Force," *NYT*, 24 Sept. 1953, 1.

69 *Canada Year Book, 1955*, 133, and Greg Donaghy, "The Politics of Accommodation: Canada, the Middle East, and the Suez Crisis, 1950–1956," *International Journal* 7, no. 2 (2016), 316.

70 Harvey Hickey, "Talks Still Open, but Won't Let U.S. Stall Seaway Plan," *G&M*, 10 Jan. 1953, 1; and Clark Davey, "50-Year Seaway Story May Reach Milestone with 1954 Work Start," *G&M*, 31 Dec. 1953, 4.

71 A.M. Rosenthal, "Canada Will Permit a Visit to Gouzenko by Senate Unit," *NYT*, 25 Nov. 1953, 1; *Chronology of International Events and Documents* 9, no. 23, 753; House of Commons, *Debates*, 14 Dec. 1953.

72 *Canada Year Book, 1955*, 121–4, 128; Hilliker and Barry, *Canada's Department of External Affairs*, 95; "The UN Report on Apartheid," *G&M*, 2 Nov. 1953, 6; John Diefenbaker, House of Commons, *Debates*, 13 Feb. 1953; Jim Byrne, House of Commons, *Debates*, 16 Feb. 1953; and "Joseph B. Salsberg: Old Line Parties Seen Violating Election Laws," G&M, 3 Aug. 1953, 4.

1954

1 Quoted in Harvey Hickey, "Opening of Parliament to Be on Television; CBC Promises Dignity," *G&M*, 22 Dec. 1954, 3.

2 *Canada Year Book, 1956*, 717; and Bert Gargrave, quoted in "Economy Said Spiralling Down to 30s Level," *G&M*, 25 May 1954, 5.

3 "Canadian Survey Affirms Forecast: Midyear Investment Report Indicates," *NYT*, 26 June 1954, 20; "Unemployment at Peak Ottawa Figures Show; Union Leaders Critical," *G&M*, 22 Apr. 1954, 17; and Dominion Bureau of Statistics, *Seasonally Adjusted Labour Force Statistics*, January 1953 – December 1966 (Ottawa: Queen's Printer, 1967), 62.

4 "On the Ground Floor," *G&M*, 4 Feb. 1954, 6; and quoted in George Bain, "Must Find Other Jobs, Howe Bluntly Advises Farm Implement Men," *G&M*, 11 Feb. 1954, 1.

5 Wilfred List, "Labor Groups Planning Nationwide Campaign to Halt Unemployment," *G&M*, 27 Jan. 1954, 1.

6 "Check on Immigration Demanded by Congress," *G&M*, 2 Oct. 1954, 5; and quoted in "Unionists Ask Switch from Budget Surplus to Deficit Financing," *G&M*, 30 Sept. 1954, 1.

7 Valerie Knowles, *Strangers at Our Gates: Canadian Immigration and Immigration Policy, 1540–1990* (Toronto: Dundurn, 1992), 135; and "Optimism Is Not Enough," *G&M*, 14 July 1954, 6.

8 Ron Haggart, "TLC Seeks Restriction on Immigrant Totals and Voice in Policy," *G&M*, 26 Aug. 1954, 3; and quoted in "Check on Immigration Demanded by Congress," *G&M*, 2 Oct. 1954, 5.

9 *Canada Year Book, 1955*, 164–5.

10 *Canada Year Book, 1956*, 181–90.

11 *Canada Year Book, 1955*, 1328; and *Canada Year Book, 1956*, 193.

12 Thomson, *Louis St. Laurent: Canadian*, 385.

13 Quoted in Harvey Hickey, "Opening of Parliament to Be on Television; CBC Promises Dignity," *G&M*, 22 Dec. 1954, 3.

14 Paul Martin, House of Commons, *Debates*, 1 June 1954; "Canada to Ban Heroin Imports after New Year's," *G&M*, 2 June 1954, 10; and

An Act to Amend the Opium and Narcotic Drug Act, *Canada Year Book, 1955*, 1326.

15 "Would Restrict Sale of Headache Tablets," *G&M*, 16 Feb. 1954, 5.

16 "Survey Indicates 1953 Polio Worst on Record in Canada," *G&M*, 12 Jan. 1954, 2; and "Doctors Hopeful Polio Beaten in Few Years," *G&M*, 18 Feb. 1954, 1.

17 "Fires and Rioting Damage Kingston Penitentiary," CBC Archives, accessed 3 Mar. 2022, https://www.cbc.ca/player/play/2312813716; Ralph Hyman, "Nothing-to-Lose Type of Convict Blamed for Riot," *G&M*, 16 Aug. 1954, 1; and Phil Jones, "Cleanup Begins at Kingston: Probers Find Evidence Mass Escape Plotted," *G&M*, 17 Aug. 1954, 1.

18 "Toronto's Subway Opens," CBC Archives, accessed 3 Mar. 2022, https://www.cbc.ca/archives/entry/torontos-subway-opens; and "The Wrath of Hurricane Hazel," CBC Archives, accessed 3 Mar. 2022, https://www.cbc.ca/archives/topic/the-wrath-of-hurricane-hazel.

19 Ryan Edwardson, *Canadian Content: Culture and the Quest for Nationhood* (Toronto: University of Toronto Press, 2008), 100.

20 "Printing Unions by a Single Vote Move to Support CCF Candidates," *G&M*, 3 May 1954, 3; and "TV Temptation of Devil, Says Anglican Layman," *G&M*, 18 Nov. 1954, 5.

21 "Unemployment, Immigration Said Top Issues," *G&M*, 24 June 1954, 5; Ken Johnstone, "How Plante and Drapeau Licked the Montreal Underworld," *Maclean's*, 1 Dec. 1954, 12–13; "Chief, 19 Police Ousted by Montreal Vice Prober," *Daily Boston Globe*, 9 Oct. 1954, 2; Canadian Institute of Public Opinion, "Only Quebec Agrees Whipping Criminals Is Best Treatment," *TDS*, 6 Feb. 1954, 3; and Lionel Groulx, "Methods of Education," in *Canadian Political Thought*, ed. Forbes, 252.

22 *Canada Year Book, 1955*, 1324–5, 1328.

23 Blair Fraser, "Backstage at Ottawa," *Maclean's*, 15 Oct. 1954, 118–19.

24 "Seaway Work Set by U.S. and Canada," *NYT*, 19 Aug. 1954, 1.

25 Harvey Hickey, "Harris New Finance Minister; Campney Takes Defense Post: G. Marler Acquires Transport," *G&M*, 2 July 1954, 1–2.

26 "Gallup Canada," MacOdrum Library, Carleton University (Nov. 1954), https://library.carleton.ca/find/data/gallup-canada.

27 Harvey Hickey, "PM Ready to Act: Call Special Session If Railwaymen Strike," *G&M*, 29 July 1954, 9; and quoted in "The Club in the Closet," *G&M*, 19 Aug. 1954, 6.

28 Ron Haggart, "CCL Supports CCF, Labor Minister Booed," *G&M*, 29 Sept. 1954, 1.

29 Thomson, *Louis St. Laurent: Canadian*, 377; "Centralization Threat to Nation Drew Tells Party," *G&M*, 17 Mar. 1954, 3; Harvey Hickey, "Vote Confidence in Drew: George Hees New President of PC National Association," *G&M*, 17 Mar. 1954, 1; and quoted in "Faith in Drew Reaffirmed: PC Student

Federation Urges Firm Policy with U.S.; Ottawa Rapped," *G&M*, 8 Feb. 1954, 3.

30 Harvey Hickey, "St. Laurent Uncertain about Asking Renewal of Emergency Powers," *G&M*, 23 Mar. 1954, 1; and George Bain, "Ottawa Drops Controversial Act: Emergency Powers Ended, PM Hopes Ordinary Law Sufficient," *G&M*, 30 Apr. 1954, 1.

31 House of Commons, *Debates*, 5 Feb. 1954; and Harvey Hickey, "Socred Wants Probe along McCarthy Lines," *G&M*, 20 Jan. 1954, 1.

32 "Coldwell Urges Trade with Russia, Red China to Ease Unemployment," *G&M*, 6 Mar. 1954, 5; Walter D. Young, *Anatomy of a Party: The National CCF, 1932–1961* (Toronto: University of Toronto Press, 1969); "Coldwell Re-elected Leader: Rhee Proposal Scored by CCFers," *G&M*, 31 July 1954, 10; "Defense Plans Held Obsolete; Cost Cut Urged," *G&M*, 24 May 1954, 1; Ronald Haggart, "MPs Proposal: More Aid to Asia Asked by CCFer," *G&M*, 12 Apr. 1954, 14; and "Why a Billion?" *G&M*, 2 Aug. 1954, 6.

33 Wilfred List, "Federation of Labor Opposes CCF," *G&M*, 18 Jan. 1954, 2.

34 "Socreds Move Here: Party Shifts National Headquarters from Edmonton, Plans to Organize East," *G&M*, 30 Jan. 1954, 4; "Limited Issue of New Money Asked by Low," *G&M*, 12 May 1954, 36; and S.R. Patterson, quoted in "The Status of Social Credit," *G&M*, 28 July 1954, 6.

35 George Bain, "The Wordiest MP in Ottawa," *Maclean's*, 15 Sept. 1954, 17, 94.

36 "A Brief History of the Atlantic Provinces Economic Council," Atlantic Provinces Economic Council, accessed 4 Mar. 2022, https://www.apec-econ.ca/about-us/briefhistory/; and Gerald Freeman, "Moncton Probable HQ: Atlantic Provinces Form Development Council," *G&M*, 29 Sept. 1954, 17.

37 Ralph Blackmore, "Seaway Problems Ahead: Maritimes May Ask Ottawa Help," *G&M*, 7 Oct. 1954, 28; and Raymond B. Blake, "Newfoundland, and Term 29: The Failure of Intergovernmentalism," *Acadiensis* 41, no. 1 (2012), 56–7.

38 Harvey Hickey, "Queen's Park, Ottawa Discuss Gas Pipeline," *G&M*, 20 Jan. 1954, 3.

39 Quoted in "Asks Proof Extra Aid Needed for B.C. Relief," *G&M*, 23 Dec. 1954, 24; and Barman, *The West beyond the West*, 301.

40 Quoted in Robert Duffy, "'Handcuffs Instead of Reins': Duplessis Hits Back at PM," *G&M*, 27 Sept. 1954, 1; Pelletier, *Years of Impatience, 1950–1960*, 60; and quoted in Thomson, *Louis St. Laurent: Canadian*, 377.

41 Robert Duffy, "Deadlock Finally Broken: St. Laurent-Duplessis Parley Points Way to Tax Changes," *G&M*, 6 Oct. 1954, 1; "Premiers Approve Plan for Tax Conference," *G&M*, 7 Oct. 1954, 2; House of Commons, *Debates*, 1 June 1954; and "St. Laurent Confident: Sure BNAA Will Be Amended," *G&M*, 31 May 1954, 3.

42 "Returns Exceed Premier's Forecast: Frost Surplus $58,400,000, Tax Rentals Boost Total for Ontario," *G&M*, 13 Feb. 1954, 1; Stephen Azzi, *Walter*

Gordon and the Rise of Canadian Nationalism (Montreal: McGill-Queen's University Press, 1999), 24; and Grey Hamilton, "Federal Projects Sought by Frost as Aid to Jobless," *G&M*, 20 Nov. 1954, 1.

43 "Optimism Is Not Enough," *G&M*, 14 July 1954, 6.

44 *Canada Year Book, 1955*, 1325; and Constitution Act, 1982, Section 43.

45 "New N.S. Premier, 39, Is Canada's Youngest," *G&M*, 11 Sept. 1954, 28.

46 Maureen Finlayson, "Cultural Sustainability of African Canadian Heritage: Engaging Students in Learning, the Past, the Present and the Future," *Improving Schools* 18 no. 2 (2015), 143.

47 John Mosher, "Blow to Newfoundland Premier: Man He Once Praised Extorted Hundreds of Thousands, Is Charged by Smallwood," *G&M*, 24 Apr. 1954, 7; "Smallwood Heard in Valdmanis Trial," *G&M*, 6 Aug. 1954, 30; "Plea Surprises Newfoundland: Valdmanis Admits $200,000 Fraud," *G&M*, 16 Sept. 1954, 10; and quoted in Bassler, *Alfred Valdmanis*, 369.

48 "Ottawa Briefs," *G&M*, 15 May 1954, 11; and James L. Kenn and Andrew Secord, "Public Power for Industry: A Re-Examination of the New Brunswick Case, 1940–1960," *Acadiensis* 30, no. 2 (2001), 99, 103.

49 "Ask Doubled Allowance: Quebec Socred Group Calls for End of Taxes," *G&M*, 7 Sept. 1954, 24; Maurice Lamontagne, *Le Fédéralisme Canadien: Évolution et Problèmes* (Québec: Presses universitaires Laval, 1954); quoted in "Quebec Tax Fight Lost, Professor's Book Holds," *G&M*, 27 May 1954, 11; and Thomson, *Louis St. Laurent: Canadian*, 377.

50 "Ontario By-Elections: Three PC Victories: Votes Show Confidence in Frost," *G&M*, 17 Sept. 1954, 1.

51 "Sickness Benefit Plan among CCF Proposals," *G&M*, 7 Apr. 1954, 12; and "Probe Party Funds, CCF Leader Urges," *G&M*, 7 Aug. 1954, 5.

52 "Liberals Pick Oliver to Lead Party Again," *G&M*, 10 Apr. 1954, 1; and quoted in "Liberal Stresses Need for Policy," *G&M*, 8 Apr. 1954, 17.

53 J.A.M. Cook, "Farm Revolt Seen Gaining Strength May Spread from Prairies to East," *G&M*, 11 Dec. 1954, 1; Carrol L. Jaques, *Unifarm: A Story of Conflict & Change* (Calgary: University of Calgary Press, 2001), 19; "Provincial Union Has 1,045 Locals," and "National Union Needed," *Leader-Post* (Regina), 1 Dec. 1954, 23; "MFU Says Banks Demanding Mortgages for Machinery," *Leader-Post* (Regina), 16 Sept. 1954, 1; "$1.50 Floor Price Sought by Farmers," *Washington Post and Times Herald*, 13 June 1954, M26; and "The Road to Depression," *G&M*, 14 Dec. 1954, 6.

54 "Paper Says PC's Would Replace Provincial Chief," *G&M*, 27 Mar. 1954, 15.

55 Michael Best, "From Manitoba," *G&M*, 16 July 1954, 6.

56 "20 Per Cent Drop in Farm Income Seen by Douglas," *G&M*, 25 Aug. 1954, 3; and Eldon Stonehouse, "Douglas Sees Province as Supplier to East," *G&M*, 9 Sept. 1954, 5.

57 "Record Alberta Budget Aids Pensioners, Blind," *G&M*, 6 Mar. 1954, 3; and Finkel, *The Social Credit Phenomenon in Alberta*, 101, 128.

58 "Fears Newsmen to Be Peddlers of Handouts," *G&M*, 13 May 1954, 5; Court Dismisses Writer's Appeal from B.C. Ruling," *G&M*, 23 June 1954, 8; and "Dangerous Precedent Seen in B.C. Court Libel Ruling," *G&M*, 6 Nov. 1954, 3.

59 Donaghy, "The Politics of Accommodation," 315.

60 Quoted in Thomson, *Louis St. Laurent: Canadian*, 364, 369.

61 Pearson, *Words and Occasions*, 128–34.

62 "Canadian Statistics in 1955," Statistics Canada, accessed 17 Feb. 2022, https://www65.statcan.gc.ca/acyb07/acyb07_0011-eng.htm; Dave McIntosh, "Korea Troops Leaving Soon for Canada," *G&M*, 20 Aug. 1954, 1; "Two More Units Canada-Bound for Christmas," *G&M*, 20 Nov. 1954, 3; and Bercuson, *Blood on the Hills*, 222.

63 "Cheering Troops Greet St. Laurent in West Germany," *G&M*, 12 Feb. 1954, 3; and "Occupation or Security? Study Canada Army Status," *G&M*, 24 Sept. 1954, 19.

64 Quoted in *Canada Year Book, 1955,* 130.

65 Dag Hammarskjöld Library, Resolutions Adopted by the General Assembly at Its Ninth Session, accessed 4 Mar. 2022, https://research.un.org/en/docs/ga/quick/regular/9; and quoted in "Canada Opposes Motion Covering Racial Question," *G&M*, 9 Dec. 1954, 28.

66 Dag Hammarskjöld Library, Resolutions Adopted by the General Assembly at Its Ninth Session, accessed 4 Mar. 2022, https://research.un.org/en/docs/ga/quick/regular/9; and quoted in "Canadians Tell Nation's Stand on UN Projects," *G&M*, 13 Oct. 1954, 32.

67 Thomas J. Hamilton, "Vishinsky Rejects Key to Arms Plan," *NYT*, 21 Oct. 1954, 4.

68 Blair Fraser, "Backstage at Ottawa," *Maclean's*, 15 Sept. 1954, 6, 94–5; and Harvey Hickey, "No Illusions about Task: Canada's Role in Indo-China Called Onerous," *G&M*, 29 July 1954, 1.

69 William Harcourt, "Pearson Supports Eisenhower: Canada Backs Atomic Pool," *G&M*, 24 Sept. 1954, 1; *Canada Year Book, 1955*, 1324; and "Gouzenko Data Revealed," *NYT*, 14 Apr. 1954, 14.

70 Quoted in Dana Adams Schmidt, "Canada Cautions U.S. on 'New Look,'" *NYT*, 16 Mar. 1954, 1; and quoted in "Unity Need Emphasized by Pearson," *G&M*, 5 June 1954, 1.

71 Canadian Institute of Public Opinion, "56 P.C. Would Sell Russia Anything but War Goods," *TDS*, 26 May 1954, 13.

72 Quoted in Azzi, *Walter Gordon*, 36.

1955

1 Quoted in Blair Fraser, "Backstage at Ottawa," *Maclean's*, 20 Aug. 1955, 6.
2 W.R. Wheatley, "Admirers Hurl Eggs, Tomatoes, Tear Gas: Richard Riot Ends Game, NHL Chief Attacked; Mob Loots 30 Stores," *G&M*, 18 Mar. 1955, 1; "Canadiens Fans Riot in Montreal over Richard Suspension," CBC Archives, accessed 4 Mar. 2022, https://www.cbc.ca/archives /entry/1955-canadiens-fans-riot-in-montreal-over-richard-suspension; and Sidney Katz, "The Strange Forces behind the Richard Hockey Riot," *Maclean's*, 17 Sept. 1955, 13.
3 "Tram Fare Riot Shut Down Streets," *Montreal Gazette*, 10 Dec. 1955. Reproduced 10 Dec. 2011, D28.
4 "Ontario Sparks Canada to 15,601,000 Growth," *G&M*, 3 Aug. 1955, 3; Statistics Canada, "Total Fertility Rate, Canada, 1926 to 2011," accessed 4 Mar. 2022, https://www150.statcan.gc.ca/n1/pub/11-630-x/2014002 /c-g/desc1-eng.htm; and Ken. W. MacTaggart, "Statistical Limb: Canadians Healthiest in 1955," *G&M*, 30 Dec. 1955, 15.
5 "The Baby Crop," *G&M*, 8 July 1955, 6; and "Population Growth Too Slow," *G&M*, 25 Aug. 1955, 6.
6 D.A. MacGibbon, quoted in "Too Much Population; Professor Broods on War from Hunger," *G&M*, 7 June 1955, 17.
7 *Canada Year Book, 1956*, 1233; and "6th Largest in Routes: CPA Launches Service over Pole to Europe, *G&M*, 4 June 1955, 9.
8 Harvey Hickey, "Ottawa Ready to Give More Aid for Building Trans-Canada Highway," *G&M*, 15 Nov. 1955, 1; and E.F. Roots, "Canadian 'Operation Franklin', 1955," *Polar Record* 8, no. 53 (May 1956), 157–60.
9 A.O.C. Cole, "Hydro Reveals Plans: Des Joachmis A-Power Site, Electricity Expected in 3 Years," *G&M*, 3 June 1955, 1; and "Up to $8,000,000 Ottawa's Share of A-Plant Cost," *G&M*, 7 June 1955, 1.
10 *Canada Year Book, 1956*, viii.
11 John LeBlanc, "TLC, CCL Ratify Terms of Merger, Select New Name," *G&M*, 10 May 1955, 1; "Stronger Labor Movement," *TDS*, 11 May 1955, 6; and Robert Duffy, "Labor Merger Said Poser for Catholic Union," *G&M*, 11 May 1955, 9.
12 "The Strike in Obsolete," *G&M*, 29 Jan. 1955, 6; James Lyle, quoted in "Ford Contract Labor Victory, Unionist Says," *G&M*, 4 Feb. 1955, 8; and "Resume Work at de Havilland on Thursday," *G&M*, 14 Nov. 1955, 1.
13 "Ottawa Scene," *G&M*, 22 Oct. 1955, 16.
14 Canadian Institute of Public Opinion, "Inadequate Say Majority of Unemployment Policy," *TDS*, 16 Mar. 1955, 27; Canadian Institute of Public Opinion, "69 P.C. See Unemployment Worse in Coming Months," *TDS*, 12 Feb. 1955, 44.

15 *Canada Year Book, 1956,* 151, 155.

16 *Canada Year Book, 1956,* 128–32; and *Canada Year Book, 1957–58,* 98–102.

17 "CBC-TV Visits a Residential School in 1955," CBC Archives, accessed 4 Mar. 2022, https://www.cbc.ca/archives/cbc-tv-visits-a-residential-school-in-1955-1.4667021; House of Commons, *Debates,* 29 Apr. 1955; and "End to Indian Schools Favored by Pickersgill," *G&M,* 1 Feb. 1955, 5.

18 Quoted in G.W. Chivers, "Financing the Trans-Canada Pipeline," *G&M,* 28 Mar. 1955, 6; and Blair Fraser, "Backstage at Ottawa," *Maclean's,* 20 Aug. 1955, 6.

19 Quoted in Blair Fraser, "Backstage at Ottawa," *Maclean's,* 20 Aug. 1955, 6.

20 House of Commons, *Debates,* 7 June 1955.

21 Harvey Hickey, "Debate Resumes Today: Socialist Issue Seen behind Howe's Powers," *G&M,* 13 June 1955, 19; and "Canada: An Advancing Opposition," *The Round Table* 45, no. 180 (1955), 373.

22 Quoted in "Senate Merely Rubber Stamp, Hees Protests," *G&M,* 9 Feb. 1955, 10; Grey Hamilton, "Opposition Parties Support PC's Proposal: Government Members Reject Drew's Plan for Reform of Senate," *G&M,* 13 July 1955, 7; House of Commons, *Debates,* 12 July 1955; and "And So to Bed," *G&M,* 27 May 1955, 6.

23 "Would Abolish Senate: Labor Asks Veto Right by Canadian Provinces," *G&M,* 30 June 1955, 3; "Would Appoint Women to 22 Senate Vacancies," *G&M,* 28 June 1955, 14; and Raymond Daniell, "13 New Senators Named by Canada," *NYT,* 29 July 1955, 5.

24 Clark Davey, "Broader Divorce Laws Turned Down by Senate," *G&M,* 24 Mar. 1955, 3.

25 "Canada: The New Session," *The Round Table* 45, no. 179 (1955), 286.

26 David Lewis, *A Socialist Takes Stock* (Toronto: Ontario Woodsworth Memorial Foundation, 1955).

27 Harvey Hickey, "Thatcher Resigns from CCF Party, Surprises House," *G&M,* 23 Apr. 1955, 1; and House of Commons, *Debates,* 2 May 1955.

28 House of Commons, *Debates,* 20 Jan. 1955; and George Bain, "CCF House Members Divided in Three Ways on Rearmed Germany," *G&M,* 22 Jan. 1955, 2.

29 "Criticism Draws Fire: Low Challenges Hees to Debate," *G&M,* 7 Nov. 1955, 4; quoted in Bruce Levett, "Maybe in 1957: Low Predicts Socreds Will Roll into Ottawa," *G&M,* 31 Oct. 1955, 3; and "Heart Attack Hits Leader of Social Credit," *G&M,* 1 Dec. 1955, 2.

30 Quoted in "CCF Harbors Reds, Liberal Leader Claims," *G&M,* 18 Apr. 1955, 5; "Budget in Brief," *G&M,* 6 Apr. 1955, 1; and House of Commons, *Debates,* 5 Apr. 1955.

31 Bothwell, Drummond, and English, *Canada Since 1945*, 168; and "But
    Competition Heavy: Another Record Year of Construction Seen," *G&M*, 18
    Jan. 1955, 20.

32 *Canada Year Book, 1956*, 1230–1.

33 "Highest Court Upholds Ottawa's Labor Code," *G&M*, 29 June 1955, 35.

34 Harvey Hickey, "Opening Gun of Conference: St. Laurent Offers Provinces
    Sliding Scale of Jobless Aid," *G&M*, 27 Apr. 1955, 1; George Bain, "Ottawa
    Letter," *G&M*, 30 Apr. 1955, 6; and Grey Hamilton, "Provinces Missed Boat
    in 1945, PM Claims; He's Glad They Did," *G&M*, 30 Apr. 1955, 1.

35 Harvey Hickey, "Ottawa and Provinces Facing Fiscal Discord," *G&M*, 15
    Apr. 1955, 1.

36 R.M. Burns, "Intergovernmental Relations in Canada," 18.

37 "Premiers Outline Provincial Proposals as Significant Conference Begins,"
    G&M, 27 Apr. 1955, 8; and "Deficit Forecast in B.C. Budget; Some Taxes
    Cut," *G&M*, 5 Feb. 1955, 13.

38 Quoted in *Proceedings of the Conference of Federal-Provincial Governments,
    October 3–6, 1955* (Ottawa: Queen's Printer, 1955), 9, 38.

39 Robert Duffy, "Premier Silent: Reaction of Duplessis No. 1 Question Mark,"
    G&M, 5 Oct. 1955, 8; and William Kinmond, "Frost Tells Conference
    Economic Facts of Life as Ontario Sees Them," *G&M*, 6 Oct. 1955, 1.

40 *Proceedings of the Conference of Federal-Provincial Governments, October 3–6,
    1955*, 67.

41 Quoted in Harvey Hickey, "Ottawa Parley Ends; Views on Value Vary,"
    G&M, 7 Oct. 1955, 1.

42 *Proceedings of the Preliminary Meeting of the Federal-Provincial Conference,
    April 26* (Queen's Printer: Ottawa, 1955); and *Proceedings of the Conference of
    Federal-Provincial Governments, October 3–6, 1955*, 23.

43 Harvey Hickey, "Ottawa Ready to Give More Aid for Building Trans-
    Canada Highway," *G&M*, 15 Nov. 1955, 1.

44 "Revenue of Provinces Rises to Record Level," *G&M*, 28 July 1955, 9.

45 Herbert L. Pottle, *Newfoundland, Dawn without Light: Politics, Power
    and People in the Smallwood Era* (St. John's: Breakwater, 1979), 13; and
    "Newfoundland Politics Likely Ottawa Subject," *G&M*, 25 Apr. 1955, 12.

46 Harvey Hickey, "Provinces Need Aid: Smallwood," *G&M*, 19 Oct. 1955, 1.

47 James L. Kenn and Andrew Secord, "Public Power for Industry: A
    Re-examination of the New Brunswick Case, 1940–1960," *Acadiensis* 30, no.
    2 (2001), 100; and Harvey Hickey, "Premier States Case: Province Needs
    Cheap Hydro," *G&M*, 27 Oct. 1955, 1.

48 Quoted in "Premiers Outline Provincial Proposals as Significant
    Conference Begins," *G&M*, 27 Apr. 1955, 8.

49 Peter MacDonald, "Engineering Feat Fulfills Dream of Late Premier,"
    G&M, 15 Aug. 1955, 3; "Canso Causeway Links Cape Breton to Mainland,"

CBC Archives, accessed 5 Mar. 2022, https://www.cbc.ca/archives
/entry/1955-canso-causeway-links-cape-breton-to-mainland; and Harvey
Hickey, "New Export Policy: Ottawa Pays Subsidy on Slack Coal in N.S.,"
G&M, 14 June 1955, 3.

50 Herbert F. Quinn, *The Union Nationale: A Study in Quebec Nationalism*
(Toronto: University of Toronto Press, 1970), 52–3; Robert Duffy, "Quebec
Opposition Unity Urged," *G&M*, 5 Nov. 1955, 3; Michael B. Stein, *The
Dynamics of Right-Wing Protest: A Political Analysis of Social Credit in Quebec*
(Toronto: University of Toronto Press, 1973), 72; and quoted in "Quebec
CCF Changes Name, Retains Policy," *G&M*, 29 Aug. 1955, 12.

51 "Ontario's Indians to Vote Thursday," *NYT*, 5 June 1955, 5.

52 Lex Schrage, "25-Point Liberal Manifesto Pledges Reforms in Ontario,"
G&M, 5 May 1955, 1; "Liberal Chances Best Since 37, Oliver Says," *G&M*,
24 Jan. 1955, 4; "Federal Machine to Help Liberals at Ontario Polls," *G&M*,
25 Apr. 1955, 1; and "Revolutionary Workers: 14 Expelled by Ontario CCF
as Members of Alien Party," *G&M*, 9 Apr. 1955, 1.

53 M.S. Donnelly, "Parliamentary Government in Manitoba," *Canadian
Journal of Economics and Political Science* 23, no. 1 (1957), 31; and quoted in
Michael Best, "Letter from Manitoba," *G&M*, 12 July 1955, 6; and Michael
Best, "Letter from Manitoba," *G&M*, 26 Nov. 1955, 6.

54 E.N. Davis, "Letter from Saskatchewan," *G&M*, 7 Sept. 1955, 6; E.N.
Davis, "Letter from Saskatchewan," *G&M*, 6 July 1955, 6; "Face to Face,"
G&M, 13 July 1955, 6; and Milton Roemer, "'Socialized' Health Services in
Saskatchewan," *Social Research* 25, no. 1 (1958), 99.

55 Advertisement, *Calgary Herald*, 25 June 1955, 8; "MLAs Had Money in Bank:
Alberta Snap Election Called after Charges by Opposition," *G&M*, 13 May
1955, 1; "Nominations for June Vote Completed by Liberals, CCF," *Edmonton
Journal*, 11 June 1955, 23; and Alvin Finkel, "The Cold War, Alberta Labour,
and the Social Credit Regime," *Labour/Le Travail* 21 (1988), 147.

56 Quoted in Harvey Hickey, "Attack on Drew Resented: National PC
Meeting Bars B.C. Party Leader," *G&M*, 9 May 1955, 1–2; and Gordon
McCallum, "Letter from British Columbia," *G&M*, 5 Oct. 1955, 6.

57 Hilliker and Barry, *Canada's Department of External Affairs*, 97.

58 Bercuson, *Blood on the Hills*, 221.

59 *Canada Year Book, 1957–58*, 113.

60 The North Atlantic Treaty (Washington D.C. 4 Apr. 1949); House of
Commons, *Debates*, 20 Jan. and 24 May 1955; and Pearson, *Mike: The
Memoirs, vol. 2: 1948–1957*, 91–2.

61 Quoted in Hilliker and Barry, *Canada's Department of External Affairs*, 112.

62 "Progress of Russians Impressive: Sinclair," *G&M*, 21 Sept. 1955, 11.

63 "Impressions of the Russians and Their Leaders," in Pearson, *Words and
Occasions*, 133–5.

64 English, *The Worldly Years*, 120.
65 House of Commons, *Debates*, 24 Mar. 1955; and "St. Laurent to Report on London Meeting," *G&M*, 14 Feb. 1955, 8.
66 Quoted in Greg Donaghy, "C'est la Guerre: The Diplomacy of Mike Pearson and Paul Martin," in *Mike's World: Lester B. Pearson and Canadian External Affairs*, ed. Asa McKercher and Galen Roger Perras (Vancouver: UBC Press, 2017), 92; and John W. Holmes, *The Shaping of Peace: Canada and the Search for World Order, vol. 2: 1943–1957*, 345.
67 Holmes, *The Shaping of Peace*, 342; and Kenneth McNaught, "Ottawa and Washington Look at the U.N.," *Foreign Affairs* 33 (1955), 673.
68 "A Word to Washington," *G&M*, 27 Aug. 1955, 6.
69 House of Commons, *Debates*, 14 Feb. 1955; "Plenty of Nothing," *G&M*, 16 Feb. 1955, 6; and Alan Harvey, "St. Laurent's View: PM's Talks of Value to All," *G&M*, 9 Feb. 1955, 1.
70 "Canada Ranks Third in Its Contributions to the Colombo Plan," *G&M*, 26 Nov. 1955, 33; and "Built by Prairie Wheat: Pearson Opens Bengal Canada Dam," *G&M*, 2 Nov. 1955, 1.
71 *Canada Year Book, 1955*, 138; and quoted in David C. Elder, "Canada's Diplomacy in Africa," in *Canada-Africa Relations: Looking Back, Looking Ahead*, ed. Rohinton P. Medhora and Yiagadeesen Samy (Waterloo, ON: Centre for International Governance Innovation, 2013), 25–6.
72 Quoted in Hilliker and Barry, *Canada's Department of External Affairs*, 114–15.
73 "Pearson's Visit Could Touch Off Third War: Low," *G&M*, 29 Oct. 1955, 8.
74 Kelley and Trebilcock, *The Making of the Mosaic*, 341–2; and Barrington Walker, "Immigration Policy, Colonization, and the Development of a White Canada," in *Canada and the Third World: Overlapping Histories*, ed. Karen Dubinsky, Sean Mills, and Scott Rutherford (Toronto: University of Toronto Press, 2016), 55.

1956

1 House of Commons, *Debates*, 14 May 1956.
2 Hilliker and Barry, *Canada's Department of External Affairs*, 181; and "TAT-1 Transatlantic Telephone Cable Links Canada and U.K.," CBC Archives, accessed 5 Mar. 2022, https://www.cbc.ca/archives/entry/1956-tat-1-transatlantic-telephone-cable-links-canada-and-uk.
3 "Massey Return Ends Aerial Trip of 10,000 Miles," *G&M*, 6 Apr. 1956, 17.
4 *Maclean's*, 28 Apr. 1956, 9.
5 *Canada Year Book, 1957–58*, xi, xiii, and xv.
6 "Money Policy Upheld: Canada Lays 'Credit Squeeze' to Expanding Economy," *NYT*, 26 June 1956, 51.

7 "Canada Ponders Smelter in West: Japan Seeks Iron, Uranium, Minister Reports," *NYT*, 13 Nov. 1956, 66.

8 House of Commons, *Debates*, 28 Nov. 1956.

9 *Canada Year Book, 1957–58*, 190–1; and "Metro Tops Houston, LA as Fastest Growing City," *G&M*, 6 Mar. 1956, 5.

10 *Canada Year Book, 1957–58*, 420–1; and House of Commons, *Debates*, 16 Jan. 1956.

11 "Cut Price Surplus Sale Backed by Farm Group," *G&M*, 27 Jan. 1956, 38.

12 "Russian Trade Group May Talk Agreement to Buy Surplus Wheat," *G&M*, 1 Feb. 1956, 1.

13 "Wheat Monopoly Outdated," *G&M*, 25 Sept. 1956, 6.

14 An Act to Promote Equal Pay for Female Employees, *4–5 Elizabeth II*, chap. 38. https://historyofrights.ca/wp-content/uploads/statutes/CN_Female_Em.pdf.

15 "Women in the Canadian Workforce," CBC Archives, accessed 5 Mar. 2022, https://www.cbc.ca/archives/entry/women-in-the-canadian -workforce-of-1956; and *Canada Year Book, 1957–58*, 769.

16 "Dress Manufacturers Claim Canada Needs Thrice as Many Women," *G&M*, 21 Jan. 1956, 36; quoted in Ralph Hyman, "Auto Firms Present Briefs: Canada's Road System Antique, Sale Charges," *G&M*, 1 Feb. 1956, 5; and "Ottawa Favors Raw Products, Inquiry Hears," *G&M*, 2 Feb. 1956, 1–2.

17 Quoted in Clark Davey, "Ontario Power Needs Alberta Gas," *G&M*, 19 May 1956, 6; and quoted William Kinmond, "Investing in the Future: Frost Declares Ontario Victim of Own Prosperity," *G&M*, 27 Jan. 1956, 1.

18 "Quebec Stand Hampers Study of Economy," *G&M*, 18 Jan. 1956, 17; and W.L. Gordon, *Preliminary Report, Royal Commission on Canada's Economic Prospects* (Ottawa: 1956).

19 "Will Not Launch Canada Council this Session: PM," *G&M*, 13 Jan. 1956, 8; and House of Commons, *Debates*, 18 June 1956.

20 Jack Dobson, "University Construction to Get Half of Canada Council's $100,000,000," *G&M*, 13 Nov. 1956, 1.

21 "A Disgraceful Comparison," *TDS*, 27 Feb. 1956, 6; and quoted in "Due in Decade: Scientist: Return of Prohibition Predicted," *G&M*, 3 Mar. 1956, 5.

22 Blair Fraser, "Backstage at Ottawa," *Maclean's*, 28 Apr. 1956, 105; "Frost's Ottawa Trip to Discuss Tax Pact Not Politics – Friends," *TDS*, 18 July 1956, 1; and Blair Fraser, "Backstage at Ottawa," *Maclean's*, 1 Sept. 1956, 8, 59.

23 "Party to Decide His Future Role, Solon Low Says," *G&M*, 9 Apr. 1956, 3; "Will Stay on Job as Party Head, Solon Low Says," *G&M*, 10 Nov. 1956, 7; and "Social Credit Quitting Toronto for Ottawa HQ," *G&M*, 22 Dec. 1956, 5.

24 "The Winnipeg Declaration of Principles (1956)," Socialist History Project, accessed 5 Mar. 2022, http://www.socialisthistory.ca/Docs/CCF /Winnipeg.htm.

25 Thomson, *Louis St. Laurent: Canadian*, 412.

26 "Finance Minister: Says Heavy Spending Is Threat to Economy," *G&M*, 9 Nov. 1956, 28.

27 Blair Fraser, "Backstage at Ottawa," *Maclean's*, 28 Apr. 1956, 105.

28 Constitution Act, 1982, Section 36.

29 House of Commons, *Debates*, 16 July 1956; and Édison Roy-César, Library of Parliament, "Canada's Equalization Formula," accessed 5 Mar. 2022, https://lop.parl.ca/sites/PublicWebsite/default/en_CA/ResearchPublications/200820E.

30 Ronald Haggart, "Final Vote on Pipeline Due: PM Gives Fourth Closure Notice," *G&M*, 5 June 1956, 1.

31 Blair Fraser, "Backstage at Ottawa," *Maclean's*, 18 Feb. 1956, 57.

32 House of Commons, *Debates*, 8 and 14 May 1956.

33 House of Commons, *Debates*, 8 May and 1 June 1956; and Harold Morrison, "'Black Friday': Exhausted Speaker Attended by Nurse after Furor in House," *G&M*, 2 June 1956, 1.

34 Hugh G. Thorburn, "Parliament and Policy-Making: The Case of the Trans-Canada Gas Pipeline," *Canadian Journal of Economics and Political Science* 33, no. 4 (1957), 528–31; and Blair Fraser, "Backstage at Ottawa," *Maclean's*, 21 July 1956, 8, 45.

35 Canadian Institute of Public Opinion, "Big Majority Still Want Private Cash in Pipeline," *TDS*, 20 June 1956, 58.

36 Thomson, *Louis St. Laurent: Canadian*, 443.

37 Quoted in "Quebec and the Speaker," *TDS*, 13 July 1956, 6.

38 George Bain, "Minding Your Business," *G&M*, 10 Dec. 1956, 6.

39 Harvey Hickey, "Balcer Says Quebec Slighted by Favorite," *G&M*, 14 Dec. 1956, 1; Raymond Daniell, "Canada Now Sees Pearson Staying: Out of Running for NATO Post," *NYT*, 16 Dec. 1956, 21; and quoted in J.E. Beliveau, "Diefenbaker Win Seen Ending Tory Chances in Quebec," *TDS*, 15 Dec. 1956, 3.

40 Clark Davey, "Ottawa Is Willing to Pay Half Cost of Health Plan," *G&M*, 27 Jan. 1956, 1; M. Taylor, *Health Insurance and Canadian Public Policy*, 220; Michael Best, "Letter from Manitoba," *G&M*, 2 Feb. 1956, 6; and "Hospital Plan Seen Introduced at Next Session," *G&M*, 12 Sept. 1956, 1.

41 William Kinmond, "Premier Presents Ontario's Case: Frost's New Tax Formula Would Bring in an Extra $250,000,000," *G&M*, 10 Mar. 1956, 9; J.W. Pickersgill, *The Liberal Party* (Toronto: McClelland & Stewart, 1962), 123; and Harvey Hickey, "Provinces Proposing Better Deal," *G&M*, 29 Feb. 1956, 1.

42 "Frost Blames Federal Tinkering for Threat to Canadian Economy," *G&M*, 26 Apr. 1956, 1.

43 Quoted in "Mr. Duplessis Says 'Yes,'" *TDS*, 27 Feb. 1956, 6; Robert Duffy, "Duplessis Proposes No Specific Demand," *G&M*, 10 Mar. 1956, 9; George

Bain, "Ottawa Letter," *G&M*, 12 Mar. 1956, 6; and quoted in "Frost's Ottawa Trip to Discuss Tax Pact Not Politics – Friends," *TDS*, 18 July 1956, 1.

44 Conrad, "The 1950s: The Decade of Development," 408.

45 "Leaders of Maritime Canada, New England Discuss Problems," *NYT*, 18 Sept. 1956, 41.

46 Conrad, "The 1950s: The Decade of Development," 404.

47 *Report of the Royal Commission of Inquiry on Constitutional Problems* (Quebec City, 1956); and Thomson, *Louis St. Laurent: Canadian*, 443.

48 E.N. Davis, "Letter from Saskatchewan," *G&M*, 19 June 1956, 6; and Blair Fraser, "Backstage at Ottawa," *Maclean's*, 4 Aug. 1956, 7.

49 Pierre Elliot Trudeau, *La grève de l'amiante* (Montréal: Éditions Cité libre, 1956); Pelletier, *Years of Impatience, 1950–1960*, 153–4; Robert Duffy, "Quebec Post-mortem: Socreds Said Poison to Liberals," *G&M*, 22 June 1956, 1; and quoted in Blair Fraser, "Backstage at Ottawa," *Maclean's*, 4 Aug. 1956, 7.

50 Quoted in Trudeau, *Federalism and the French Canadians*, 110–1.

51 Statutes of Quebec, 1–2 Elizabeth II, c. 32; and Quinn, *The Union Nationale*, 148–51.

52 "N.B. Voters Re-elect PC's by Big Margin," *G&M*, 19 June 1956, 1; "Voting for Dollars," *G&M*, 19 June 1956, 6; "PC Faith in Voters for Re-election Today Based on N.B. Record," *G&M*, 18 June 1956, 3; and quoted in "Socred Leader Says Candidates Victims of Fears," *G&M*, 20 June 1956, 3.

53 Quoted in "Newfoundland Again Strong for Liberals," *G&M*, 3 Oct. 1956, 1; and "Candidates Confident: Newfoundland Voters Go to Polls on Tuesday," *G&M*, 1 Oct. 1956, 7.

54 Quoted in Torchy Anderson, "B.C.'s Bennett Angles for Liberal, Tory Votes in War on 'Socialists,'" *TDS*, 20 Aug. 1956, 6; and "No B.C. Upset Expected," *TDS*, 17 Sept. 1956, 6.

55 Quoted in "B.C. Election: Votes Given Doukhobors, 19-Year-Olds," *G&M*, 18 Sept. 1956, 23; and "One Week to Go: Name Calling, Smears Mark Campaign in B.C.," *G&M*, 12 Sept. 1956, 7.

56 Conrad, "The 1950s: The Decade of Development," 387.

57 "Upset in Nova Scotia," *TDS*, 31 Oct. 1956, 6.

58 Quoted in James D. Morrison, "Around the Provinces: Post-Election Firings Are Out of Date," *G&M*, 30 Nov. 1956, 6.

59 James D. Morrison, "Around the Provinces: Maritime Liquor Laws," *G&M*, 13 Dec. 1956, 6.

60 M.S. Donnelly, *The Government of Manitoba* (Toronto: University of Toronto Press, 1963), 79–80; Michael Best, "Letter from Manitoba," *G&M*, 15 Mar. 1956, 6; Robert Collins, "The Splash Oil's Making in Manitoba," *Maclean's*, 29 Sept. 1956, 18–19; and "INCO Will Expand Nickel Output 50%," *NYT*, 6 Dec. 1956, 68.

61 Hilliker and Barry, *Canada's Department of External Affairs*, 105–6, 217; and Lindesay Parrott, "U.N. Completes 2 Councils," *NYT*, 21 Oct. 1955, 1.

62 Hilliker and Barry, *Canada's Department of External Affairs*, 128; and "Canada Ponders Smelter in West: Japan Seeks Iron, Uranium, Minister Reports," *G&M*, 13 Nov. 1956, 66.

63 "New Immigrant Source?" *G&M*, 14 Apr. 1956, 6; and quoted in "Hungarian Refugees Immigration Dream, Pickersgill Reports," *G&M*, 24 Dec. 1956, 13.

64 Major-Gen. W.H.S. Macklin, "The Costly Folly of Our Defense Policy," *Maclean's*, 18 Feb. 1956, 20–1, 51–7, quoted on 57.

65 "Atom Interchange Pact Signed by 3 Nations," *G&M*, 25 Sept. 1956, 15.

66 *Canada Year Book, 1957–58*, 1270.

67 "Ottawa Slightly Puzzled," *NYT*, 24 Feb. 1956, 5; George Bain, "Eisenhower Welcomes St. Laurent, Cortines at Goodwill Meeting," *G&M*, 27 Mar. 1956, 1; W.H. Lawrence, "Canada and Mexico Accept Bid by U.S. to Aid New Nations," *NYT*, 28 Mar. 1956, 1, 15; and Hilliker and Barry, *Canada's Department of External Affairs*, 365.

68 Thomson, *Louis St. Laurent: Canadian*, 444; Harvey Hickey, "Views of Prime Ministers Vary on Soviet New Look," *G&M*, 29 June 1956, 1; and House of Commons, *Debates*, 9 July 1956.

69 House of Commons, *Debates*, 28 July and 1 Aug. 1956.

70 Hilliker and Barry, *Canada's Department of External Affairs*, 124.

71 Geoffrey Pearson to Lester Pearson, 1 Nov. 1956, "Private Letters, Public Matters: the Pearsons, Father and Son, Correspond about Suez, NATO and the French," Presentation by Landon Pearson to the Retired Heads of Mission Association (RHOMA), Ottawa, 20 April 2011.

72 Quoted in Philip Deane, "Pearson Held Top Hope by Washington Circles to Revitalize NATO," *G&M*, 7 Sept. 1956, 1; "NATO Report Pushed: Committee of Three Plans Meeting in New York," *NYT*, 25 Sept. 1956, 28; "NATO Will Seek to Unify Policy," *NYT*, 15 Dec. 1956, 12; and Raymond Daniell, "Canada Now Sees Pearson Staying: Out of Running for NATO Post," *NYT*, 16 Dec. 1956, 21.

1957

1 "Senators' Views for and against Canada Council, *G&M*, 22 Feb. 1957, 7.

2 "Supersonic Routine for Arrow: Pearkes," *G&M*, 5 Oct. 1957, 5; and quoted in "Round the World in 96 Minutes," *NYT*, 6 Oct. 1957, 193.

3 "Find Eskimos Lived 500 Miles from Pole," *G&M*, 30 Aug. 1957, 13; Conrad, "The 1950s, The Decade of Development," 392; "The First Official Run," *G&M*, 25 Nov. 1957, 1; and "'Thinkers' Retreat," *G&M*, 13 July 1957, 6.

4 "Flu in Ontario Is Asian: Ottawa," *TDS*, 20 Sept. 1957, 1; "Classes Empty 4,300 Have Flu at Sudbury," *TDS*, 17 Sept. 1957, 25; and "Flu Halves Attendance at Camporee," *TDS*, 7 Oct. 1957, 8.

5 *Canada Year Book, 1957–58*, xi, xiii.

6 "Quebec Unionist Asks Eisenhower Block Alcan Aid," *G&M*, 24 May 1957, 25.

7 CBC Archives, "Trans-Canada Airlines Goes Non-stop," accessed 5 Mar. 2022, https://www.cbc.ca/archives/entry/trans-canada-airlines-goes-non-stop.

8 "Crash Worst in Canada," *G&M*, 12 Aug. 1957, 7.

9 Thomson, *Louis St. Laurent: Canadian*, 504, and Clark Davey, "Warm Welcome for Leader: PC Gain in Maritimes Expected," *G&M*, 6 May 1957, 1–2.

10 Canadian Institute of Public Opinion, "Only One in Five Think U.S. Influence Too Great," *TDS*, 29 June 1957, 36.

11 Peter Stursberg, "Gordon Report Delights Opposition," *TDS*, 12 Jan. 1957, 6.

12 "Glances at 1980," *G&M*, 11 Jan. 1957, 1.

13 *Canada Year Book, 1957–58*, 119.

14 Canadian Institute of Public Opinion, "Prosperous Canada No Major War in '57 View of 73 Per Cent," *TDS*, 2 Mar. 1957, 25; and "Distrust of Russia Drops from '50 Peak Among Canadians," *TDS*, 27 Nov. 1957, 8.

15 *Canada Year Book, 1957–58*, 146–9.

16 "Political Education Seen Lack," *G&M*, 16 Feb. 1957, 23; and "Close of Nominations Finds 868 Candidates in 265 Federal Seats," *G&M*, 28 May 1957, 1.

17 Herbert Whittaker, "Hamlet Death Scene Magnificent Climax at Stratford Opening," *G&M*, 2 July 1957, 1; House of Commons, *Debates*, 13 and 14 Feb. 1957; and "Senators' Views for and against Canada Council," *G&M*, 22 Feb. 1957, 7.

18 "*Billboard* Year-End Top 50 Singles of 1957," Wikipedia, accessed 5 Mar. 2022, https://en.wikipedia.org/wiki/Billboard_year-end_top_50_singles_of_1957.

19 "Commons Is Nearly Empty While Elvis Plays to 8,000," *G&M*, 4 Apr. 1957, 7.

20 Whitaker, *The Government Party*, 420.

21 Quoted in "Save Parliament PC Party's Aim, Michener States," *G&M*, 12 Mar. 1957, 5; Thomson, *Louis St. Laurent: Canadian*, 501–2; Fraser Robertson, "Plan Scored: Office Boys for Ottawa, Says Banker," *G&M*, 12 Mar. 1957, 1; and House of Commons, *Debates*, 28 Mar. 1957.

22 M.J. Coldwell, John Diefenbaker, and Solon Low, House of Commons, *Debates*, 11 Feb., 28 Mar., and 2 Apr. 1957; "Low Mortgage Rates Goal of Social Credit, Election Letters State," *G&M*, 18 Apr. 1957, 7; "$100 Old Age Pensions, 30 p.c. Income Tax Cut Social Credit Promise," *G&M*, 19

Apr. 1957, 1; and Clark Davey, "Favors Control of Finance Companies: CCF Five-Point Plan Calls for Action on Coyne's View of Bank's Use of Savings," *G&M*, 14 Mar. 1957, 3.

23 Quoted in Thomson, *Louis St. Laurent: Canadian*, 498; Liberal Election Pamphlet, "This Record Proves That Liberal Action Policies Get Results," accessed 5 Mar. 2022, https://www.poltext.org/sites/poltext.org/files /plateformesV2/Canada/CAN_PL_1957_LIB.pdf; quoted in Peter C. Newman, *Renegade in Power: The Diefenbaker Years* (Toronto: McClelland & Stewart, 1973), 49; House of Commons, *Debates*, 8 Apr. 1957; and "Liberal in Newfoundland: First Member of New Parliament Acclaimed," *G&M*, 14 May 1957, 1.

24 Canadian Institute of Public Opinion, "Tory Gains Slight in Ontario, Quebec West Shows Loss," *TDS*, 24 May 1957, 1; Robert Taylor, "See Liberal Victory 'Absolute Minimum' of 140 Safe Seats," *TDS*, 3 June 1957, 1; and Canadian Institute of Public Opinion, "Voting Blocs Divide among All Parties Much as in 1953," *TDS*, 5 June 1957, 27.

25 Michael Best, "Around the Provinces: Why Manitoba Premier Boycotted Mr. St. Laurent," *G&M*, 7 May 1957, 6; Clark Davey, "Diefenbaker Hailed By 3,800 in Victoria," *G&M*, 22 May 1957, 1; Clark Davey, "Diefenbaker Receives His Greatest Acclaim in Vancouver Overflow," *G&M*, 24 May 1957, 1–2; and Thomson, *Louis St. Laurent: Canadian*, 506.

26 Quoted in Cory Baldwin, "The Branding of the Prime Minister: 'Uncle Louis' and Brand Politics in the Elections of Louis St. Laurent, 1949–1957," master's thesis, Trent University (2017), 158.

27 Bruce Hutchison, *Mr. Prime Minister, 1867–1964* (New York: Harcourt, Brace & World, 1964), 316.

28 Meisel, *The Canadian General Election of 1957*, 272–3.

29 Clark Davey, "Magic Word: Power Is Main Question as Major Parties Campaign," *G&M*, 4 May 1957, 3; and Conrad, "The 1950s, the Decade of Development," 412.

30 "$100 Old Age Pensions, 30 p.c. Income Tax Cut Social Credit Promise," *G&M*, 19 Apr. 1957, 1.

31 "Government Changes Advertising Agencies," *G&M*, 9 Aug. 1957, 7; quoted in "Backstage with the PM's Team," *Maclean's*, 23 Nov. 1957, 3; and Speech from the Throne, House of Commons, *Debates*, 14 Oct. 1957.

32 Blair Fraser, "Backstage at Ottawa," *Maclean's*, 7 Dec. 1957, 2; and Blair Fraser, "Backstage at Ottawa," *Maclean's*, 23 Nov. 1957, 2.

33 Statistics Canada, Table H92–112, "Provincial Governments, Net General Revenue by Major Source, Selected Years, 1933 to 1969," and Table H75–91, "Federal Government, Net General Revenue by Major Source, Selected Years, 1933 to 1969," https://www150.statcan.gc.ca/n1/pub/11-516-x /sectionh/4057752-eng.htm.

34 "Brief to Prime Minister: Business Group Asks Permanent Federal-Provincial Conference," *G&M*, 25 Nov. 1957, 25; Harvey Hickey, "Taxes Head Agenda at Ottawa Meeting," *G&M*, 25 Nov. 1957, 1–2; and quoted in "Red Sputniks Alert, West, PM Believes," *G&M*, 6 Nov. 1957, 1.

35 Conrad, "The 1950s, the Decade of Development," 411–12; "B.C.'s Bennett Seeks Tax Payment Boost with New Formula," *G&M*, 26 Nov. 1957, 27; Penny Bryden, *A Justifiable Obsession: Conservative Ontario's Relations with Ottawa* (Toronto: University of Toronto Press, 2013), 96; and Langevin Coté, "Duplessis Stand Unchanged: Quebec's Tax Issue Left up in Air," *G&M*, 27 Nov. 1957, 8.

36 Mark Harrison, "Diefenbaker Offers Housing, Jobless Cash Medical Care Payment," *TDS*, 25 Nov. 1957, 1; and Clark Davey, "Tax Formula to Await New Parley," *G&M*, 26 Nov. 1957, 1–2.

37 Clark Davey, "Provinces in Accord on Fringe Benefits," *G&M*, 27 Nov. 1957, 1–2.

38 Quoted in "Newfoundland Broke, $44,000,000 in Debt after 8 Years' Union," *G&M*, 29 May 1957, 2.

39 William R. Callahan, *Joseph Roberts Smallwood: Journalist, Premier, Newfoundland Patriot* (St. John's: Flanker Press, 2003), 186; House of Commons, *Debates*, 14 Nov. 1957; and Clark Davey, "Maritimers, PM Discuss Power Problems," *G&M*, 15 Aug. 1957, 7.

40 Brian O. Connell, "The Atlantic Provinces' Horde," *G&M*, 6 July 1957, 7; and quoted in "P.E.I. Aid in Doubt," *G&M*, 1 Mar. 1957, 7.

41 Langevin Coté, "Union Nationale Scores Sweep in By-Elections," *G&M*, 19 Sept. 1957, 1.

42 Quoted in Pelletier, *Years of Impatience, 1950–1960*, 60; and Quinn, *The Union Nationale*, 155–6.

43 Quoted in Switzman v. Elbling and A.G. of Quebec [1957] SCR 285; and Robert Duffy, "Duplessis Restrained in Comment on Ruling," *G&M*, 9 Mar. 1957, 1.

44 Elizabeth Quinlan and Andrea Quinlan, "Textually Mediated Labour Activism: An Examination of the Ladies Auxiliary of the Canadian Mine Mill & Smelter Workers Union, 1940s–1960s," *Journal of International Women's Studies* 16, no. 3 (2015), 146.

45 "Always Backs a Winner: Frost Pledges Support to Diefenbaker Drive," *G&M*, 26 Apr. 1957, 5; and Wilfred List, "Ontario Premier's Aid Could Help Turn Tide," *G&M*, 4 May 1957, 7.

46 "Frost Says Hospital Plan Nation's Best," *G&M*, 27 Mar. 1957, 1.

47 "Frost, Liberal Leader Tangle in Legislature Over Federal Budget," *G&M*, 16 Mar. 1957, 1.

48 "Parties and Principles," *G&M*, 7 Sept. 1957, 6.

49 "The Week across the Land," *G&M*, 26 Oct. 1957, 7.

50 Paul Barber, "Manitoba's Liberals: Sliding into Third," *Manitoba Politics and Government: Issues, Institutions, Traditions*, ed. Paul G. Thomas and Curtis Brown (Winnipeg: University of Manitoba Press, 2010), 136.

51 Michael Best, "Is a Swing Portended? Manitoba's Premier Campbell Has a Problem," *G&M*, 15 June 1957, 7; and David Queen, "Roblin's Ready to Move In," *G&M*, 14 Sept. 1957, A8–9.

52 "2,000 Pour in to Hear Douglas-Thatcher Tilt in Gala Prairie Town," *G&M*, 21 May 1957, 11; Dale Eisler, *Rumours of Glory: Saskatchewan & the Thatcher Years* (Edmonton: Hurtig, 1987), 19–32; and "Barbed Words at Mossbank," *Leader-Post* (Regina), 22 May 1957, 17.

53 Thomson, *Louis St. Laurent: Canadian*, 502.

54 "64% Vote 'Yes' in Liquor Vote," *Edmonton Journal*, 31 Oct. 1957, 1, 10.

55 "3 of 4 Alberta Cities Will Not Fluoridate," *G&M*, 18 Oct. 1957, 10.

56 Douglas Collins, "More at Stake in B.C. than a Baseball Team," *G&M*, 5 June 1957, 7; and "Sunday Sport Gets Majority in Vancouver," *G&M*, 13 Dec. 1957, 8.

57 Bercuson, *Blood on the Hills*, 221; "Regular Shipping between Canada and China Again," *G&M*, 9 Sept. 1957, 2; "Canada Gives India $4,000,000 Power Plant," *G&M*, 10 July 1957, 7; and Hilliker and Barry, *Canada's Department of External Affairs*, 172.

58 Hilliker and Barry, *Canada's Department of External Affairs*, 96; and Omar Hayyat Khan, "Instruments of Influence: Canada and Arms Exports to South Asia, 1947–1971," master's thesis, Dept. of History, Carleton University (2005), 129.

59 "Ottawa Briefs," *G&M*, 3 Apr. 1957, 8; "Ottawa Briefs," *G&M*, 13 Apr. 1957, 17A; and James Joseph McCann, House of Commons, *Debates*, 12 Apr. 1957.

60 "Canada, B.W.I. Relations Slated for Discussion," *G&M*, 29 July 1957, 3.

61 Raymond Daniell, "Canada, Britain Differ over U.N.," *NYT*, 26 Mar. 1957, 16; Philip Deane, "Howe Seeks Fixed Prices for Uranium," *G&M*, 26 Mar. 1957, 1; House of Commons, *Debates*, 27 Mar. 1957; and "Canada to Let U.K. Postpone Loan Payments," *G&M*, 7 Mar. 1957, 1.

62 Quoted in "Norman's Death Brings Sorrow to Britain," *G&M*, 5 Apr. 1957, 7; "Norman Suicide Deeply Stirs Australia Press," *G&M*, 6 Apr. 1957, 4; and House of Commons, *Debates*, 4 Apr. 1957.

63 Quoted in "Canada, U.S. Agree to Share Salmon Catch," *G&M*, 4 July 1957, 7.

64 House of Commons, *Debates*, 27 Nov. 1957.

65 Leonard Ingalls, "Arms Talks Open in London Today," *NYT*, 18 Mar. 1957, 4.

66 Jack Bravely, "Canadians in Big Role in Occupation of Gaza," *G&M*, 11 Mar. 1957, 13; "Canada's Lester B. Pearson Wins Nobel Peace Prize," CTV News,

accessed 9 Mar. 2022, https://www.ctvnews.ca/5-things/flashback-friday
-canada-s-lester-b-pearson-wins-nobel-peace-prize-1.2695910?cache=%2F5
-things-to-know-for-tuesday-november-26-2019-1.4702572; and "An
Unstuffy Diplomat: A Trouble-Shooter a Superb Conciliator: Lester Bowles
Pearson," *NYT*, 15 Oct. 1957, 14.

67 Quoted in George Bain, "Warm Welcome for New PM: Economic Topics
First, Diefenbaker Tells U.K. Trade Talks in Ottawa Proposed," *G&M*, 25
June 1957, 1–2; and Hilliker and Barry, *Canada's Department of External
Affairs*, 210.

68 Quoted in Harvey Hicks, "Favor Talks By 11 PMs about Trade," *G&M*, 1
Oct. 1957, 1–2.

69 Quoted in Clark Davey, "PM Suggests Canada Quit Arms Group," *G&M*,
24 Sept. 1957, 1–2.

70 House of Commons, *Debates*, 1 Nov. 1957.

71 "Canadian Departs for Pre-NATO Talks," *NYT*, 13 Dec. 1957, 6; and
"Diefenbaker Wins Mention of Captive People's Plight," *G&M*, 19 Dec.
1957, 2.

1958

1 Paul W. Fox, "What's the Future of Our Political Ideas," *G&M*, 16 Aug.
1958, A13.

2 Quoted in "Policies Stupid or Dishonest – Professor," *TDS*, 25 Mar. 1958, 1.

3 *Canada Year Book, 1959*, ix.

4 "Canada in Trouble," *NYT*, 27 Apr. 1958, E4; and *Canada Year Book, 1959*, ix.

5 Gordon W. Stead, "Patterns of Government Expenditure," *Canadian Public
Administration* 1, no. 1 (1958), 1.

6 House of Commons, *Debates*, 19 May 1958; Bruce MacDonald, "Tories
Hopeful? Immigrant Curb Stays," *TDS*, 9 Aug. 1958, 7; and "Bitter
Medicine," *TDS*, 27 June 1958, 6.

7 *Canada Year Book, 1959*, 162, 175–6.

8 Lower, *Canadians in the Making*.

9 Quoted in Rhodri Windsor Liscombe, "A Study in Modern(ist) Urbanism:
Planning Vancouver, 1945–1965," *Urban History* 38, no. 1 (2011), 137.

10 "City Hall Plan Is Won by Finn," *TDS*, 26 Sept. 1958; Rhodri Windsor
Liscombe and Michelangelo Sabatino, *Canada: Modern Architectures in
History* (London: Reaktion Books, 2016), 218; and Beverly Gray, "Need 3
Days to Open New Montreal Hotel," *G&M*, 16 Apr. 1958, 3.

11 *Canada Year Book, 1960*, 347–8; and *TDS*, 16 Apr. 1958, 1.

12 Michiel Horn, *Academic Freedom in Canada: A History* (Toronto: University
of Toronto Press, 1999), chap. 9; "Professor Dismissed after Letter Written,"
G&M, 17 Sept. 1958, 2; D.G. Creighton, et. al., "The Troubles at United

College," *G&M*, 12 Dec. 1958, 6; and "5 More Quit College on Eve of Statement," *G&M*, 8 Dec. 1958, 1.

13 "Television Set Sales Reflect Completion of Microwave System," *G&M*, 29 Aug. 1958, 20; "Color Television 1959 Possibility, CBC Man Says," *G&M*, 4 Dec. 1958, 5; "The Truth Will Out," *G&M*, 19 Feb. 1958, 6; and Winifred Kalis, "How to Harness TV for Education," *G&M*, 20 Nov. 1958, 6.

14 "They Talk Most in Cold Climates," *Manchester Guardian*, 18 Dec. 1958, 7; "Elegant Colored Phones Room Styling Feature," *TDS*, 4 Sept. 1958, 23; "Pester Emergency Line: Dial for Plumber Pick-Up Bottles," *TDS*, 17 Mar. 1958, 2; and "Start Direct Dialing for U.S. Cities Sunday," *G&M*, 31 Dec. 1958, 11.

15 Yves Thériault, *Agaguk: Roman Esquimau* (Paris: Bernard Grasset, 1958).

16 Paul Perron, *Semiotics and the Modern Quebec Novel: A Greimassian Analysis of Thériault's Agaguk* (Toronto: University of Toronto Press, 1996), 17, 31.

17 Colin McDougall, *Execution* (Toronto: Macmillan, 1958).

18 *Canada Year Book, 1959*, 1231–5.

19 Bruce MacDonald, "Force an Early Election Said Pearson Policy," *TDS*, 17 June 1958, 1; and L.B. Pearson, "Introduction," in Pickersgill, *The Liberal Party*, ix–x.

20 House of Commons, *Debates*, 20 Jan. and 1 Feb. 1958; and Blair Fraser, "Backstage at Ottawa," *Maclean's*, 1 Feb. 1958, 2.

21 Bruce MacDonald, "Diefenbaker Tries to Get Jump on Foes, Vote Mar. 31," *TDS*, 3 Feb. 1958, 1–2; and House of Commons, *Debates*, 1 Feb. 1958.

22 William Kinmond, "Pearson Plugs Peace Plan as Martin Gets Applause," *G&M*, 15 Feb. 1958, 1; William Kinmond, "B.C. Airport Crowd Encourages Pearson," *G&M*, 24 Feb. 1958, 1; Clark Davey, "Liberal Leader Finds Political Climate Cold in Atlantic Province," *G&M*, 14 Mar. 1958, 1; "Liberal Stalwarts Rally to Pack Massey Hall," *G&M*, 22 Mar. 1958, 4; and Clark Davey, "Coldwell Hopes CCF to Take Over from Liberals as Official Opposition," *G&M*, 7 Feb. 1958, 1.

23 Clark Davey, "5,000 Crowd Record for PM at Winnipeg," *G&M*, 13 Feb. 1958, 1; William Kinmond, "Crowds Total 10,000 to Greet Diefenbaker," *G&M*, 10 Mar. 1958, 1; and Clark Davey, "Cape Breton Crowd: N.S. to Get New Deal, Diefenbaker Pledge," *G&M*, 1 Mar. 1958, 1.

24 Blair Fraser, "Backstage in the Campaign," *Maclean's*, 29 Mar. 1958, 2.

25 "Diefenbaker's Statements & Promises 1959," Poltext, accessed 6 Mar. 2022, http://poltext.org/sites/poltext.org/files/plateformesV2/Canada/CAN_PL_1958_PC.pdf; and quoted in Robert Taylor, "Diefenbaker Called Canada Abe Lincoln Is Cheered in B.C.," *TDS*, 13 Mar. 1958, 1–2.

26 "For Peace … For Jobs: Canada's Liberal Path to Prosperity, Progress and Peace: The Pearson Plan," 5, Poltext, accessed 6 Mar. 2022, http://poltext.org/sites/poltext.org/files/plateformesV2/Canada/CAN_PL_1958_LIB_en.pdf.

27 "Let's Go Forward (The National CCF Program)," Poltext, accessed 6 Mar. 2022, https://www.poltext.org/sites/poltext.org/files/plateformesV2/Canada/CAN_PL_1958_CCF.pdf.

28 "There's Something Better," Poltext, accessed 6 Mar. 2022, https://www.poltext.org/sites/poltext.org/files/plateformesV2/Canada/CAN_PL_1958_SC.pdf.

29 "13 of 100 'On Fence' 56 P.C. Favor Tories Gain of 6 in Month," *TDS*, 15 Mar. 1958, 3; and quoted in "Polls Don't Govern," *TDS*, 5 June 1958, 6.

30 William Kinmond, "Party Was Too Smug, Liberal Leader Claims," *G&M*, 19 Apr. 1958, 5; and Paul W. Fox, "What's the Future of Our Political Ideas," *G&M*, 16 Aug. 1958, A13.

31 E.N. Davis, "Will Douglas Replace Coldwell?," *G&M*, 5 Apr. 1958, 7; "CCF Ponders Future as Knowles Sought for High Labor Post," *G&M*, 10 Apr. 1958, 3; and Stanley Knowles, *The New Party* (Toronto: McClelland & Stewart, 1961).

32 Clark Davey, "Full of Vigor, Socreds Say," *G&M*, 9 Apr. 1958, 17.

33 "Follows Liberal Pattern: PM Refuses to Table Report of Economists," *G&M*, 19 June 1958, 3.

34 House of Commons, *Debates*, 5 Sept. 1958; and "Lawyers Brand Rights Bill Dangerous, Political Show," *G&M*, 11 Sept. 1958, 1.

35 "Diefenbaker's Sales Pitch," CBC Archives, accessed 6 Mar. 2022, https://www.cbc.ca/archives/entry/diefenbakers-sales-pitch-1958; House of Commons, *Debates*, 16 June 1958; and Robert Duffy, "Minding Your Business," *G&M*, 29 Jan. 1958, 6.

36 House of Commons, *Debates*, 16 June and 14 July 1958.

37 Quoted in Langevin Coté, "Prospects Bright for Development in New Brunswick," *G&M*, 26 Feb. 1958, 22; "The Week in the Capital," *G&M*, 1 Feb. 1958, 7; quoted in William MacEachern, "PEI Want Causeway, Did Tories Kill Plan? It Haunts Them Now," *TDS*, 19 Mar. 1958, 10; and "Newfoundland Needs $8,000,000 Annual Aid Commission Finding," *G&M*, 26 July 1958, 4.

38 "Would Share Municipal Costs: Diefenbaker Offers 50–50 Plan Designed to Create Winter Jobs," *G&M*, 28 Oct. 1958, 1; Langevin Coté, "Duplessis Will Allow Federal Works Aid," *G&M*, Dec 6, 1958, 3; and Langevin Coté, "Angry Duplessis Slams the Door on Federal Aid to Universities," *G&M*, 26 Nov. 1958, 9.

39 Clark Davey, "Diefenbaker Favors Tri-Level Tax Talks," *G&M*, 8 Feb. 1958, 1; Harvey Hickey, "Frost Statement Used by Ottawa Liberals but PM Not Budging," *G&M*, 17 May 1958, 3; and House of Commons, *Debates*, 2 June 1958.

40 Ben Rose, "New Plan Is Needed for Old Age Pensions All Politicians Say," *TDS*, 8 Jan. 1958, 3; and Harvey Hickey, "Defense, Welfare Cost Curbs Cash to Cities, PM Warns Mayors," *G&M*, 7 Oct. 1958, 1.

41 Ostry, "The Foundations of National Public Hospital Insurance," 261–81; "Hospital Plan Starts Today in Five Provinces," *G&M*, 1 July 1958, 3; "Roblin Presents PC Program for Manitoba," *G&M*, 8 Nov. 1958, 4; and "$160,000,000 '59 Ottawa Cost of Hospital Plan," *G&M*, 16 Dec. 1958, 4.

42 Clark Davey, "Eight Provinces Urge Subsidy: Cabinet Action on Rail Crisis Possible Today," *G&M*, 25 Nov. 1958, 3.

43 Anthony Thompson, "The Nova Scotia Civil Service Association, 1956–1967," *Acadiensis* 12, no. 2 (1983), 81–105; and Harold Shea, "Nova Scotia Gives Economy Big Push," *NYT*, 8 Jan. 1958, 78.

44 Bren Walsh, "The Rise and Fall of Joey Smallwood's Visions of Empire," *G&M*, 18 Jan. 1958, 7.

45 William MacEachern, "PEI Want Causeway, Did Tories Kill Plan? It Haunts Them Now," *TDS*, 19 Mar. 1958, 10; "Hunt for Oil Reaches Prince Edward Island," *G&M*, 26 Feb. 1958, 25; and Langevin Coté, "Prospects Bright for Development in New Brunswick," *G&M*, 26 Feb. 1958, 22.

46 Langevin Coté, "Quebec MLA Explains Diefenbaker Support," *G&M*, 24 Mar. 1958, 9; and Langevin Coté, "Diefenbaker Consistent on Quebec," *G&M*, 3 Mar. 1958, 7.

47 Langevin Coté, "Lesage Asks Inquiry in Quebec Gas Deal," *G&M*, 17 June 1958, 2; quoted in Langevin Coté, "Lesage Sees Quebec as Shame of America," *G&M*, 12 July 1958, 4; and quoted in Langevin Coté, "Lesage Turns Tables on Autonomy Issue," *G&M*, 14 July 1958, 8.

48 Quoted in Quinn, *The Union Nationale*, 168–9; and Pierre Elliott Trudeau, "Advances in Politics," in H.D. Forbes, *Canadian Political Thought*, 329.

49 Quoted in Langevin Coté, "Duplessis Set a Bear Trap: If It Doesn't Fight Elections, Has an Opposition Abdicated?," *G&M*, 3 Oct. 1958, 7.

50 "Thirteen Candidates Fight 4 By-Elections," *G&M*, 29 Apr. 1958, 5.

51 Quoted in "MacDonald Presses Pipeline Issue Attack," *G&M*, 10 May 1958, 1–2; Graham, *Old Man Ontario*, 346; "Brands Wintermeyer Real Conservative," *G&M*, 29 May 1958, 5; and William Kinmond, "Ontario Liberals Choose Wintermeyer New Leader," *G&M*, 21 Apr. 1958, 1–2.

52 Wiseman, *Social Democracy in Manitoba*, 70–1.

53 Fred Cleverley, "He was 'Some Boy Scout,'" *Winnipeg Free Press*, 1 June 2010, https://www.winnipegfreepress.com/opinion/analysis/he-was-some-boy-scout-95297404.html; and "Roblin Presents PC Program For Manitoba," *G&M*, 8 Nov. 1958, 4.

54 "Alberta PCs Elect Red Deer Lawyer," *G&M*, 18 Aug. 1958, 12.

55 E.N. Davis, "Prairie PCs Choose Underdog Candidate," *G&M*, 1 Nov. 1958, 7; and "PM Offers Aid for Winter Jobs," *Leader-Post* (Regina), 27 Oct. 1958, 1.

56 Blair Fraser, "Backstage: Who'll Lead the Tory Tide in B.C.?" *Maclean's*, 10 May 1958, 2; "Finlayson PC Choice By 11-Vote Edge in B.C.," *G&M*, 15

Sept. 1958, 16; "B.C. Tories Retain Finlayson as Chief," *Edmonton Journal*, 15 Sept. 1958; and Douglas Collins, "The Outlook for B.C. Is Right Versus Left," *G&M*, 20 Sept. 1958, 7.

57 "Macmillan Revives Free Trade Proposal," *G&M*, 14 June 1958, 1; Clark Davey, "Canada Asks Council Meet as First Step to Summit," *G&M*, 30 July 1958, 1–2; and Harold Callender, "20 Nations Urge Steps to Reduce Curbs on Trade," *NYT*, 19 Oct. 1958, 1.

58 Clark Davey, "Troops Stay, PM Assures Dr. Heuss," 3 June 1958, 1; and Raymond Daniell, "President Begins Talks in Ottawa," *NYT*, 9 July 1958, 1, 3.

59 Blair Fraser, "Backstage at Ottawa," *Maclean's*, 27 Sept. 1958, 2.

60 Harvey Hickey, "Tariff Concession by Canada Aids British Industrial Export," *G&M*, 24 Sept. 1958, 1–2; Harvey Hickey, "33,000 Miles by Phone: Canada Backs Coaxial Cable to Link All Commonwealth," *G&M*, 25 Sept. 1958, 1–2.

61 Hilliker and Barry, *Canada's Department of External Affairs*, 135.

62 Quoted in "Mr. Diefenbaker's Great Journey," *G&M*, 29 Oct. 1958, 6.

63 "Pakistan Next on PM's Tour; Visited Pope," *G&M*, 13 Nov. 1958, 1; "PM Goes Sightseeing in Land of Mogul Emperors," *G&M*, 17 Nov. 1958, 11; Walter Gray, "Diefenbaker to Talk New Zealand Trade," *G&M*, 13 Nov. 1958, 7; Robert R. Wilson, "Commonwealth as Symbol and as Instrument," *American Journal of International Law* 53, no. 2 (1959), 393; and "Real Hope for Peace," *South China Morning Post*, 23 Dec. 1958, 19.

64 Quoted in Clark Davey, "Canada to Ask UN Endorse Arctic Patrol," *G&M*, 29 Apr. 1958, 11.

65 Clark Davey, "Canada Asks Council Meet as First Step to Summit," *G&M*, 30 July 1958, 1–2; Lebanon – UNIGOL, Facts and Figures, accessed 6 Mar. 2022, https://peacekeeping.un.org/mission/past/unogilfacts.html; and "Toward a Constructive Program," *G&M*, 28 July 1958, 6.

66 "Rocket Expert Says CF-105 Too Expensive," *G&M*, 22 Oct. 1958, 2; quoted in Palmiro Campagna, *Requiem for a Giant: A.V. Roe Canada and the Avro Arrow* (Toronto: Dundurn, 2003), 101; Clark Davey, "Pearkes Denies Decision Made on Arrow Jet," *G&M*, 26 Nov. 1958, 1; "Text of Diefenbaker Statement," *G&M*, 24 Sept. 1958, 8; and Graham, *Old Man Ontario*, 357.

67 Raymond Daniell, "President Backs Policy on Trade in Canadian Talk," *NYT*, 10 July 1958, 1, 5; Robert Taylor, "'Inexcusable' Protest on Oil by Fleming Shocks, Angers U.S.," *TDS*, 17 Jan. 1958, 1; Tillman Durdin, "Red China Buying Canadian Wheat," *NYT*, 1 Apr. 1958, 11; "Visit to Peking: Push for China Trade Seen Canada's Goal," *G&M*, 5 July 1958, 2; and "Canada Not Planning Recognition of China, Fleming Tells Japan," *G&M*, 8 Nov. 1958, 1.

68 Quoted in "Better U.S. Ties to Canada Urged," *NYT*, 5 May 1958, 14.

69 *Canada Year Book, 1960,* 158–9; John Diefenbaker, House of Commons, *Debates,* 23 Jan. 1958; "Canada Offers Gift of Ship," *G&M,* 11 Mar. 1958, 15: and Clark Davey, "West Indies to Get Two Ships as Part of $10,000,000 Offer," *G&M,* 24 Sept. 1958, 1.

1959

1 "Some Changes Have Been Made," *G&M,* 19 Sept. 1959, 6.
2 Bothwell, Drummond, and English, *Canada Since 1945,* 11; *Canada Year Book, 1961,* 168, 170–1, 183–4; *Canada Year Book, 1959,* 169; *Canada Year Book, 1960,* 205; and "Walpole Indians Granted Control of Expenditures," *G&M,* 7 Oct. 1959, 8.
3 Anthony Wilson-Smith, "Aboriginals' Fight for the Franchise," *Diplomat & International Canada* (Summer 2015), 81; Wendell H. Oswalt and James W. Van Stone, "The Future of the Caribou Eskimos," *Anthropologica* 2, no. 2 (1960), 156–7; and "Colonel Leonard Hanson Nicholson, OC, MBE, GC St J, LLD," accessed 6 Mar. 2022, http://canadianprovostcorps.ca/pm .nicholson.htm.
4 Quoted in Peter C. Newman, "Are New Canadians Hurting Canada?" *Maclean's,* 18 July 1959, 19, 55.
5 *Canada Year Book, 1960,* 382, 392; Statistics Canada, "Table W1–9 Summary of Total Full-Time Enrolment, by Level of Study, Canada, Selected Years, 1951 to 1975," https://www150.statcan.gc.ca/n1/pub/11-516-x/sectionw /4147445-eng.htm; and "$52 Million for U of T's Future," *TDS,* 23 May 1959, 6.
6 "Mrs. Fairclough Again Woman of the Year," *G&M,* 30 Dec. 1959, 11; and quoted in "Backstage with Women in Politics," *Maclean's,* 3 Jan. 1959, 3.
7 "Interest Rates and Exchange Rates," Statistics Canada, accessed 6 Mar. 2022, https://www150.statcan.gc.ca/n1/pub/11-210-x/2010000/t098-eng.htm; "Historical US Treasury Bond Rates," Forecast Chart, https://www.forecast -chart.com/rate-treasury-10.html; *Canada Year Book, 1959,* xiii, xiv; *Canada Year Book, 1960,* xii; "Farmers Get Protection of Tariffs," *G&M,* 10 Apr. 1959, 1; and quoted in "Free Trade with U.S. Seen Helping Canada," *G&M,* 1 Apr. 1959, 2.
8 "Some Changes Have Been Made," *G&M,* 19 Sept. 1959, 6.
9 E.A. Ingram, "Drop Arrow: Layoff Stuns Thousands at Malton," *G&M,* 21 Feb. 1959, 1; Cartoon, *TDS,* 24 Feb. 1959, 6; "Across the Land: Tumult Born of Dead Arrow," *G&M,* 28 Feb. 1959, 8; quoted in Chris Gainor, *Arrows to the Moon: Avro's Engineers and the Space Race* (Burlington, ON: Apogee Books, 2001), 39; and Nigel Dunn, "8,000 Still Lack Employment," *G&M,* 28 Apr. 1959, 1.
10 "Backstage with the CBC Strike," *Maclean's,* 14 Mar. 1959, 3; and Clark Davey, "CBC Strike Sees Cabinet at Odds," *G&M,* 28 Jan. 1959, 1.

11 "Stampede Week Gate Hits Record 591,000," *G&M*, 13 July 1959, 17; James Senter, "20,000 See Highlanders' Review," *G&M*, 30 June 1959, 12; and "Trim Prison Terms to Mark Royal Tour," *G&M*, 23 May 1959, 1.

12 "Vanier Sees Canada French Culture Source," *G&M*, 11 Dec. 1959, 12.

13 James M. Ham, "The World of Learning: Use of Electricity Doubled Since '47," *G&M*, 6 Oct. 1959, 7; "Telephone Veteran Sees Change," *G&M*, 2 Feb. 1959, 13; "Preview: A Look at Tomorrow in Terms of Today," *Maclean's*, 3 Jan. 1959, 2; "Ford of Canada Compact Cars Prices Listed," *G&M*, 8 Oct. 1959, 38; and E.W. Kenworthy, "Eisenhower Greets Canada via Moon," *NYT*, 7 June 1959, 1.

14 "Across the Land," *G&M*, 20 June 1959, 8.

15 Northrop Frye, "Letters in Canada 1959: Poetry," *University of Toronto Quarterly* 29, no. 4 (July 1960), 459.

16 Gregory Betts, Paul Hjartarson, and Kristine Smitka, eds., *Counter-Blasting Canada: Marshall McLuhan, Wyndham Lewis, Wilfred Watson, and Sheila Watson* (Edmonton: University of Alberta Press, 2016), xvii.

17 (Québec: Institut littéraire du Québec, 1959).

18 Morton, "Canadian Conservatism Now," 7–8.

19 "Native Son Protests: Ensign Said Insult to Canadians," *G&M*, 9 Jan. 1959, 5.

20 House of Commons, *Debates*, 26, 27 Jan. 1959; and "Backstage with the CBC Strike," *Maclean's*, 14 Mar. 1959, 3.

21 Blair Fraser, "Backstage at Ottawa," *Maclean's*, 9 May 1959, 2.

22 Ray Argyle, *Joey Smallwood: Schemer and Dreamer* (Toronto: Dundurn, 2012), 104; and House of Commons, *Debates*, 16 Mar. 1959.

23 Blair Fraser, "Backstage at Ottawa," *Maclean's*, 17 Jan. 1959, 2.

24 House of Commons, *Debates*, 23 Feb. and 16 Mar. 1959.

25 "Two Orders from U.S. Valued at $8,200,000 Confirmed in House," *G&M*, 24 Feb. 1959, 1; Harvey Hickey, "'Won't Be Satisfied with Promises': PM Declares Canada Insisting U.S. Share Orders for Defense," *G&M*, 4 Mar. 1959, 1–2; and House of Commons, *Debates*, 8 Aug. 1958.

26 Harvey Hickey, "Farmers Fail to Gain Promise of Deficiency Payment on Grain," *G&M*, 11 Mar. 1959, 15; E.N. Davis, "Farmers' Ottawa Trek May Start Next Month," *G&M*, 3 Jan. 1959, 7; and "1,100 Move on Ottawa but Harkness Blasts Grain Subsidy Bid," *G&M*, 7 Mar. 1959, 3.

27 Newman, *Renegade in Power*, 13; and quoted in Blair Fraser, "Is Diefenbaker Running a One-Man Government?" *Maclean's*, 14 Mar. 1959, 13.

28 John LeBlanc, "Won't Water Down Policy: Argue," *G&M*, 31 Aug. 1959, 15; and Canadian Institute of Public Opinion, "'Stay Out of Politics' Public Tells Unions," *TDS*, 28 Nov. 1959, 7.

29 Andrew Snaddon, "Social Credit Feels History on Its Side," *G&M*, 5 Dec. 1959, 7.

30 Clark Davey, "Energy Board to Be Watchdog," *G&M*, 20 May 1959, 3; "Cabinet Split on Energy Bill, Liberal Declares," *G&M*, 2 June 1959, 9; "The National Energy Board," *G&M*, 12 Aug. 1959, 6; and House of Commons, *Debates*, 27 May 1959.

31 Harvey Hickey, "Changing the Criminal Code: Obscenity Definition Would End 1868 Test," *G&M*, 12 June 1959, 3.

32 Clark Davey, "Extra Aid to Jobless Subsidy for the Idle, Contractor Tells MPs," *G&M*, 20 May 1959, 1.

33 Kenneth Smith, "A Matter of Personal Dedication: PM Says Bill of Rights Coming by Statute Early Next Session," *G&M*, 7 Sept. 1959, 1.

34 House of Commons, *Debates*, 28 Apr. 1959; and Blair Fraser, "Backstage at Ottawa," *Maclean's*, 6 June 1959, 2.

35 Canadian Institute of Public Opinion, "Conservative Rating down but Holds Firm," *TDS*, 7 Nov. 1959, 7; and Denis Smith, *Rogue Tory: The Life and Legend of John G. Diefenbaker* (Toronto: Macfarlane Walter & Ross, 1995), 304.

36 Harvey Hickey, "Ottawa Rejects 1960 Boost in Tax Share of Provinces," *G&M*, 16 Oct. 1959, 1–2; and Clark Davey, "May Force More Loans by Ontario," *G&M*, 16 Oct. 1959, 1–2.

37 Langevin Coté, "Maritime Premiers Study New Financial Requests for Ottawa," *G&M*, 16 Sept. 1959, 9; Robert Duffy, "Minding Your Business," *G&M*, 28 Mar. 1959, 8; and House of Commons, *Debates*, 25 Mar. 1959.

38 Langevin Coté, "'Where Are My Fiscal Rights?': Duplessis Is Due for Comeback, on National Scene," *G&M*, 8 May 1959, 7; and Langevin Coté, "PM Seen Paving Way for Sauvé to Accept School Grants Offer," *G&M*, 25 Dec. 1959, 4.

39 "Across the Land: Tumult Born of Dead Arrow," *G&M*, 28 Feb. 1959, 8; and Graham, *Old Man Ontario*, 351–2, 357, 368.

40 Ted Byfield, "All Not Bliss in Ottawa-Manitoba Marriage," *G&M*, 31 Oct. 1959, 7; quoted in "Ottawa Meeting 'Disappointing' to Duff Roblin," *G&M*, 19 Oct. 1959, 25; and quoted in Clark Davey, "May Force More Loans by Ontario," *G&M*, 16 Oct. 1959, 1–2.

41 Harvey Hickey, "PM Requests House Pass Energy Bill," *G&M*, 27 May 1959, 1–2; House of Commons, *Debates*, 26 May and 2 Mar. 1959: and Kenneth Smith, "Briggs' Post: Socred Opponents Pleased," *G&M*, 14 Aug. 1959, 13.

42 Bert Burgoyne, "Fall Vote for New Brunswick," *G&M*, 26 Sept. 1959, 7; and "Stanfield Ends Election Rumor in Nova Scotia," *G&M*, 31 Aug. 1959, 15.

43 H. Landon Ladd, *Only the Strong Are Free* [Video Recording] (St. John's: Memorial University Television and Committee on Canadian Labour History, 1985); and Langevin Coté, "PC Leader Is Ousted; Labor Loses," *G&M*, 21 Aug. 1959, 1–2.

44 "PEI Awaits Election: Free Texts Pledge by Liberals," *G&M*, 27 Aug. 1959, 11.

45 Ian Stewart, "Friends at Court: Federalism and Provincial Elections on Prince Edward Island," *Canadian Journal of Political Science* 19, no. 1 (March 1986), 132.

46 Graham, *Old Man Ontario*, 361–3.

47 Quoted in Wiseman, *Social Democracy in Manitoba*, 72.

48 Christopher Adams, "Realigning Elections in Manitoba," in *Manitoba Politics and Government*, ed. Thomas and Brown, 164.

49 Lee Belland, "Disillusioned at Dief Alberta Goes Socred," *TDS*, 19 June 1959, 1; "Tory Collapse Ottawa Fault Says Bennett," *TDS*, 19 June 1959, 3; and Canadian Institute of Public Opinion, "Tories are Slipping from Record High," *TDS*, 16 May 1959, 3.

50 Langevin Coté, "Sauve Is Appointed as Quebec Premier," *G&M*, 11 Sept. 1959, 1.

51 Alexandre Turgeon, "De la création à la commémoration: le 'Désormais…' de Paul Sauvé dans l'histoire du Québec, 1959–2010," *Canadian Historical Review* 98, no. 4 (2017), 765–97; Langevin Coté, "Sauvé Defends School System in Quebec," *G&M*, 5 Oct. 1959, 15; and Langevin Coté, "Quebec to Continue to Press for Rights, Sauvé Policy Pledge," *G&M*, 5 Oct. 1959, 1.

52 Kenneth McRoberts, *Quebec: Social Change and Political Crisis* (Toronto: McClelland & Stewart, 1988), 83.

53 E.N. Davis, "Merging of CCF Opposed," *G&M*, 25 July 1959, 7; and quoted in E.N. Davis, "Saskatchewan's Cabinet Is Fading Away," *G&M*, 27 June 1959, 7.

54 Douglas Collins, "Ten Premiers' Shopping Lists Would Be Ready If Ottawa Should Call Tomorrow," *G&M*, 19 Sept. 1959, A11; "Across the Land," *G&M*, 25 July 1959, 8; and Douglas Collins, "Communists Hang on Grimly in British Columbia," *G&M*, 11 Apr. 1959, 7.

55 June Helm, *Prophecy and Power Among the Dogrib Indians* (Lincoln, NE: University of Nebraska Press, 1994), 27; "Alberta Faces Education Challenge," *G&M*, 21 Nov. 1959, 7; "Yukon Territory Has First Oil Find, *NYT*, 19 Aug. 1959, 37; and "MP Asks New Power for Yukon's Council," *G&M*, 12 Aug. 1959, 21.

56 An Act to Amend the Bretton Woods Agreements Act; Canada-Finland Tax Convention Act, 1959; "Gen. Burns Resigns as UNEF Head: Gets Canadian Post," *Herald Tribune* (New York), 5 Dec. 1959, 4; and Ian Vorres, "Canadian Chairman of Red Cross Group," *G&M*, 5 Oct. 1959, 39.

57 "Freedom Pledge Urged by PM," *G&M*, 13 Jan. 1959, 1–2; Alan Freeman, "Trailblazing Ex-diplomat Peter Dobell Gave Policy Advice to Parliamentarians," *G&M*, https://www.theglobeandmail.com/canada /article-trailblazing-ex-diplomat-peter-dobell-gave-policy-advice-to/;

William J. Jorden, "NATO Allies Back West's Big Three on Berlin Stand,"
NYT, 4 Apr. 1959, 1, 3; C.L. Schulzberger, "Foreign Affairs: The Illness of
Our Grand Alliance," *NYT*, 16 Dec. 1959, 40; "Hopes for Summit – Five
Views," *NYT*, 29 Mar. 1959, E5; George Bain, "London Report: Canadian
Influence Diminishing," *G&M*, 27 June 1959, 1–2; "'Middle Power' Role,"
G&M, 7 Nov. 1959, 8; and quoted in Jamie Glazov, *Canadian Policy Toward
Khrushchev's Soviet Union* (Montreal: McGill-Queen's University Press,
2002), 136.
58 Albert Legault and Michel Fortmann, *A Diplomacy of Hope: Canada and
Disarmament, 1945–1988* (Montreal: McGill-Queen's University Press,
1992), chap. 5; "Green Says Canada Opposed to French on Plan for
Atom Explosion in Sahara," *G&M*, 11 Nov. 1959, 1; Hilliker and Barry,
Canada's Department of External Affairs, 238, 150–2; and Rod Bantjes, *Social
Movements in a Global Context: Canadian Perspectives* (Toronto: Canadian
Scholars' Press, 2007), 80.
59 Bruce Smardon, *Asleep at the Switch: The Political Economy of Federal Research
and Development Policy Since 1960* (Montreal: McGill-Queen's University
Press, 2014), 143; House of Commons, *Debates*, 3 July 1959; Blair Fraser,
"Backstage at Ottawa," *Maclean's*, 28 Mar. 1959, 2; and "Canada, Bonn to
Plan Plane Standardization," *G&M*, 24 Sept. 1959, 11.
60 House of Commons, *Debates*, 29 Jan. 1959; "Agreement on the Columbia,"
G&M, 21 Dec. 1959, 6; Tania Long, "U.S. and Canada Get Power Plans,"
NYT, 31 Dec. 1959, 37; and Clark Davey, "Canada Acts for British in Trade
Bid," *G&M*, 6 Jan. 1959, 1.
61 "Urges Canada, Russia Plan More Contacts," *G&M*, 6 Nov. 1959, 5;
"Opening the Door," *G&M*, 1 Apr. 1959, 6; "Canada Trade Said Welcomed
by Chinese," *G&M*, 7 May 1959, 12; "Green Outlines Canada's Role in
Controversy," *G&M*, 14 Nov. 1959, 3; Thomas J. Hamilton, "Poland has
Lead in U.N. Balloting for Council Seat," *NYT*, 13 Oct. 1959, 1, 3; and
James Feron, "Poland Rejects U.N. Compromise," *NYT*, 17 Nov. 1959, 11.
62 "Freedom Pledge Urged by PM," *G&M*, 13 Jan. 1959, 1–2; and Walter Gray,
"Soviet Still Same, PM Tells Canada," *G&M*, 1 Dec. 1959, 1.
63 House of Commons, *Debates*, 19 Mar. 1959.
64 Howard Green, House of Commons, *Debates*, 3 July 1959; and "Help
Commonwealth, Education 'Talks' Aim," *G&M*, 8 July 1959, 24.

Conclusion

1 House of Commons, *Debates*, 4 July 1952, and 19 June 1950.
2 "The Royal Visit and Joyce Davidson," *TDS*, 20 June 1959, 6; Judy
Stoffman, "TV Personality's Remark on a Royal Visit Drew Backlash in a
Narrow-Minded Era," *G&M*, 20 May 2020, B24; "Joyce Quits 'To Save the

CBC from Grief,'" *TDS*, 20 June 1959, 1; and "Joyce, Two Children among Tour Crowds," *TDS*, 29 June 1959, 4.

3 Statistics Canada, Series A164–184: "Principal Religious Denominations of the Population, Census Dates, 1871 to 1971," accessed 7 Mar. 2022, https://www150.statcan.gc.ca/n1/pub/11-516-x/sectiona/4147436-eng .htm#A164_184; "A Toronto Pastor and a Professor Contribute to Biblical Knowledge," *G&M*, 4 Apr. 1953, 7; and "IODE Urges St. Laurent Ban Sex and Love Comics," *G&M*, 30 May 1950, 13.

4 Kingsley Davis, "Analysis of the Population Explosion," *NYT*, 22 Sept. 1957, 15; Alfred Sauvy, "Évolution récente des idées sur le surpeuple-ment," *Population* 15, no. 3 (1960), 467–84; and "Rail Parley Called by Canada Premier," *NYT*, 25 Aug. 1950, 1.

5 Statistics Canada, "Table R1–22 General Statistics for All Manufacturing Industries," https://www150.statcan.gc.ca/n1/pub/11-516-x/sectionr /R1_22-eng.csv.

6 Historic Inflation Canada - CPI Inflation, https://www.inflation.eu /inflation-rates/canada/historic-inflation/cpi-inflation-canada.aspx.

7 Livio Di Matteo, "A Federal Fiscal History, Canada, 1867–2017," Fraser Institute (Feb. 2017), 50, accessed 7 Mar. 2022, https://www.fraserinstitute .org/sites/default/files/federal-fiscal-history-canada-1867-2017.pdf.

8 Porter, *The Vertical Mosaic*, 166; Statistics Canada, "Table W439-455: Full-Time University Undergraduate Enrolment, by Field of Specialization and Sex, Canada, Selected Years, 1861 to 1975," accessed 7 Mar. 2022, https:// www150.statcan.gc.ca/n1/pub/11-516-x/sectionw/4147445-eng.htm#3; Jack Dobson, "University Construction to Get Half of Canada Council's $100,000,000 *G&M*, 13 Nov. 1956, 1; and "Table W519-532: Operating and Capital Expenditures of Universities, by Source of Funds, Canada, Selected Years, 1920 to 1974," accessed 7 Mar. 2022, https://www150 .statcan.gc.ca/n1/pub/11-516-x/sectionw/W519_532-eng.csv.

9 Harold Innis, *Empire and Communications* (Oxford: Clarendon Press, 1950); Harold Innis, *The Bias of Communication* (Toronto: University of Toronto Press, 1951); and Marshall McLuhan, *The Mechanical Bride* (New York: Vanguard, 1951).

10 Northrop Frye, *Anatomy of Criticism* (Princeton: Princeton University Press, 1957), and "Just What Was Said: Who Cheated the Children," *G&M*, 22 Oct. 1959, 7.

11 Treaties and Historical Research Centre, P.R.E. Group, Indian Affairs and Northern Development, "The Historical Development of the Indian Act" (1978).

12 Herman Bakvis, *Regional Ministers: Power and Influence in the Canadian Cabinet* (Toronto: University of Toronto Press, 1991).

13 C. Baldwin, "The Branding of the Prime Minister," 158.

14 Quoted in Reginald H. Roy, *For Most Conspicuous Bravery: A Biography of Major-General George R. Pearkes, V.C., through Two World Wars* (Vancouver: University of British Columbia Press, 1977), 258.

15 Quoted in "Lauds Ukrainians for Contribution; Music Is Praised," *G&M*, 1 April 1957, 5.

16 "Canada: Mr. Diefenbaker's Triumph," *The Round Table* 48, no. 191 (June 1958), 290.

17 House of Commons, *Debates*, 26 and 27 Jan. 1959; and "Backstage with the CBC Strike," *Maclean's*, 14 Mar. 1959, 3.

18 House of Commons, *Debates*, 23 June 1959; Ron Johnson and Morris Duff, "31 Top Men Quitting, CBC Meets in Crisis," *TDS*, 24 June 1959, 1–2; and "Committee to Study CBC Resignations," *Edmonton Journal*, 24 June 1959, 2.

19 British North America Act, 1951, 14–15 Geo. VI, c. 32 (UK).

20 "Legislature Urges Nat'l Labor Code," *Leader-Post* (Regina), 8 Apr. 1953, 11; and "Duplessis Vetoes Hit by Corman," *Leader-Post* (Regina), 18 Feb. 1958, 10.

21 Richard M. Bird, "Section H: Government Finance," Series H52–74 and Series H92–112, accessed 7 Mar. 2022, https://www150.statcan.gc.ca/n1/en/pub/11-516-x/pdf/5500098-eng.pdf?st=QxAW58RR; and Statistics Canada, "Federal Government Transfers to Provinces and Territories, 1947 to 1975," Table H474–493 H474–493, accessed 7 Mar. 2022, https://www150.statcan.gc.ca/n1/pub/11-516-x/sectionh/4057752-eng.htm#3.

22 Quinn, *The Union Nationale*, 148–51; "Vote Official Beaten over Election Probe," *Edmonton Journal*, 29 June 1957, 1; "Tories Turn Out Liberals in Nova Scotia Election," *Regina Leader-Post*, 11 Oct. 1956, 5; and Eric Seymour, "Out of Date Election List Hot Issue in Newfoundland," *G&M*, 28 Nov. 1951, 2.

23 Hugh MacLennan, *Two Solitudes* (New York: Duell, Sloan & Pearce, 1945).

24 Graham, *Old Man Ontario*, 410; and Noel, "The Ontario Political Culture: An Interpretation," 60.

25 Statistics Canada, "Factors in the Growth of Population, 1951 to 1961," accessed 8 Mar. 2022, https://www65.statcan.gc.ca/acyb02/1967/acyb02_19670184002-eng.htm.

26 Douglas Collins, "Ten Premiers' Shopping Lists Would Be Ready If Ottawa Should Call Tomorrow," *G&M*, 19 Sept. 1959, A8; "Saskatchewan Plans Prepaid Medical Care," *G&M*, 30 Dec. 1959, 10; and Paul G. Thomas and Curtis Brown, "Introduction: Manitoba in the Middle," in *Manitoba Politics and Government*, ed. Thomas and Brown, 5.

27 Sally Morphet, "Resolutions and Vetoes in the UN Security Council: Their Relevance and Significance," *Review of International Studies* 16, no. 4 (1990), 346.

28 Quoted in Thomson, *Louis St. Laurent: Canadian*, 369.
29 Quoted in Thomson, *Louis St. Laurent: Canadian*, 364.
30 *Canada Year Book, 1952–53*, 933; and *Canada Year Book, 1961*, 970.
31 *Canada Year Book, 1957–58*, 113.
32 Sidney Smith, quoted in Douglas G. Anglin, "Canada and Apartheid," *International Journal* 15, no. 2 (1960), 123.
33 Michael Gauvreau, *The Catholic Origins of Quebec's Quiet Revolution, 1931–1970* (Montreal: McGill-Queen's University Press, 2005), 105; and Cook, *Canada and the French-Canadian Question*, 115–16.

Index